No Choice
but War

ALSO BY ROLAND H. WORTH, JR.
AND FROM MCFARLAND

Biblical Studies on the Internet: A Resource Guide, 2d ed. (2008)

Shapers of Early Christianity: 52 Biographies, A.D. *100–400*
(2007, paperback 2012)

Messiahs and Messianic Movements through 1899 (2005)

Congress Declares War: December 8–11, 1941 (2004)

*Alternative Lives of Jesus: Noncanonical Accounts
through the Early Middle Ages* (2003)

World War II Resources on the Internet (2002)

*Secret Allies in the Pacific: Covert Intelligence and
Code Breaking Cooperation Between the United States,
Great Britain, and Other Nations Prior to the
Attack on Pearl Harbor* (2001)

*Pearl Harbor: Selected Testimonies, Fully Indexed,
from the Congressional Hearings (1945–1946) and Prior
Investigations of the Events Leading Up to the Attack*
(1993, paperback 2013)

ALSO OF INTEREST BY ERNIE GROSS
AND ROLAND H. WORTH, JR.

This Day in American History, 4th ed. (McFarland, 2012)

No Choice but War

The United States Embargo Against Japan and the Eruption of War in the Pacific

Roland H. Worth, Jr.

McFarland & Company, Inc., Publishers
Jefferson, North Carolina

The present work is a reprint of the library bound edition of No Choice but War: The United States Embargo Against Japan and the Eruption of War in the Pacific, *first published in 1995 by McFarland.*

LIBRARY OF CONGRESS CATALOGUING-IN-PUBLICATION DATA

Worth, Roland H., 1943–
    No choice but war : the United States embargo against Japan and the eruption of war in the Pacific / by Roland H. Worth, Jr.
        p.   cm.
    Includes bibliographical references and index.

    ISBN 978-0-7864-7752-4
    softcover : acid free paper ∞

    1. World War, 1939–1945—Campaigns—Japan.
2. Economic sanctions—Japan.   3. United States—
Economic policy.   I. Title.
D767.2.W67 2014
940.54'25—dc20   95-8392

BRITISH LIBRARY CATALOGUING DATA ARE AVAILABLE

© 1995 Roland H. Worth. All rights reserved

No part of this book may be reproduced or transmitted in any form or by any means, electronic or mechanical, including photocopying or recording, or by any information storage and retrieval system, without permission in writing from the publisher.

On the cover: the USS *Arizona* burning after the Japanese attack on Pearl Harbor (National Archives and Records Administration)

Manufactured in the United States of America

McFarland & Company, Inc., Publishers
    Box 611, Jefferson, North Carolina 28640
    www.mcfarlandpub.com

To Professor R. Barry Westin:
How large two pages
in a research paper have grown!

TABLE OF CONTENTS

	Preface	ix
	Introduction	1
1	America's Growing Alienation from Japan: The 1930s	7
2	The Slaps on the Wrist Grow Stronger: 1940	26
3	Buildup to Confrontation: January to July 1941	44
4	An Appearance of Totality—The Embargo Becomes Official: July 1941	62
5	Gambling on Economic Strangulation: Appearance Becomes Reality, August to December 1941	82
6	Impact of the 1940 Embargo Measures on Japan	100
7	Impact of the 1941 Embargo Measures on Japan	107
8	The Petroleum Supply Crisis of 1941	123
9	The Public Stance of the Japanese Government	136
10	Top Echelon Dialogue: The Liaison and Imperial Conferences of the Japanese Government	157
11	Internal Diplomatic Communications of the Japanese Government	163
12	Confidential American Evaluations of the Embargo's Impact	175
13	The American Recognition of the War-Making Potential of an Embargo	187
14	Disavowing the Linkage Between Embargo and War	203
	Conclusion	217
	Bibliography	221
	Index	227

PREFACE

The Japanese attack on Pearl Harbor, both in its immediate setting and in its broader historical context, can be approached in either of two ways. The "conventional" approach considers from a detached perspective the events leading up to the beginning of the war, the attitudes, the tactics, the individual politicians, government leaders, and military officers in their respective strengths and weaknesses. The "controversial" approach singles out one or more aspects of the event for consideration from a point of view that has not, at least, at the time of this writing, become part of the general consensus. (If it ever reaches that level of broad acceptance, it will become part of the new orthodoxy and the new conventional approach.)

At one extreme, the "controversial" approach adopts a total revisionist perspective, such as the view that President Franklin D. Roosevelt "plotted" to get the United States attacked by the Japanese or that the British connived to withhold vital intelligence that would have alerted the American forces to the forthcoming attack. In its more moderate form, it zeroes in on some aspect that is more or less generally acknowledged but whose true significance is held to have been glossed over or minimized by the dominant orthodoxy. Likewise, the actual supporting evidence may vary immensely: from conjecture, speculation, and innuendo to a mountain of supporting data where the only question is whether the interpretation put on the data is the best and most credible one.

My earlier book, *Pearl Harbor: Selected Testimonies* (McFarland, 1993), was in the tradition of conventional Pearl Harbor historiography, being designed as a detached culling of the most significant, interesting, and relevant testimony that was presented to the various U.S. government investigative committees that probed the events surrounding the beginning of the war. In contrast, this book is one of advocacy, of singling out a central theme that is often mentioned only in passing. By presenting a wide range of information from diverse sources, it is the purpose of this book to thoroughly document the pivotal role of the U.S.–led economic embargo in pushing Japan over the edge into overt hostilities against the West. In other words the U.S. decision to embargo 90 percent of Japan's petroleum and two-thirds or more of its trade led directly to the attack on Pearl Harbor on December 7, 1941.

Whether war was ultimately inescapable is an irrelevancy; it was this effort to economically destroy Japan that guaranteed U.S. involvement. It was not just a matter of Japanese imperialism; the misjudged American response sealed off the possibility of a peaceful solution or even of "hot cold war" in which each side annoyed and angered the other without pushing the other beyond the point of no return.

I do not share the frequently expressed conviction that the internal dynamics and failures of the Japanese political system made such a war inescapable—though I concede that it represents one reasonable scenario of what might have occurred. But even assuming that Japan would ultimately have launched an attack southward against the Philippines and beyond, one is still amazed at a decision that forfeited six or more vital months that would have produced major reinforcement of the U.S. military posture in the Far East. Certainly these months would have vastly increased the price in blood the Japanese would have shed in the effort at expansionism, slowed the campaign down, and quite probably reduced the area that had to be recaptured with the inevitable saving of thousands of American lives.

The thesis of this book in no way makes the Americans villains and the Japanese heroes. Japanese militarism was arrogant, abrasive, and minimally restrained by considerations of prudence and even common sense. At a time when the United States was preparing to abandon its own Far East colony of the Philippines, Japan was attempting to erect a major empire with extreme brutality and lack of concern for the local populations it incorporated. I can express no sympathy for its aggression.

Even so, would it not have been better to avoid the war entirely if possible? Lobbying against aggression, hanging a massive onus of international guilt on the foe, and enacting limited economic restrictions (as had been undertaken already prior to the American escalation to total embargo) were all means of making known the profound anguish and anger of the American people. Even so, shameful as were Japan's aggression and occupation tactics in China, no American security interests were affected.

The facts of an embargo are well known, but its war-provoking nature is less commonly recognized. When the subject of the U.S. embargo of Japan is discussed, it is normally embedded in a broader discussion of the intricacies of diplomacy that led up to the decision or is mentioned as part of the prelude to hostilities. Here we single in on the actual effects of the embargo and the recognition by both sides of the war it would lead to. The impact of the embargo was not a deep, dark secret. It was explicitly recognized by high ranking officials in both governments and repeatedly discussed in the American press. The American decryption program confirmed from the secret Japanese diplomatic messages that the total embargo was devastating the Japanese economy and that the opportunity for peace was evaporating almost as quickly as the morning dew on a hot day.

To paint this picture in proper detail required the accumulation of data from a wide variety of sources. The Inter-Library Loan Department of the University of Richmond provided invaluable assistance. As with other research projects, they were able to obtain scarce and rare books with a degree of success that continues to leave me amazed. This book could be as polemical without their assistance but it could never be as well documented.

No Choice but War directly grows out of a short section of a research paper prepared in Professor Barry Westin's graduate seminar on Twentieth Century America at the University of Richmond. Directly or indirectly, this paper led also to my previously published compendium on *Pearl Harbor* and to several works currently in progress related to the beginning of the conflict. Although Professor Westin in no way bears responsibility (or blame!) for the conclusions of the current work, I owe a great debt for the opportunity of preparing that research paper: It clarified and codified a number of strains of thought that had been in my mind for many years, and the additional research made plain related aspects that I had not previously been aware of.

Roland H. Worth, Jr.
Spring 1995

INTRODUCTION

Over fifty years have passed since the great American humiliation on December 7, 1941. The foe had crossed, unseen, a supposedly "American" ocean. It had launched, undetected, six carrier loads of attack aircraft. As the enemy closed upon their target, the Hawaiian Islands, an American radar sighting of the carrier planes was dismissed as unimportant by the untrained officer in charge of the newly opened aircraft information center.

The first people to observe the planes overhead did not recognize their nationality and thought they were perhaps the expected bombers due in from the mainland or were fighters arriving ahead of their American carrier. Others heard explosions from a distance and thought it was a maneuver of some kind.

Instead, a skillful, well-trained, and daring adversary had risked more than half of its carriers on what could easily have turned into a fiasco. Serious losses were anticipated, but fortune smiled upon the Japanese that day as everything went their way. The "impregnable" Pearl Harbor was shattered and the fleet devastated at only token losses to the attacker. The minimal losses of the enemy made the catastrophe ten times more shocking and unbearable, producing a fear of possible future "sneak attacks" that would permanently scar the collective American psyche.

Yet the damage to the American fighting capacity was not as overwhelming nor as long lasting as first appeared. Most of the sunken vessels were salvageable and could be returned to combat. Far more important, most of the crews survived to man the vessels that would ultimately hunt down and sweep the seas clean of the entire Japanese navy.

That the Japanese military attacked and decisively defeated the United States at Pearl Harbor is dire historical fact. But why did they do so on that bright Sunday morning of December?

Looking back at the event from the perspective of the late twentieth century, the Japanese (I use the term to mean those in control of their government and their military) remain the "bad guys." They had demonstrated a record of cruel imperialism in Korea and had betrayed the idealistic element originally present as one of the factors behind their occupation of Manchuria. The regimes they attempted to establish in the Far East represented clear-cut colonialism at its worst, absent only the white skin traditionally associated with the phenomena.

Yet many an aggressor has coexisted with the United States without ever feeling the need or desirability of directly attacking its territories or citizens. On the other side of the coin, a goodly number of foreign regimes have been passionately despised by much of the American people—and for good cause—without producing a policy that so collided with the other nation's perceived self-interest that bloody carnage resulted. Such restraint did not mean that either the people or the leaders of the United States government necessarily respected the character of the dictator or the repressive regime. It simply meant that the American administration "held its nose" while hoping for, working for, and (sometimes) even plotting for a change in the rival's power structure. Compared to such governments of the past and present, Japan was no better and no worse. Hence we must look for some factor beyond moral or political fault to explain the eruption of war between the two powers. What made this situation different? What pushed a tense and difficult relationship over the edge into international conflict?

Although there were other points on the way at which the slide into war could have been prevented, late July to early August, 1941, can be viewed as a pivotal period. At this time, policies were adopted on both sides of the Pacific that were resolved only by an armed struggle.

The crucial dividing point between peace and war, from the Japanese standpoint, can best be placed at Japan's decision to strong-arm the Vichy French into permitting expansion from northern Indochina into the entire French colony. Although word of what was afoot was well publicized in the Western media and protests were fervently made, Japan went ahead and carried out its intention.

From the American side, this event was also critical. American indignation was so deep that it produced a total trade freeze and a complete petroleum embargo. This placed Japan in an intolerable situation for it struck a dagger into its economic heart: without trade much of its citizenry faced a devastating loss of employment and without petroleum neither business nor the military could long function in this oil-poor nation.

If the American side had shown the flexibility it had demonstrated in earlier years, even this dangerous step might not have resulted in the Pacific War of 1941–1945. Indeed, more constructively approached, it might even have produced the much desired rollback of the Japanese empire out of Indochina and much (though not all) of China. This would not have been sufficient to please the bungling Nationalist regime of China nor its fervent advocates in the United States, but it could have been adequate to guarantee the security interests of the Western powers in that part of the world.

Introduction   3

Unfortunately, American demands were so stringent for the restoration of trade and petroleum—and the time frame for negotiation was so tight—that the Japanese were convinced that there were only two basic courses open to them: a "surrender" to American demands or war against a power they knew was much stronger than they. An analysis of the full scope of the U.S.-Japanese negotiations is a fascinating subject in itself but would at least double the length of this book. Hence we have chosen to concentrate on what we regard to be its most inflammatory aspect, the comprehensive trade cutoff. One could argue that it was the failure of the general negotiations rather than the abolishment of economic relationships that produced the war but this would miss the key point: without the termination of trade even unsuccessful negotiations need not have led to war; with the trade termination frozen in place the unsuccessful negotiations left Japan with little or no option but to play its war card.

Oddly enough, the central role of the American embargo in producing war has been generally overlooked or downplayed. When it is mentioned at all, the significance of the either-or position it placed Japan in is often ignored or minimized—or the reader is left to make the necessary deduction. The average reader is unlikely to even think about the matter, however, unless the subject's significance is explicitly pointed out.

The specialist in modern Japanese or twentieth-century Far Eastern diplomatic history is the type of individual most likely to be aware of the economic significance of the embargo and its potential for igniting international war. Even in these circles, it is unusual for the embargo and the war to be linked in an explicitly condemnatory way, perhaps because of the natural unpleasantness of the conclusion for American pride or because of a sense that such explicitness is contrary to scholarly objectivity. As one ventures further afield, one is less and less likely to discover the embargo emphasized at all, and when it is mentioned, it is most typically narrated as if it were merely another of the many steps toward war rather than as the uniquely decisive action it was. If this bleak summary be challenged, one need only scan the texts of a variety of representative works to discover its validity or consider the scarcity of mention of the boycott in the indexes to such volumes.

In spite of this general situation, the careful reader will discover at least a resonable amount of attention devoted to the embargo in a minority of works and an explicit awareness of the explosiveness of the decision in a yet smaller number. An admirable step in the right direction, though it stops just short of such explicit war linkage, is found in Robert J. Maddox's recent history of the war:

> The president regarded the Japanese action with great apprehension because
> Japan's leaders had secured an excellent staging area to strike out against targets

in Southeast Asia. On July 26, he issued an executive order freezing all Japanese funds and assets in the United States.

FDR's response had unforeseen consequences. He believed sanctions should be applied gradually to enable the Japanese to weigh the effects without provoking them to rash action. He had intended his freeze order to further limit sales of strategic materials through licensing, not to cut them off altogether. But his jealous subordinates interpreted his order to mean banning entirely all exports of oil and gasoline to Japan. FDR was dismayed by this construction when he learned of it but did not rescind it because he was afraid he would appear irresolute. The Japanese were shocked by his action, which, as one newspaper put it, amounted to "a declaration of economic war." The freeze not only strengthened the argument that Japan must seize its own resources but emphasized the need to do so quickly, before existing stocks became depleted.[1]

Unlike the authors who merely mention the boycott in passing, as one of a multitude of ministeps to war, Maddox puts sufficient stress upon the boycott and its inherent danger to Japan to make the alert reader aware that this was a highly important step. Even this admirable summary does not quite pose the war-making potential of the act in explicit terms, however.

Surely the most restrained judgment one can make on the relationship between the embargo and the outbreak of hostilities is that offered by Donald F. Drummond in his *The Passing of American Neutrality*. He notes the overwhelming reliance of Japan on foreign petroleum and comments: "The American government held a powerful economic weapon and was now using it freely for the first time. But since it confronted Japan with a choice between surrender and new aggressions, the decision was made at [the] cost of bringing war a good deal closer."[2] But doesn't even this very restrained presentation of cause and effect require the deduction that the action of the United States dramatically intensified an inflammatory relationship and therefore deserves at least partial blame for the situation ultimately degenerating into total war?

John K. Emmerson, at the time a minor official at the American embassy in Tokyo, later recalled how dramatically the U.S.-led embargo affected the Japanese government not only on the economic plane but also on the ever-vital psychological level: "Freezing meant the termination of all financial transactions, the virtual cessation of trade, and the ending of direct Japanese-American steamship service. *In Tokyo we knew that this was the beginning of the end.* No move by either government had so shaken the other. The Japanese recognized that time was not on their side" [emphasis added].

Again, do not such admissions require us to elevate the United States embargo to a level of being at least the co-precipitating cause of the Pacific war? Indeed, since the American trade limitations were not a response to any direct or immediate threat to the United States or its territories, could not a reasonable interpreter go even a step further and elevate these limitations to the role of major or dominant cause for the war? Nor would such an analyst have to be afflicted with a bad case of anti–Americanism. An individual could be quite friendly to the United States and yet still come to such a conclusion. Writing in a year-end "Political Review for 1941," the British ambassador to the United States had no doubt of the preeminent role played by the embargo in producing the war and sounds cynically amused at the prevalent misunderstanding of what caused the war:

> That the United States Government had, in fact, imposed a total blockade upon Japan by an adroit exploitation of its freezing order was scarcely appreciated by the general public. It is worth recording that the Government of the British Commonwealth and of the Netherlands East Indies followed the United States lead in this forward policy without asking for any prior military guarantee. The United States public do not to this day understand how severe were the measures of economic pressure imposed upon Japan, and still believe implicitly in the official doctrine of the Japanese "stab in the back" at Pearl Harbor.[4]

"Blaming everything on the Americans" has been a popular international pastime since the sixties. Usually (though not always) this has been a thoroughly unjust practice aimed at besmirching the reputation of a powerful nation attempting to protect itself (and, indirectly, the rest of the world) from what was, indeed, an "evil empire." This does not mean that every decision and every policy was necessarily wise or astute, only that it was normally well intended.

The same is true in regard to 1941. For all its faults, the United States was the "good guy." It had no expansionist aims; with small territorial exceptions, what little "empire" it had, it was ready to give away. (The date for Philippine independence had already been announced.) Any war that did occur would cost considerable blood and treasure of the United States. So convinced was he that the outcome of the Anglo-German war was vital to America's long-term interests that President Franklin D. Roosevelt was determined to get the nation into it at virtually any cost. In this context, the Far Eastern crisis was a dangerous sideshow that diverted attention from the central danger posed by a triumphant Nazi Germany. If war did erupt in that quarter, it could easily produce disastrous losses for the British and the diversion of vital supplies from the European theater to the Pacific. For all these reasons, Roosevelt did not want a war with Japan.

On the other hand, Japan's policies had long annoyed and angered the president, and pressure had remained upon him to take far stronger action than he had prior to the total embargo. Key elements in his administration pressed for a throw-down-the-gauntlet policy that he privately favored but was reluctant to embrace lest it make the situation uncontrollable and ignite a Pacific war when the greater danger was perceived as coming from Germany.

It is the thesis of this volume that at this point the United States made a fatal policy miscalculation: it knowingly, willingly, and even enthuasiastically inflicted upon the major military empire of Japan a devastating embargo that left it no alternative but to choose between what it perceived as a humiliating surrender or launching a retaliatory war. The Japanese actions up to this point were, at most, an indirect and potential threat against the United States and its possession the Philippines. In contrast, the American embargo was a direct and immediate threat against the survival of the Japanese empire. It aimed a devastating body blow at both Japan's military prowess (via the elimination of all petroleum imports) and the ability of the Japanese economy to survive (by the elimination of petroleum and all trade).

The embargo was so successful that it denied Japan the bargaining time that might have encouraged it to continue negotiations rather than opt for a risky war against the major Western powers. Beyond being urged to rely blindly upon American goodwill, Japan was offered no concessions concrete or substantial enough to encourage its desperate negotiators to believe that a long-term solution could be reached. By placing a major military power in such dire straits and with such a limited time frame before irrevocable economic disaster arrived, the American leaders foolishly and needlessly created a situation in which war seemed the only way out.

Probably the Anglo-German war would still have produced American participation in the European conflict, but the avoidable war in the Pacific resulted in thousands of needless American casualties—the sons of the past generation and the fathers of the emerging one. International politics consists not just in being "right," but also in being prudent. American policy toward Japan in the last six or seven months before Pearl Harbor abandoned that essential prudence and caution. The result was a war. To the extent that we can make such judgments, a needless war.

NOTES

1. Robert J. Maddox, *The United States and World War II* (Boulder, Colo.: Westview, 1992), 88.
2. Donald F. Drummond, *The Passing of American Neutrality* (1995; reprint, 1968), 273.
3. John K. Emmerson, *The Japanese Thread: A Life in the U.S. Foreign Service* (New York: Holt, Rinehart and Winston, 1978), 113.
4. [Halifax, Lord, a.k.a. Edward Frederick Lindley Wood], *Confidential Dispatches: Analyses of America by the British Ambassador, 1939–1945* (Evanston, Ill.: New University Press, 1974), 33. This is a reprint, with a new introduction, of the British edition entitled, *Confidential Dispatches: Analysis [sic] of America by the British Ambassador* (London: H.M.S.O., 1975). With the exception of the 1939 report, all of these dispatches were submitted by Lord Halifax.

Chapter 1
AMERICA'S GROWING ALIENATION FROM JAPAN: THE 1930s

We are primarily concerned with the embargo measures of 1940 and 1941, but in order to place them in their historical context, it would be useful to provide a background of the deteriorating American-Japanese relationship that ultimately produced such actions. Although the Washington administration dramatically overreacted in the summer of 1941, it should never be forgotten that the Japanese unwillingness (or inability) to rein in its empire builders over a period of a decade created the atmosphere of distrust and disgust that weakened the hand of those Americans who might otherwise have backed a policy of continued restraint.

Japan's Expansionism in Asia

During the First World War, Japan had eagerly grasped the opportunity to play a role on the world scene. A joint Anglo-Japanese expedition seized the German-controlled city of Tsingtao in China while the unfortified Marshall and Caroline Islands quickly fell to Japanese forces. The Japanese navy energetically scoured the Pacific for any German shipping that had escaped seizure by the British.[1]

When the central European powers were decisively defeated, the question arose of how to divide the modest foreign possessions of the losers. Japan was permitted to retain the Carolina and Marshall Islands and to assume the special national "rights" previously exercised by Germany in China. This way Nippon was able to obtain much desired inroads on the Asiatic mainland itself without bearing the international censure of having forced new concessions on an unwilling Chinese government; she had inherited, if you will, the loser's spoils.

A decade later in September 1931, the "Mukden Incident" provided the justification for the Japanese army to go on the march without the excuse of defeating a faraway foe. Chinese troops were said to have attacked the railroad station in that town, and Japanese officials insisted they were forced to protect their rights in that Japanese-occupied sector. This "Manchurian Affair," as the entire series of events was more commonly called in the West, provided the excuse for Japan to cement regional control and establish a puppet regime. Although this pseudo-independent country of Manchukuo provided a paper veneer of protection against accusations of imperialism, it fooled no one. Nor were Western powers reassured when Japanese operations were expanded into other areas as well, including Shanghai.

Japan forcefully affirmed the reasonableness of its actions: they were brought about by the necessity of "protecting" its businessmen and their possessions from those who were hostile. Whatever element of truth there was in this, there were other underlying political and economic considerations that encouraged the Japanese to seize the opportunity to solidify their position in northern China.

> Externally, the steady development of Chinese nationalism loomed as a threat to Japan's influence on the mainland while the resumption of Sino-Russian relations late in 1932 appeared as a prophetic warning to the Tokyo government. Internally, Japan's pressing needs for raw materials, in addition to finding outlets for its surplus population and industrial exports, strengthened the position of Japanese chauvinists and militarists who sought to eliminate the economic distress at home and to re-establish the country's prestige abroad.[2]

On the scene reportage quickly began to outweigh the limited information available from Tokyo.[3] The image of a vigorous offensive was soon replaced with a picture of barbaric excess. Newspapers around the world condemned Nippon for unleashing such extreme and seemingly unconcerned slaughter upon a weaker foe.

In May 1932, Japan finally agreed to accept the League of Nations' proposed ceasefire. This simply meant the end of hostilities and not a withdrawal from occupied positions. Japan itself retained a firm hold on the territories it had conquered.

For the purpose of analysis, we might divide the Japanese military and governmental personnel into three broad categories: unrestrained militarists, restrained militarists, and accommodationists. The accommodationists were especially strong within the government (though not totally unknown in the military). They candidly recognized the vastly superior economic resources of the Americans and British and regarded a peaceful relationship with the West as the only practical, long-term policy. However enticing an empire might be, it was not sustainable over any prolonged period without at least a tacit understanding with these foreign powers. A smaller, more compact empire—one that the Western powers could at least grudgingly tolerate—was far preferable to a vaster reign that would agitate the relationship into ultimate conflict. Some accommodationists also had serious moral qualms about the renewed expansionism and the military excesses used to carry it out. The fact that the expansionists were willing to lie brazenly both to the government and to their own military superiors and equals widened the breach.

The militarists were divided between the realists and the gung ho dreamers. The former believed that militarism had to operate within a framework of practicality; the latter were so absorbed in the sought-for result that the attainability and sustainability of the expansionism was a virtual irrelevancy. The realists balanced potential value versus risk, while the unrestrained militarists only thought of the glory it would bring. These "ultras" were especially common among the lower rank officers, but their superiors were often all too willing to tolerate them if not to openly or bluntly embrace their goals.

The dominant approach varied within the General Staff, the War Ministry, and the various field commands throughout the 1930s as ongoing events influenced attitudes and individuals were transferred from one assignment to another.[4] New options even caused individuals to reverse their previous commitments. For example, some who played major roles in the incursion into Manchuria were strongly opposed when the Marco Polo Bridge Incident of July 1937 created a new war in China proper.[5]

The chief accommodationist was Hirohito himself. Because he was opposed to the expansionism in Manchuria and, even more so, in China proper, those supporting these policies did their best to keep the true situation from him. Although theoretically he held definitive power over both the military and the government, there was no actual tradition of the emperor personally wielding that power, especially in reversing any approach openly embraced by the military. Everything was done in his name, but there was no system to enforce obedience if he decided to oppose what the military was doing. Without such precedents to go by, and perhaps because of his own personal psychology, Hirohito was unwilling to assume the role of absolute ruler that theory bestowed upon him. As a result, he was only able to restrain the military rather than dramatically reverse their actual policy. Furthermore, the zealots pledged their loyalty to the emperor and not to Hirohito personally. If he pushed them beyond modest changes, there was a very real danger that he would be assassinated and a more cooperative emperor would take his place, one more understanding of the "true" interests of both his throne and his nation.[6]

In 1937 the Japanese military leadership in China decided that it was once again time to strike out in a major way. The preceding victories had been relatively simple ones, increasing the hope that future ones would be equally easy. Those desiring such action could point to the fact that the economic problems of the homeland economy had not been solved and potential opponents (such as the United States and Britain) were preoccupied by their own economic difficulties. At the Marco Polo Bridge near

Peking, a minor battle occurred that provided the militarists with the publicly needed justification for the latest effort to expand the boundaries of Nipponese control.

For both domestic and foreign consumption, Japan once again attempted to provide some type of reasonable explanation for its renewed expansionism as it built upon its past efforts at intellectual self-defense.

> The justifications advanced by Japan [during the thirties] were multiple: the protection of interests acquired fighting Russia in 1904–1905; the need to have access to raw materials which would otherwise be looted by Western capitalists; the need to protect investments (and, later, citizens, in the well-known extension); access to markets, and their protection; the desire for a "Japanese sphere of influence" which was easy to argue since Japan's expansion, unlike that of the European and U.S. imperialists, was limited to geographically adjacent areas; geo-political arguments, which were used vis-à-vis the U.S.S.R., first over the invasion of Siberia, and later in Korea and China; general statements about the need to control Manchuria and Korea, sometimes combined with a plea that Japan was actually improving the territory; solidarity with the non-white peoples of Asia against the Caucasians; population pressure.[7]

At home, such reasoning had considerable appeal, but in other parts of the Far East, there were deep suspicions. In the Western world there was outright rejection.

There was a clear-cut racist element to Japan's policy as well. To assume that whatever racial stock one may be descended from is superior to all others seems a universal temptation, at least when a powerful nation is attempting to rationalize its foreign adventures. Just as the assumption of white racial superiority easily justified the possession of colonies inhabited by other ethnic groups, the claim of fighting racism became a handy cover for imposing nonwhite colonialism. Major Kametaro Tominaga of the War Ministry's Press Bureau delivered a highly publicized speech in mid–September of 1941 that freely used such antiwhite sentiments to justify Japan's own new colonialism:

> It may be thus clear to all that the Manchurian Affair and the China Affair, coming after the Russo-Japanese War, have one distinct ideology that runs through both. These events are demonstrations of an attempt to free the oppressed Oriental races from the clutches of the White, and put them on complete, independent political status. These are in fact racial wars. Japan has been fighting for years, as the leader of the Oriental races, wars of emancipation against aggression and oppression and is resolved to carry on to the finish.[8]

Anti–white/foreign sentiment certainly made sense to many Asians, but Japan's own harsh policy toward non–Japanese ethnic strains (viewed as inferior to the Japanese, of course) undermined the credibility of such assertions. Japan came to be viewed as simply another foreign oppressor, one who had no more legitimate claim to an Asian mainland empire than did the Western powers.

After the Manchurian Incident cre ited a new status quo, both China and Japan tolerated the new situation in which "peace" existed. The China Affair had no such tidy ending to satisfy the Japanese. This time the combat was destined to continue off and on until 1945. This is one reason why some historians prefer to date the beginning of World War II not with the German invasion of Poland in 1939 but with the Japanese advance two years earlier. On the other hand, the Atlantic and Pacific wars began independently of each other and out of dramatically different reasons. They were really two separate wars that only merged into one in December 1941. Hence one could describe it either way, according to the center of one's interest. From the Oriental perspective it would be quite natural to date the Second World War as beginning in 1937, expanding into Europe in 1939, and becoming one war in late 1941. For Americans and Europeans, to whom the stagnant war in China was brutal but inconclusive (and ten times less important than Nazi adventurism in Europe), it was all a dangerous sideshow. Hence, from their perspective, the real war began in 1939 and expanded to the Pacific in 1941 when Japan dropped its penny-ante warring in Asia and began waging the kind of conflict that the Western powers recognized as the genuine article. Furthermore, history is normally written from the standpoint of the victors. Offensive as it may be to regional pride, no Asian power won the Pacific war. An extraordinary alliance of British-American sea-land power swept Japan back into its home islands, the Russian army (not the Chinese) finally crushed the Japanese forces on the Asian mainland, and the American nuclear bomb crunched out the last dying embers of resistance. Since the Western Anglo-American-Russian coalition was the true winner of the war, it seems inevitable that World War II will always "start" in 1939 even though conflict in China itself was never fully settled in the two preceding years.

What is important in this context, however, is the vital fact that because of a combination of factors, the new stage of the China war could not be brought to a successful conclusion. It is one thing to expect the Western powers to be reconciled to a triumphant expansionist regime; it is something else to foolishly demand reconciliation when the "defeated" native power refuses to turn over and die. Weak and incompetent as independent China was, until it collapsed, there would remain an ongoing rival for control of the southern Asian mainland.

The Estrangement with the United States

During the thirties, the American image of Japan became increasingly negative. This was accelerated by the renewed war that began in 1937. In September 1937, Americans were asked by the George Gallup Institute of

Public Opinion which side of that war they favored. Only a meager 2% favored Japan, 43% favored China, and 55% refused to commit themselves to either side. By June 1939 the Japanese percentage remained frozen at 2%, while almost three-quarters (74%) now favored China, with the remainder undecided.[9] Gallup Poll figures revealed Americans shifting from 63% opposed to a campaign to stop buying Japanese goods in October 1937 to 66% supporting it in June 1939.[10]

Japan's bellicose policies in the early forties only served to intensify this hostility. In an article published in July 1941, Raymond Clapper called attention to the dramatic difference in attitudes he had recently noted at an anti-interventionist rally on the West Coast. The guest speaker was a strict pacifist and was asked if the United States should go to war if attacked by the Germans. His fervent answer of "no" was greeted with vigorous applause. The question of whether to respond militarily to a Japanese assault brought forth a second "no," but this one the audience reacted to with only stony, nonapproving silence. Clapper commented: "Senator Hiram Johnson of California may deplore every step the Administration makes in the European war. But if there is trouble with Japan, you know where Senator Johnson and every other Western senator and representative will stand."[11] Speaking of the pre–Pearl Harbor period of 1941, the British ambassador reported home, "Japan was more strongly disliked and distrusted than any other nation in the world."[12]

The Gallup Poll monitored a rise in those willing to go beyond anger to taking concrete steps that would increase the risk of war. In late July 1941, a poll taken largely before the Japanese expansion into all of Indochina was completed showed some 51% of Americans were willing to "take steps now to keep Japan from becoming more powerful, even if this means risking a war with Japan." Not even a third (only 31%) opposed this approach.[13]

Between February and March of 1941, those willing to risk war to keep Japan out of Singapore and the Dutch Indies had increased an unimportant amount (from 39% to 40%), while those opposing such a course had decreased significantly from 46% to 39%. In a later poll (which Gallup in July only called "recent"), 60% perceived a Japanese takeover of those colonies as dangerous to the United States, while only 20% rejected that interpretation. By July 1941 a majority was even willing to support the establishment of American naval bases in Singapore, New Zealand, and Australia, a half-world away.[14]

A number of factors had combined to produce this utter repudiation of Japan. No one of them might have done it alone, but the presence of each of them over a prolonged period of time reinforced the negative portrait.

The religious "investment" in China predisposed many Americans to hostility toward the invader. For many years, American missionaries had sought to convert the locals, had engaged in cultural efforts such as the building, maintenance, and staffing of schools, and had promoted humanitarianism in the form of hospitals and charitable relief. In addition to the destruction of their long-term efforts, the need of resident Americans (including missionaries) to leave the Japanese-occupied sectors produced an element of personal anger toward the expansionary effort.[15]

Detailed knowledge of what was going on came primarily from the daily newspapers. Even neutral reporting could hardly avoid implying a disparaging image of Japan. The ongoing headlines, "JAPS BOMB..." were inescapable, while the perpetual weakness of China and its inability to mount meaningful retaliation resulted in all the negative coverage relating to the Japanese side.[16]

The Japanese did not help themselves by severely limiting the flow of information to Tokyo-based reporters.[17] The reporters with the greatest access to information were filing from Chinese-defended territories and were sympathetic to the Chinese cause.[18] No matter how objective one tries to be, there is an inevitable judgment aspect to reporting that causes one thing to be stressed above another and shapes the word choices used in describing a particular event. Add to this personal preference the inability to find anything favorable to say about the other side and one finds a media presentation of Japan that could only reduce its reputation abroad.

In September 1937, Japan began major aerial bombing of Chinese cities. As Americans came face to face with the plain verbal and visual pictures of mass civilian destruction, they were horrified at the inevitable result of any war and roundly placed the blame on the Japanese. There was a widespread conviction that even war did not have to be this nasty, and the Japanese again were given the blame and the guilt.

In that age before television, movie newsreels had a major impact upon those who paid little attention to the printed media. What might even be tedious in a verbal description jumped off the screen to convey the living horror of war. Newsreels repeatedly showed the brutal impact of the hostilities upon the Chinese civilian population. After viewing one such newsreel in September 1937, American Admiral William Leahy commented that the images shown represented "powerful publicity in favor of the Chinese."[19]

Cinematic fiction reinforced the same picture. An estimated twenty-three million Americans viewed *The Good Earth* when it first appeared in 1937. A Japanese visitor of that year attended a showing and observed (and on this point none were likely to challenge his evaluation): "First comes Pearl Buck's "The Good Earth," which shows the Chinese at their best—polite, diligent and honest. Then comes the bombing of the Cathay Hotel [in Shanghai]. The bodies of the Chinese are seeen strewn about the streets. The captions tell of the ravages of war and Japanese aggression."[20]

Secretary of State Hull referred to the growing indignation at Japanese war tactics in a September 1937 telegram to Ambassador Grew in Tokyo: "American public opinion has been outraged by the methods and strategy employed by the combatants, particularly by the Japanese military, and has become gradually more critical of Japan."[21] By the end of the month, the United States government had lodged what the secretary of state called "repeated protests to the Japanese Government against aerial bombing of noncombatants." In one case, the department had even published the text of a protest delivered "in objection to and condemnation of such bombing." He noted that on September 28, the State Department had issued a public statement further denouncing such conduct.[22]

In early October, President Roosevelt surely had Japan's conduct in China in mind when he lamented:

> The present reign of terror and international lawlessness began a few years ago. It began through unjustified interference in the internal affairs of other nations or the invasion of alien territory in violation of treaties and has now reached a stage where the very foundations of civilization are seriously threatened. The landmarks and traditions which have marked the progress of civilization toward a condition of law, order, and justice are being wiped away.
>
> Without a declaration of war and without warning or justification of any kind, civilians, including women and children, are being ruthlessly murdered with bombs from the air. In times of so-called peace ships are being attacked and sunk by submarines without cause and notice.[23]

On December 12, 1937, Americans were given a far more personal reason to resent the latest bout of Japanese belligerence. While it was clearly flying the American flag, Japanese naval aviators repeatedly assaulted the American gunboat *Panay*. Two seamen were killed, as was a prominent Italian newsman. Twelve men received serious injuries and thirty-eight received lesser wounds.[24] Although some American newspapers advocated direct American intervention, many were dubious as to why such a vessel was in an area of probable military hostilities.[25] What was shared in common by all shades of opinion was indignation that American blood had been shed.

The crisis was defused by the Japanese accepting responsibility even though they insisted that their pilots had not realized that an American vessel was on the receiving end of their assault. Over $2,200,000 was paid the American government in compensation for sinking the *Panay* and three oil-carrying vessels. Included in this sum was over a quarter million dollars for the injured parties and the estates of those who perished—very large sums of money for that time.[26]

Regardless of the superficial reconciliation, few Americans could view the Japanese side with anything short of repugnance. After all, if they had done this to *us*, who could doubt what worse atrocities they might commit upon the semihelpless Chinese?

The Imposition of a "Moral Embargo"

As the months sped by after the China Incident erupted, nothing convincing occurred to reverse the American drift away from Japan. The issue quickly became not whether something should be done but the form that something should take.

One quickly rejected option was that of proceeding under the Third Neutrality Act of May 1937. That legislation provided that after a presidential proclamation of the existence of a war, it would "be unlawful to export, or attempt to export, or cause to be exported, arms, ammunition, or implements of war from any place in the United States to any belligerent state named in such proclamation, or to any neutral state for transshipment to, or for the use of, any such belligerent state" (Section 1[a]). To attempt to send any military supplies into either belligerent country carried a penalty of five years imprisonment and a ten thousand dollar fine, a huge sum in those days (Section 6[a]). In short, the legislation put both warring parties on the same level even when one was clearly being victimized and the other was engaging in blatant empire building. Any action under this law would cut off all of China's access to American military goods while doing little to harm Japan's ability to continue the war. By so doing, it would have substantially hurt China and have been of minimal use in restraining Japan.

Furthermore, the legislation also called for a cutoff of all sales within the United States of the warring parties' "exchange bonds, securities, or other obligations."[27] Only humanitarian transactions could be exempted and limited sums for commercial transactions. The end result of invoking this law would be to deny China not only the arms it needed to defend herself but also the ability to borrow the money to buy arms from other sources.

Hence China avoided forcing the American president's hand by declining to officially declare a state of war. In spite of its preponderant impact upon China, the application of the law would also have been an inconvenience to Japan, so it also never bothered to declare formally that a state of hostilities existed. Technically neither had to do so. The actual wording of the legislation (Section 1[a]) simply refers to "whenever the President shall find that there exists a state of war"; in other words, only presidential certification was required, not a formal declaration of war by the involved powers. Roosevelt was far from desirous of exercising his power because of the harm certain to be inflicted upon the Chinese nation.[28]

Reservations existed on other grounds as well. Those fearing the potential for American involvement in foreign wars—the major philosophical underpinning for enacting the law—were afraid that actually implementing its provisions would increase the danger of such a scenario becoming reality.[29] From a practical standpoint, there were also concerns that the step would effectively reduce the protection available to Americans residing in China.[30]

Rhetoric could not force Japan to reverse its policy, but it might just be able to create an American consensus for stronger and more direct action. On October 5, 1937, President Roosevelt delivered his "Quarantine the Aggressors" speech before an audience in Chicago, Illinois. While repeatedly insisting that the United States desired to avoid war, he emphasized that the degree of military conflict then present in the world carried a threat to all nations everywhere. "The peace, the freedom, and the security of 90 percent of the population of the world is being jeopardized by the remaining 10 percent, who are threatening a breakdown of all international order and law."[31]

In a thrust clearly aimed at Japan, Roosevelt argued:

> It ought to be inconceivable that in this modern era, and in the face of experience, any nation could be so foolish as to run the risk of plunging the whole world into war by invading and violating in contravention of solemn treaties the territory of other nations that have done them no real harm and which are too weak to protect themselves adequately. Yet the peace of the world and the welfare and security of every nation is being threatened by that very thing.[32]

Sumner Welles, using his own firsthand knowledge of the president's intentions, wrote of how a "trade embargo" and "quasi blockade" were in Roosevelt's mind when he gave this speech.[33] Although Welles was uncertain what caused the president to back away from this more militant and confrontational policy, a consideration of the American reaction to the speech provides much of the answer. Americans were still too preoccupied with their domestic economic problems to be rallied to a fighting attitude toward faraway nations. Although one might make the philosophical case that American interests were endangered, it was hard to convince most Americans at this early point, that this was any more than a theoretical danger.

What happened behind the scenes sounded the death knell to any possibility that the administration would boldly strike out, trusting that Americans would automatically rally to their government in the hour of crisis. The president sounded out the British to see if they would cooperate in joint action, and Anglo-American naval meetings were held to discuss the practical problems of a naval blockade. Anthony Eden warned that "no one should contemplate action of that kind in the Far East unless he is convinced that he has an overwhelming force to back that policy.[34] Obtaining such commitments was impossible. The Americans declined to follow Anthony Eden's recommendation that their Far Eastern fleet be substantially strengthened. The Chamberlain government in London backed away from a blockade policy because of the prime minister's fear of a multifront war far beyond Britain's ability to handle. With neither side willing to provide the necessary firm support, any remaining slim chance that a blockade would be implemented was removed by Eden's resignation as foreign secretary.[35]

Unable to rally American opinion around a militant policy and unable to obtain British support for an aggressive blockade, Roosevelt had few remaining options. About the only alternative left was to establish an officially backed, privately implemented "moral embargo" in the hope that this might either slow down or hinder Japan's adventurism on the Asian mainland. By denying Japan military equipment it needed from American suppliers, at least the quantities of such material would be reduced and Japan's war-making capacity toned down to that limited degree.

Many put a great deal of faith in such a policy. As early as the spring of 1937, Freda Utley published her *Japan's Feet of Clay*, in which she effectively argued that the Nipponese economy was so fragile that an economic embargo by the Western powers would force Japan to reverse any aggression that had been undertaken. This provided a philosophical framework within which private individuals and companies could individually act to undermine Japan's course in China, above and beyond any official demand of the United States government.[36]

Emotionally satisfying as such a policy would be, its ability to seriously alter Japan's battlefield success and war-making capacity was open to serious challenge. In the spring of 1939, one scholar publicly warned against putting too much faith in such a scenario: "[A] survey of Japan's economic horizon reveals many clouds. But I strongly doubt whether these difficulties, serious as they are, portend a speedy collapse of the war effort. It is remarkable on how little an individual can live when he is overtaken by misfortune. And a nation's economy, like an individual's, possesses more elasticity than one would suspect in advance."[37]

This writer also warned that any limitation of trade strong enough to have the chance of forcing a policy reversal was more likely to provoke a further expansionism to obtain the embargoed products:

> Sanctions, however, could not be applied safely without taking full measures for the protection of the Oriental possessions and dependencies of the participating Powers. For it is hardly likely that the Japanese Army and Navy would bow to economic pressure from other Powers and accept defeat without a struggle. It is far more probable that they would strike out desperately for the Netherlands Indies, French Indo-China, the Philippines, Malaya—any places within naval range which could provide the necessary iron, oil, rubber, tin. Economic sanctions cannot be considered a safe and easy halfway house between neutrality and war. Weak sanctions will scarcely prove effective: a nation keyed to war pitch will find means of evading or overcoming them. Strong sanctions, in all psychological probability, will lead to war.[38]

Even so, an embargo at least gave Americans the feeling of doing something to express pent-up frustration and indignation. In October 1937 the AFL-CIO endorsed a boycott of all products made in Japan.[39] Soon after the *Panay* attack in mid–December, over fifty American hosiery manufacturers shifted from utlizing silk to replacement substances. Four of the United States' largest retail chains (Woolworth, McCroy, Kress, and Kresge) also announced that they were no longer buying Japanese goods. (In 1939, these retailers backtracked slightly from their absolutist cutoff.)[40]

On June 11, 1938, Secretary of State Cordell Hull put the prestige of the United States behind a "private" cessation of sales abroad of offensive military aircraft. According to the official government summary of Hull's press conference, a correspondent opened the subject by inquiring about a report published that morning asserting that "the Secretary was considering some plan" to discourage aerial assaults. Part of this effort was reported to include "discouraging the sale of American bombing planes abroad."

The secretary responded by stressing the upcoming joint British-American investigation "of bombings in Spain." He went beyond this narrow context, however, and emphasized "that he was continuing to maintain" opposition to "the bombing of civilian populations or its material encouragement" in any part of the world. "He declared that he was saying this abroad and saying it at home to the American people and especially to the manufacturers of bombing planes."[41]

> A correspondent asked whether this meant that the Administration or the Government would frown on all future sales of American airplanes that could be used for bombing purposes or whether the Government would encourage them to pick their customers. The Secretary replied that his public statements condemning the bombing of civilian populations would discourage sales to regions where they would be used to bomb civilian populations.[42]

It is clear from the context that the bombings in Spain were considered, for public consumption at least, the straw that broke the camel's back and produced the decision to discourage the sale of bombers overseas. Although the policy was aimed primarily at Japan, the administration preferred to go out of its way to avoid admitting that the Japanese were the central target of the decision.

On July 1, the State Department's Office of Arms and Munitions Control sent out a letter to all manufacturers and exporters of aircraft and aircraft equipment to guarantee that none of them would be under any doubt of how seriously the department viewed its "request" that such items not be sold abroad:

> In view of the fact that the Secretary's statement definitely condemned bombing of civilian populations from the air, it should be clear to all concerned that the Government of the United States is strongly opposed to the sale of airplanes or aeronautical equipment which would materially aid or encourage that practice in any countries in any part of the world. Therefore, in view of this policy, the Department would with great regret issue any licenses authorizing exportation, direct or

indirect, of any aircraft, aircraft armament, aircraft engines, aircraft parts, aircraft accessories, aerial bombs or torpedoes to countries the armed forces of which are making use of airplanes for attack upon civilian populations.[43]

There seems in this statement to be the clear hint that a policy of at least calculated delay would greet any future effort to export such proscribed armaments. This impression is reinforced by the fact that it was "suggested" that any shipments required by preexisting contracts be clearly described as such when shippers requested the necessary export licenses.[44]

Although this approach lacked the clout of an openly imposed, official boycott, it provided the government a convenient shield of deniability: it was, after all, the individual companies who were making the decision to sell or not. The government had neither explicitly prohibited them from doing so nor prohibited the necessary licenses. And if any firm should attempt to defy both public and government opinion and exercise its freedom to sell offensive military weaponry, the licenses might, strangely enough, be inordinately delayed. Since procrastination is inevitable in even more efficient governments, how could the Japanese place inordinate blame on the American administration?

This element of deniability was clearly in isolationist Senator George W. Norris's mind when he endorsed the moral embargo: it combined retaliation for Japanese expansionism with the inability to pin explicit blame on the United States government. This would avoid the danger of American involvement in the Chinese conflict but "would result in Japan's being compelled to cease her warlike acts."[45]

Laying the Foundation for an Official Embargo

American ethical leaders were aroused by the injustices brought about by the war in China and cast their case for positive action in moral terms. In order to rally moral support, the administration leaders, who also viewed Japanese policy as fundamentally immoral, cast their own arguments in similar terms. Yet there were other issues that deeply annoyed the State Department and gave quite practical, down-to-earth reasons for opposing the spread of Japanese control.

Just as the United States had a pronounced economic self-interest in maintaining trade with Japan, it also had a strong self-interest in preserving unrestricted commerce with China. The first worked to discourage strong restrictive action, while the latter worked to encourage it. Japan's policies in the middle and late thirties convinced key policymakers that not only was Japan interested in military domination (if not outright control) of most or all of Asia, but it also desired to exercise that control in a way that would be extremely hostile to the commercial interests of the United States. This interpretation was already deeply ingrained prior to the bout of expansionism that began in 1937. For example, Secretary of State Hull summarized a summer 1936 conversation with the Japanese ambassador to Great Britain in which he laid great stress upon this perception:

> I told Mr. Yoshida that I would speak frankly but in the friendliest possible spirit and say that the impression among many persons in this country was that Japan sought absolute economic domination, first of eastern Asia, and then, of other portions as she might see fit; that this would mean political as well as military domination in the end; that the upshot of the entire movement would be to exclude countries like the United States from trading with all of those portions of China thus brought under the domination of controlling influence so-called of Japan; that this presented a serious question to first-class countries with commercial interests in every part of the world.[46]

A formal diplomatic note on December 30, 1938, again stressed the American disgruntlement with seeing its business firms being treated in a manner in defiance of past agreements and practices:

> With reference to such matters as exchange control, compulsory currency circulation, tariff revision, and monopolistic promotion in certain areas of China the plans and practices of the Japanese authorities imply an assumption on the part of those authorities that the Japanese Government or the regimes established and maintained in China by Japanese armed forces are entitled to act in China in a capacity such as flows from rights of sovereignty and further in so acting to disregard and even to declare nonexistent or abrogated the established rights and interests of other countries including the United States.
>
> The Government of the United States expresses its conviction that the restrictions and measures under reference not only are unjust and unwarranted but are counter to the provisions of several binding agreements, voluntarily entered into, to which both Japan and the United States, and in some cases other countries, are parties.[47]

In a perceptive analysis of the roots of the American-Japanese dispute over China, the United States State Department noted in an internal study of summer 1941 that economic competition and dramatically different world views were combining to drive the two nations further apart:

> The troubled relations between the two countries are due to two basically opposed points of view involving principles as well as self-interest, and the outlook for compromise or reconciliation is not bright.
>
> Briefly stated, Japan's aim is to create an economic empire in the Far East which will be self-sufficient and capable of resisting the application of sanctions by any power or group of powers. In other words, Japan looks forward to an economic order which will be independent of the British Empire or the United States. In pursuing this aim the Japanese have not had scruples in discarding or ignoring treaties, agreements and the established rights of third parties.
>
> The Far Eastern policy of the United States is based on two principles, the sanctity of treaties and the equality of economic opportunity in China. That of Japan, on the contrary, is to upset the status quo. As a result, American relations with Japan during the past two years have been characterized by a steadily increasing

pressure upon Japan. On July 26, 1939, without warning, the United States informed the Japanese Government of its intention to terminate the Treaty of Commerce and Navigation of 1911. This action constituted the first blow struck in defense of American policy. However, by a temporary arrangement, commercial relations remained as before, without benefit of treaty.[48]

The last three sentences refer to the next step of American escalation, which laid the foundation that would make legal and official the right to ban exports to Nippon. The imposition of such a policy would have violated the requirements of the 1911 Treaty of Commerce and Navigation between the two nations.

In April 1939, the chairman of the Senate Foreign Relations Committee publicly endorsed giving the president broadened authority to prohibit shipments to nations violating certain international agreements and engaging in warfare endangering American citizens. Because trade prohibitions would be inconsistent with the 1911 treaty, these could only be carried out by its abrogation. In July, Arthur H. Vandenberg, a leading Republican, specifically advocated the end of the agreement, which was almost three decades old.[49] These public pleas reinforced a policy drift already favored by what we today would call "hardliners" in the administration, such as the State Department's Stanley K. Hornbeck. Ambassador to Japan Joseph C. Grew, however, urged avoidance of such a step because it would increase the danger of war by strengthening the militarists inside the Tokyo governing structure.[50]

In July 1939, the government finally acted to revoke the long-standing pact. Publicly the administration insisted that the reason lay in the need to update the agreement. The announcement scrupulously avoided the slightest hint that it was retaliation for the Japanese policy in China.[51] No matter how the actual motive was obscured for public relations purposes, the six months required termination notice had been delivered. As Myra Wilkins rightly notes, "With the end of the treaty on January 26, 1940, the State Department could place actual—not only moral—embargoes on sales to Japan."[52]

During this moral embargo phase, there were already strong voices being raised that oil exports be included among the prohibited merchandise. A July 1941 internal State Department historical retrospective summarized the types of arguments that were made by the policy extension advocates:

> First, this step was favored as a punitive measure against Japan. Some persons believed that war, declared or undeclared, was from the point of view of international society unmoral except when waged in self-defense and that a responsibility existed on the part of all other nations to punish international lawbreakers. Other persons believed that, even apart from the wider interests of international society as a whole, Japan's acts in and against China were of such a character as to deserve punitive action by other nations.

> Second, this step was favored in the belief that it would result in the military collapse of Japan in the campaign in China.
>
> Third, this step was favored because of a conviction that the trade in a commodity which was the means of bringing death or suffering to a people fighting in self-defense was morally wrong and should not be tolerated under the conditions of modern warfare, a nation's entire economic, political and social life was directed to the prosecution of war and no moral distinction could be drawn between trade in petroleum products and trade in any other commodity with a country engaged in hostilities. Those who advocated the cutting off of oil shipments to Japan also in general favored non-involvement in the hostilities in the Far East.[53]

What several of these views held in common was the evaluation of petroleum as a nonviolent de facto military weapon that could be used against resented expansionism. To the extent that a potential foe regarded such a weapon as decisive, would he not regard it as irrelevant whether it was violent or not? Would he not regard it as unconsciencesable meddling in his affairs to a degree that (if feasible) a military response would be essential?

Opposition to the League of Nations and its internationalist policies, especially its inability to carry out a successful embargo, played a key role in justifying opposition to any similar American-initiated policy, according to State Department documents:

> By far the larger group of opinion in this country during the period in question was opposed to the cutting off of oil shipments to Japan by this Government. This opposition was in part due to the connection which many persons felt between such an embargo and the sanctions which formed a part of the system of the League of Nations. Aversion to any move by this country in the direction of collective security was strong in this country. Aversion to sanctions in particular was in general widespread. It was remarked that the sanctions applied by the League of Nations against Italy had not served to stop Italy's program of conquest in Ethiopia but had served to create a large measure of international ill-will to no purpose.[54]

The nation's traditional nonembargo policy was introduced as a strong historical precedent that should be set aside only if the strongest conceivable reasons existed. To carry out severe trade restrictions in the lack of such circumstances would only produce needless (and legitimate) outrage upon the part of Japan, with all the inherent dangers that such a confrontation would produce:

> Strong opposition to an oil embargo was also expressed on the ground that such a measure would be contrary to the established commercial policies of this Government and to the generally accepted principles of international law. This country, it was said, throughout its history had been the champion of the principles of freedom of international commerce and of non-discrimination in trade.
>
> So long as the United States possessed an ample supply of oil and so long as the United States was at peace with Japan it was held that the cutting-off of oil shipments in the absence of any treaty or agreement envisaging such an embargo would give Japan cause for legitimate complaint and retaliation. Retaliation would

lead to counter retaliation and to inflamed popular feeling with the end impossible to foresee. It was pointed out that not only did no treaty or agreement authorize our taking such measures against Japan but our treaty with Japan concluded in 1911 expressly precluded the imposition of such an embargo upon trade with Japan, and no justification in general was perceived for the giving of notice to Japan for a termination of the treaty at the period in question.[55]

In addition to taking into consideration such vigorous opposition arguments, the pragmatic problems connected with any petroleum cutoff weighed heavily upon the State Department. A successful embargo would require the full support of other major oil-producing nations. Without it, a ban on petroleum would inflict financial harm to American firms, enrich competitors abroad, and do nothing to change Japan's aggressive Asian policy.

NOTES

Japan's Expansionism in Asia

1. For a concise study of the war that provides due attention not just to the central action in Europe but also to subsidiary theaters such as the Far East, see Hanson W. Baldwin's *World War One* (New York: Grove, 1962).
2. Manny T. Koginos, *The Panay Incident: Prelude to War* (Lafayette, Ind.: Purdue University Studies, 1967), 2.
3. Ernest R. May discusses the limitation upon the accuracy of the reportage that came from Japan itself in his chapter "U.S. Press Coverage of Japan, 1931–1941," in *Pearl Harbor as History: Japanese-American Relations, 1931–1941*, ed. Dorothy Berg and Shumpei Okamoto (New York: Columbia University Press, 1973), 512–17.
4. John Hunter Boyle discusses the impossibility of totally accurate generalizations that would fit the entire decade in regard to pro- and anti-expansionist Army elements (*China and Japan at War, 1937–1945: The Politics of Collaboration* [Stanford, Calif.: Stanford University Press, 1972], 44).
5. For examples, see Edwin P. Hoyt, *Hirohito: The Emperor and the Man* (New York: Praeger, 1992), 110.
6. A major theme of Hoyt's book (note 5) is the effort of Hirohito to preserve peace while maintaining the traditional hands-off policy expected of emperors.
7. Jon Halliday, *A Political History of Japanese Capitalism* (New York: Pantheon Books, 1975), 129–30.
8. Major Kametaro Tominaga, "Warning Bell Peals in East" (text of speech), *Japan Times and Advertiser*, 18 September 1941 (Morning Edition), 6.

The Estrangement with the United States

9. George Gallup, "Public Would Risk War to Check Japan," *Richmond Times Dispatch*, 3 August 1941, IV-7; George Gallup, "Voters Approve Check on Japan," *New York Times*, 3 August 1941, I-20. Although these two published versions contain essentially the same text, the way the data are presented (tables versus summaries) and the order in which identical paragraphs are presented varies for unknown reasons. The Richmond paper is, visually, the better organized of the two.

10. Ibid.
11. *Watching the World*, ed. Mrs. Raymond Clapper (New York: McGraw-Hill/Whittlesey House, 1944), 277.
12. [Halifax, Lord, a.k.a. Edward Frederick Lindley Wood], *Confidential Dispatches: Analyses of America by the British Ambassador, 1939–1945* (Evanston, Ill.: New University Press, 1974), 33.
13. Gallup, "Public Would Risk War," IV-7.
14. Ibid.
15. The newspaper staff of *Asashi Shimbun* discusses the impact of such matters but conspicuously omits any discussion of the way the conduct of the Japanese army inflamed an already negative opinion of the conqueror (*The Pacific Rivals: A Japanese View of Japanese-American Relations* [New York: Weatherhill/Asashi, 1972; English translation, first edition, 1972], 86–87).
16. William L. Neumann, *America Encounters Japan: From Perry to MacArthur* (Baltimore: Johns Hopkins University Press, 1969), 258, notes the power of the ongoing press coverage to shape the image of Japan's conduct in China.
17. May, "U.S. Press Coverage," 522.
18. Ibid., 523.
19. Neumann, *America Encounters Japan*, 258.
20. Ibid.
21. For the text of the entire telegram, see "90. The Secretary of State to the Ambassador in Japan (Grew), Washington, September 2, 1937—2 p.m.," United States Department of State, *Peace and War: United States Foreign Policy, 1931–1941* (Washington, D.C.: United States Government Printing Office, 1943), 377–80; the quotation comes from 379. "All paraphrases" are by State Department.
22. "92. The Secretary of State to the Minister in Switzerland (Harrison) (Paraphrased), Washington, September 28, 1937—10 p.m.," in *Peace and War*, 380–83; quote comes from 381.
23. "93. Address Delivered by President Roosevelt at Chicago, October 5, 1937," in *Peace and War*, 384.
24. Koginos, *Panay Incident*, 29. A vivid collection of photographs taken during and after the attack is found between pages 38 and 39.
25. For a survey of American press reaction, see Koginos, *Panay Incident*, 31–38.
26. Koginos, *Panay Incident*, 54–76, 73, provides a detailed account of how the settlement was reached and an itemized listing of the compensation promised by Japan.

The Imposition of a "Moral Embargo"

27. For the entire text, see "83. 'Neutrality Act' of May 1, 1937," in *Peace and War*, 355–65.
28. Koginos, *Panay Incident*, 126.
29. Ibid., 11.
30. Ibid.
31. "93. Address Delivered by President Roosevelt at Chicago, October 5, 1937," *Peace and War*, 386. For entire text see 383–87.
32. Ibid., 386–87.
33. Sumner Welles, *Seven Decisions that Changed History* (New Yotk: Harper & Bros., 1950, 1951), 71–72. Welles' remarks on the subject are also found in an extract from the book published under the title "Roosevelt and the Far East," *Harpers* (February 1951): 29–30.
34. Koginos, *Panay Incident*, 75.
35. For a detailed study of the proposed blockade and why it was not imposed, see

John McVicker Haight, Jr., "Franklin D. Roosevelt and a Naval Quarantine of Japan," *Pacific Historical Review* 40 (May 1971): 203-26.
  36. Neumann, *America Encounters Japan*, 241.
  37. William Henry Chamberlain, "Japan at War," *Foreign Affairs* 17 (April 1939): 487.
  38. Ibid.
  39. Neumann, *America Encounters Japan*, 241.
  40. Mira Wilkins, "The Role of U.S. Business," in *Pearl Harbor As History*, 346.
  41. "Document 108. Memorandum of a Press Conference of the Secretary of State [Extract], June 11, 1938," in *Peace and War*, 421.
  42. Ibid.
  43. "Document 109. [Letter text] The Chief of the Office of Arms and Munitions Control (Green), Department of State, to One Hundred Forty-eight Persons and Companies Manufacturing Airplane Parts, Washington, July 1, 1938," *Peace and War*, 422.
  44. Ibid.
  45. Wayne S. Cole, *Roosevelt & the Isolationists, 1932-1945* (Lincoln: University of Nebraska Press, 1983), 346.

Laying the Foundation for an Official Embargo

  46. "72. Memorandum by the Secretary of State Regarding a Conversation with the Japanese Ambassador to Great Britain Yoshida, [Washington] June 12, 1936," in *Peace and War*, 319-20; for the entire memorandum, see 319-22.
  47. "123. The Ambassador in Japan (Grew) to the Japanese Minister for Foreign Affairs (Arita)," in *Peace and War*, 442; for the entire text, see 441-47.
  48. "Political Estimate, August 20, 1941," State Department document 894.00/1132, page 40. *Records of the U.S. Department of State Relating to the Internal Affairs of Japan, 1940-1944, Document File 894* (Scholarly Resources Microfilms).
  49. Norman A. Graebner, "Hoover, Roosevelt, and the Japanese," in *Pearl Harbor as History*, 42.
  50. Ibid.
  51. The incredible text of this bland and misleading notification amply verifies the cynical definition of a diplomat as "one who is sent abroad to lie for his country." For the text, see "Document 135: The Secretary of State to the Japanese Ambassador (Horinouchi) Washington, July 26, 1939," as reprinted in *Peace and War*, 475.
  52. Wilkins, "The Role of U.S. Business," in *Pearl Harbor as History*, 350.
  53. "Oil Shipments to Japan: A Survey of This Government's Policy, July 31, 1941," State Department document 894.24/1587, pages 8-9. *Records of the U.S. Department of State Relating to the Internal Affairs of Japan, 1940-1944, Document File 894* (Scholarly Resources Microfilms).
  54. Ibid., 9-10.
  55. Ibid., 10-11.

Chapter 2

THE SLAPS ON THE WRIST GROW STRONGER—1940

*Praise for the Moral Embargo
and Pleas for Yet Firmer Action*

The new year brought with it the continuation of the well-established, semiofficial moral embargo against the export of a number of items of direct military usefulness. The *Christian Century*, a major Protestant religious publication and a staunch supporter of the ban on offensive hardware, applauded its accomplishments early in 1940:

> The moral embargo is a complete success, where applied, in cutting off supplies from invading nations, yet it involves none of the political dangers implicit in an official, legal embargo. It is no more than an unwritten understanding that American exporters will not take orders to supply aggressor nations with certain goods. Yet the moral embargo has proved airtight.
>
> Not long ago, the outcry against American responsibility for China's suffering emphasized the part that American planes and American bombs and American shrapnel were playing in killing Chinese. That charge is not heard any more; the moral embargo has ended such exports. Of the $86,000,000 worth of arms, ammunition and implements of war shipped from the United States during January only airplane parts under an old contract to a total of $1,651 went to Japan.[1]

Based upon the precedent of this success, the magazine called for a major expansion of the restrictions: "If the moral embargo has done this in the case of munitions, it can do as much to control scrap iron, copper, cotton and airplane gasoline. It should be expanded to cover every important export item which is helping Japan to continue the war."[2]

Any believer in the reality and pervasiveness of human greed would find such heady optimism difficult to embrace. That some—or many—individuals could be convinced to follow such a course is comprehensible; to think that the vast majority would do so is something else again. Furthermore, it is one thing to utilize public pressure and indignation to prohibit a modest number of items; to expand the list dramatically would be to vastly increase the temptation to defy the policy, even if only in a discreet and cautious manner. Too many people's private and corporate self-interest would be threatened to make it a viable general and long-range policy.

This is not merely a matter of retrospective judgment. Even at the time, the alert reader of the press would have grasped the unwillingness of segments of American business to agree voluntarily to any further major limitation on their right to do business where and when they pleased. In mid–January, J. F. Pemberton, a spokesman for the oil industry, testified before Congress that during the preceding month in excess of 110,000 barrels of petroleum a day had been exported to Japan. This represented a substantial increase over the earlier figure of 77,000 barrels daily. Pemberton contended that it was "good business" to continue such exports. He denied that it was the responsibility of business to impose any restrictions; "it's up to the government to make changes in trade agreements."[3]

A number of months later, a business reporter for the *New York Times* noted that both the moral embargo and changed government policies had caused disgruntlement among commercial enterprises. These "developments of a fairly recent past . . . have been disturbing alike to United States merchants and foreign importers, including the Japanese."[4]

The pressure to procede further along the road to trade limitation flowed from the anti–Japanese sentiments we analyzed in Chapter 1. Reinforcing these emotions was the widely shared perception that it was time to upgrade dramatically both the quantity and quality of the American military capacity. From the outbreak of war in Europe in 1939 and throughout the calendar year of 1940, a very modest congressional majority (pushed on by a prointerventionist President Franklin D. Roosevelt) adopted various proposals to enlarge and strengthen the American forces. There were intense and bitter debates over their adoption because of the precedent they might be setting for future overt belligerent action. Out of the same sentiment, any measures that suggested help to Britain were even more bitterly opposed. The strengthening of American forces could be defended as an action of self-defense, but aid to Britain represented a commitment to one specific side in a highly dangerous European war. Opponents remembered all too well the allegations that the British had lied to try to draw the United States into World War I and how the munitions industry had pressured the administration into intervention to protect American investments on the Allied side. These opponents remembered that in less than two years of active involvement in the First World War, over a hundred thousand Americans had been killed and almost a quarter million wounded; they were passionate in their determination not to let it happen again.[5]

Saving the substantial pacifist element, many of these isolationists could at least abstractly concede the need for a clear-cut American superiority that could guarantee continental defense, and their attitude allowed those with wider aspirations to pick up key support for military expansion. The strongest supporters of an improved and strengthened national defense became more concerned during the year as to whether the nation possessed an adequate supply of raw materials and resources if the ultimate step of direct intervention in Europe finally occurred. Even within the more limited context of supplying the American military machine with all it needed short of such intervention, the specter of massive exports of war-related supplies raised the question of whether the United States was compromising its own defense capacity.

Hence the desire to punish Japan for her unrelenting expansionism was reinforced by the need to assure the United States an adequate reserve for her own rearmament programs and possible future military action. Even permitting the transhipment (through the United States) of vital minerals and ores was open to challenge upon the same grounds. Did not this nation need these resources far more than potential enemies?

The *Christian Century* article quoted at the beginning of this chapter was not the only influential source of pressure for strengthening the embargo. Although that publication desired to do so by adding items to the list of voluntarily prohibited exports, others sought to have the United States government openly enforce such an expanded agenda. As the new year began, many informed Americans were still discussing a mid–December radio program, "Town Meeting of the Hour" by Dr. Walter H. Judd. The *Reader's Digest* early 1940 reprint of an abridgment gave even wider circulation to what the publication called this "widely discussed radio broadcast." The long-term medical missionary to China emphasized that American resources had made possible the Japanese conquests on the Asian mainland. "Over 90 percent of Japan's scrap iron and steel and copper she gets from the United States. . . . Over 90 percent of Japan's aviation gasoline is American. An embargo on this item alone would practically stop the bombing of open cities which we so piously condemn." He insisted that this could be done with minimal risk since the probability of an embargo producing a war was "remote." Furthermore, "If she is having all she can do trying to defeat the Chinese with our assistance, just how would she defeat those same Chinese *and* the United States, without our assistance?"[6]

Such religious advocates of an official embargo also had their religious opponents. The *Christian Century*, though, conceded that "in opposing such an embargo we have probably gone counter to the views of a majority in the American churches."[7] The magazine was surely referring to the *leadership* of the various churches since their views have traditionally (and sometimes misleadingly) been taken to represent the dominant opinion of their membership.

Whether or not the *Christian Century*'s approach represented a minority view among the Protestant religious leadership of America, there were others quite willing to stand up for it. A written response to the article concurred in the magazine's approach. The correspondent argued that "an embargo would certainly" produce "reprisals" of some sort and, "to put it bluntly, Americans would not 'take anything' from the Japanese." Hence a cycle of counterreprisals would ensure that could hardly avoid escalating into outright armed conflict. In addition to such utilitarian objections, there were also moral difficulties in the proposed enhancement of the boycott. The writer contended that the call for such an extension did not seem "to be consistent with the Christian pacifism of those who advocate such action."[8]

While the public debated, the government bureaucracy slowly made concrete decisions. Although the revocation of the trade treaty with Japan went into effect in January 1940, the administration proceeded cautiously. In that same month, the Army-Navy Munitions Board compiled a list of twenty-nine vital materials essential to America's defense interests.[9] Even so, real teeth had not been put into any such lists. During the first half of the year, there was no official prohibition of friend or foe purchasing any amount of such materials that it desired. True, verbal arm-twisting could be utilized, but such tactics could not be guaranteed to work in all cases and might conceivably be embarrassing if brought to public attention.

During the first months of 1940, an energetic American Committee for Non-Participation in Japanese Aggression lobbied for strong restrictions on the large volume of trade still being carried out with that nation. Although proponents convinced a number of key congressmen to support such action, the secretary of state's influence prevented the legislation from emerging from committee. In late April, Hull informed the group that far more modest limitations were now acceptable to him. Far from pleased with his unwillingness to go as far as they wished, the organization still supported Hull's approach as the only feasible means to obtain any type of trade restriction legislation.

In May 1940, the triumphant advance of Hitler through Western Europe convinced the Congress that the president vitally needed explicit control over defense-related exports that could potentially harm this nation's own defense efforts. It was also recognized that this approach could be used as a method to covertly deny to potential enemies resources that were only "useful" to America rather than absolutely "essential." By casting the measure in broad terms, the administration was given maximum flexibility as well as maximum deniability, depending upon how energetically it chose to exercise its power.

House Resolution 9850 ("To Expedite the Strengthening of the National Defense") passed the House on May 24 by a vote of 392 to 2. The

Senate modified it to assure that petroleum supplies were clearly included within the presidents' prerogative. The congressional debate made it plain that the legislation was intended to permit the president to embargo a given item either to all countries or to whatever specific nations he deemed appropriate. Differences between the House and Senate versions were worked out in a joint committee and then passed without a recorded vote. (No isolationists are known to have opposed the measure.)[10]

On July 2 the president signed what was now known as the National Defense Act. This legislation was entirely permissive in nature. It did not exclude any product (including petroleum and scrap metal) from its provisions; on the other hand it did not require the president to include any item. It was all left to administrative action by the executive branch. The administration had a preliminary list ready to be announced the same day. Some forty types of war-related items were prohibited from exportation. The list, notably, omitted the two most explosive options, petroleum and scrap metal in general.[11]

Although this act was naturally publicized as a defensive measure to protect the United States, it invariably carried offensive overtones as well. Understandable as it was to restrict vital exports when the international situation was so intense, the very limiting of shipments built up the American military potential to act abroad while simultaneously denying other nations the opportunity to utilize those resources for their own commercial (or military) purpose. Justifiable as such a policy clearly was, it was the type of action that could only create foreboding in Japan about what lay in the future.

The Growing Pressure for Petroleum Exportation Limitations

Although petroleum and general scrap metal exports had not been initially limited, these were items that generated intense discussion within the White House and supporting bureaucratic agencies. Even those who might be expected to favor a strong prohibitive policy had severe misgivings. General George C. Marshall (chief of staff of the army) and Admiral Harold R. Stark (chief of naval operations) were convinced that the advocates of a total cutoff were making a severe error. Such an action would provoke a prompt Japanese invasion of Malaysia and the Dutch East Indies to gain replacement supplies. On this occasion, Sumner Welles also came out for moderation. "I opposed it because I believed that in a moment of such supreme danger to the United States as the summer of 1940 it was unwise to risk goading an already berserk Japanese Army into an attack upon an almost crippled Britain and an almost defenseless Netherlands that would probably involve the United States herself in war."[12] Although

Roosevelt supported the more militant approach at first, when he saw the intense opposition it had aroused among such members of the administration he backed away from his initial preference.

Even so, less extreme limitations came to be quickly adopted. In late July 1940, it was announced that aviation-grade oil exports to Japan would be curbed. On August 6, the prohibition of exporting aviation fuel to that nation was further clarified by defining it as being 87 octane or higher.[13] At the time, this appeared to be a very logical cutoff point. American planes normally utilized 100 octane fuel and defining the substance at a substantially lower level seemed to guarantee that the petroleum most useful for Japanese civilian and military aviation would be retained in North America.

In an apparent measure to protect against the negative consequences of the fuel curb that was under debate, in mid–July Japan flooded the commercial market with orders for tons of lubricating oil (for aircraft use) and 17 million gallons of aviation-grade fuel. Virtually every significant seller of petroleum products in the United States received purchase orders seeking prompt delivery.[14] Although this was a natural self-protective action, it also revealed the vulnerability of the United States to runs on one of its most precious resources.

The rationale for banning aviation gas, asserted the Undersecretary of State Sumner Welles, was to assure America's own supply. The increasing exports, the State Department asserted, justified the restriction of aviation gas shipments to the Western Hemisphere.[15]

Figures reported on August 3, 1940, by Dr. B. B. Sayers, director of the Bureau of Mines, indicated that available supplies of petroleum provided a modest six months reserve. Sayers' official figures allowed one to argue for or against the government position.[16] In May 1940 his data had indicated that the United States produced 940,000 barrels of petroleum. Of this, 44.1% was exported to various foreign destinations, 48.4% was consumed domestically, and the remainder built up the national reserve. In contrast, in October 1939, 33.4% went abroad. On the other side of the coin, however, "the total [exported] for the first five months of this year [1940] was 1,246,000 barrels, 42 percent lower than in the same period last year." Furthermore, the American reserve had increased more than fifty percent, from 2,400,000 barrels in October 1939 to 3,942,000 barrels in May 1940, the latter representing the six-month reserve Sayers had pointed to. Computing the percentages based upon the report's figures (Table 2.1), Japan's percentage of the total exports was surprisingly modest even though it was the object of the most concern.

What American officialdom was apparently unaware of was that Japanese planes could commonly run on the still unrestricted 86 octane. The fact that additives could be utilized to increase the octane rating permitted

Table 2.1. Selected American Petroleum Exports: May 1940

	Barrels	Percentage
Japan	29,000	7.0
France	152,000	36.6
United Kingdom	148,000	35.7
Other European	7,000	1.7
W. Hemisphere	28,000	6.7
Other countries	51,000	12.3
Total	415,000	100.0

Source: Calculated from government data provided by Bertram D. Hulen, "Washington Gets Tokyo Complaint," *New York Times*, 4 August 1940, 19.

even lower octane products to be utilized for aviation. The Americans had at least some inkling of this danger, though they underestimated its seriousness, because the July 26 prohibitions included the exportation of tetraethyl lead, which was vital to the enhancing process.[17]

It did not take long for officials to suspect that they had left open a far bigger loophole in their regulations than they had imagined. On August 14, 1940, "numerous officials" of the Tidewater Associated Oil Companies and Standard Oil held a conference with cabinet secretaries Knox, Ickes, and Morgenthau in which they provided detailed information concerning "the location of refineries in Japan and other foreign countries." In addition to discussing non–American sources of petroleum that Japan might utilize, the company representatives noted that the official ban on selling aviation gasoline would obviously be circumvented. The only question was how difficult it would be. As Morgenthau summarized in a memorandum sent to the president: "The Japanese will probably be able to make most of their aviation gasoline if they can obtain tetraethyl lead. They may be able to purchase tetraethyl lead (which is produced in England, France, Germany, Italy, Mexico, U.S.S.R.) or may be able to make it. Both Standard Oil and Tidewater officials believe that Japan can make tetraethyl, though the experts disagree as to the difficulty involved."[18]

Japan was also attempting another means of carrying out an end run around the recent prohibition. The director of naval intelligence addressed a memorandum to the chief of naval operations on August 26, 1940, pointing to the fact that Japan was negotiating to purchase a "special blend of crude" from the United States sources. Although this blend was "rated at 89 octane," it was technically not aviation fuel and therefore was exempt from the recent restrictions. This fuel would also be enhanced for plane use. "It is contemplated that by suitable leading of this special blend with ethyl, practically all Japanese requirements for high octane fuel can be met regardless of export control."[19]

Publicly, the government pleaded surprise when the capacity of Japan to engage in such upgrading was publicly reported in a *New York Times* dispatch of August 30. According to a slightly later statement by an unidentified official, this was the first the government became aware of Nippon possessing this ability. Perhaps out of embarrassment either at the existence of the loophole or the publication of its existence, the informant "refused ... to reveal how much gasoline has been shipped from this country to Japan since the licensing regulations became effective."[20]

In early October, the same publication reported that it had again confirmed examples of lower grade products being shipped to Japan. "This lower grade aviation gasoline can be stepped up by the Japanese into a higher grade airplane fuel, but it is a very expensive process and the resultant fuel is still inferior."[21]

Joseph G. Utley notes that, "Japan was able to buy 550 percent more 86-octane 'aviation' fuel during the five months following the embargo than during the five months preceding it."[22] Waldo Heinrichs presents the data in an even more impressive form:

> In the ten months after the aviation-gas embargo the Japanese took away almost four times as much gasoline as they had taken in 1939 and almost three times as much lubricating fluid. Five million licensed gallons awaited shipment. Two million more gallons had been applied for [at the time of the total fuel embargo the following year]. Shipments from California in May [1941] were the highest in ten months—over two million barrels—on account of a coincidence in tanker sailings, according to the board chairman of Stavac.[23]

As is so often the case, statistics can be read two ways. In such citations as these, the impression is left that exports were mushrooming in spite of governmental restrictions, which is, indeed, a partial truth. This impression among American observers spread far and wide and increased the demand for sterner action. The rest of the statistical story will be examined in our chapter on the effects of the petroleum restrictions: there were strong contradictory trends at work by the spring of 1941 that paint a considerably different picture than the export increase data we have examined. The important thing to note in the current context is that there "were" increases in the short term (fall and winter 1940) and that these increases bred stringent demands that the pattern be reversed.

Especially in the early months after the restrictions were imposed, it was natural for those in the know to ask, "Where is the boycott?" In a naval intelligence report submitted to the director of naval intelligence under the date of November 2, 1940, it was noted that Commerce Department figures indicated that though the export volume of aviation gasoline had decreased from 40,938 barrels (July) to only 8,540 (in August), that it had promptly skyrocketed to 115,051 barrels one month later (in September). In a situation reminding one of medieval Jesuits splitting theological hairs, the amount of aviation petroleum had both increased *and* decreased, according to whose definition of terms was accepted: "The Division of Controls (State Department) informs us that while the Commerce Department figures are accurate they are based upon the presumption that any gasoline suitable for use or actually used in aeroplanes is 'aviation' gasoline; the Controls Office uses a stricter definition in terms of octane count."[24]

The report went on to concede that much Japanese-bound petroleum was being upgraded upon receipt but that for political reasons the Division of Controls was believed to prefer to ignore the fact,

> It is recognized in that office [of the Commerce Department] that a *very large proportion* of the gasoline now being sent to Japan is actually used in planes and can be stepped up by "boosters" to high octane count. It is also stated that the question is essentially political insofar as the Controls Office is under instructions, following a lenient policy designed to appease Japan and relieve the Netherlands East Indies of pressure. [emphasis added][25]

The ironies inherent in the July limitations did not escape the notice of those pleading for a more comprehensive ban. Within a few weeks, one liberal periodical was noting: "The new oil ban does not apply to gasoline for tanks, trucks, and passenger cars. As the situation stands, we refuse to supply the Japanese with planes and aviation gas to bomb the Chinese, but we continue to supply them with steel and machine tools to make the planes and with at least part of the chemicals for the bombs. We hope the Chinese appreciate these fine distinctions."[26] The following spring, the same periodical noted that even from the military standpoint, the exclusion solely of aviation fuel made little sense: "It is unfortunate that public attention has been centered on aviation gas, for war with Japan would be a naval war, and fuel oil runs battelships."[27]

An unintentional side of effect of the European war prevented the short-term outflow of petroleum from becoming even worse during the fall and winter. During that period, Japan was faced with the inability to obtain tanker capacity for all the petroleum it could still legally purchase. As of June 30, 1939, there were some 1,731 tankers in the world (defined as a vessel of one thousand or more gross tons). Of these tankers, 24.3% were American flag, 25.1% British Empire (including Canada and the dominions). In bleak contrast, Japan had only forty-seven tankers in its entire maritime fleet.[28] After the European war broke out in the fall of 1939, Italian and German merchantmen were no longer entering the Pacific, so that important potential source of assistance was quickly denied to the Nipponese economy.

Rising Asian tensions and the desire to please the United States naturally inclined the British toward severely limiting Japan's access to empire shipping. The intensity of the submarine warfare in the Atlantic removed all doubts and left Britain with no realistic option but to concentrate all its own shipping in that nearer ocean. Although that did not mean that all of the dominions completely followed suit, it still permanently removed substantial shipping capacity that was irreplaceable from any source.[29] So desperate were the Japanese to overcome their fuel shipping difficulties that by the summer of 1941 at least three whale oil ships/factories had been converted into petroleum-carrying vessels.[30]

Even the limited fuel ban of summer 1940 convinced the Pacific fleet commander-in-chief, James O. Richardson, that a major step had been taken toward war and that this had been done without the American citizenry being aware of the significance of what had happened. As he wrote many years later, after his retirement

> On July 26, the President put aviation gasoline and certain classes of scrap iron on the control list. This further decreased the possibility of any amicable settlement with the Japanese. This embargo action seemed to me a good indication that the political leaders in the United States were more and more intent on war with Japan, unless Japan was willing to back down pretty completely. I did not believe that the people of the United States were being prepared for this contingency.[31]

Increasing Support for Scrap Export Limitations

Another vital concern of Japan (for both economic and military reasons) was the continued flow of an ample supply of scrap metal. A U.S. government survey of foreign economic developments covering 1939 and the first part of 1940 drew attention to already existing Japanese problems in this area:

> Although production in the iron and steel industry reached a record level, the supply of iron and steel materials was admittedly short throughout the year—a factor partly responsible for the slow progress in expanding other industries. Shortage of steel for building purposes held up the construction of many projected factories and workshops, while the lack of adequate quantities of special steel greatly restricted activities in the machine tool, automobile, and metal manufactures industries.[32]

The report referred to the "fear of a cessation of scrap-iron imports from the United States." It noted that the Japanese government was implementing various measures to minimize the impact, including centralized control over the distribution of scrap metals.[33]

The law that permitted the president to ban defense-related exports partially or completely also established the National Defense Advisory Commission (NDAC) to provide expert nongovernment advice on such matters. The executive secretary of the American Iron and Steel Institute,

Walter S. Tower, was responsible for providing expert insight to NDAC in regard to the resources required to maintain and expand steel manufacture.[34] After the establishment of the NDAC, Tower pushed for strict regulatory controls on all scrap metal exports so that the government could quickly move from regulation to prohibition when the crunch between resources and needed output finally arrived. Since there was not yet any domestic scarcity of scrap metal, it was decided, however, that any action on his request for comprehensive regulation should be postponed.

Even so, at the end of July a more limited ban was adopted which applied only to "heavy melting scrap," the top grade of steel and iron scrap.[35] Although this ban certainly hindered Japan, it increased its low- and medium-grade imports to compensate for part of the loss. Other factors that came into play were pointed out by a close student of British wartime economic embargoes: "The restriction on the export of iron and steel scrap did not affect [Japan] seriously. She was already buying less of these products than in 1939, for she found it cheaper to buy steel ingots and rolled products; as the ban of 26th July concerned only the highest grade of scrap she proceeded to increase her purchases of other iron and steel products."[36]

It was also possible to nibble away at the edge of the prohibition without engaging in an open repudiation of the restrictions. A business commentator was quick to point out this danger of abuse shortly after the restrictions went into effect: "The joker in our present dispositions is that only a hairbreadth divides the description of No. 1 [prohibited] and No. 2 [permitted] scrap steel. Indeed, there is almost always a quantity of first-grade scrap in each shipment of the second quality. Dealers will wink more and more at a rising percentage of the higher grade if the price received for No. 2 scrap is adequate, some observers contend."[37]

Greater vigilance could eliminate some such scheming, and old-fashioned patriotism (or anti-Japanese bias) might hold it down even more. Yet the total suppression of such schemes (barring overt war) would seem to have been an impossible ideal. And by their very nature, any successful efforts to dodge the regulations would be unlikely to come to public attention. This type of potential dodging was permitted to exist for only a few months and was eliminated by later, broader prohibitions (see below).

In the middle of August, the crunch between needed output and available resource input proved Tower's warnings to have been valid. In spite of the difficult situation, the government remained divided about what policy to pursue. The State Department was grudgingly willing to proceed with a proposed total prohibition only if it were absolutely certain that this was essential to maintain the American defense programs. Henry Morgenthau, Jr., secretary of the Treasury, had no such reservations and pushed for immediate adoption. The steel industry found itself squeezed between government pressure to keep down the price of steel and a declining supply of scrap that pushed the price upwards. Faced with that harsh dilemma, the industry shifted to support of Tower's regulatory approach.

Although there was growing support for more comprehensive restrictions (from both within and outside the government), Roosevelt retained reservations about the wisdom of the approach. A wider ban was also held up by the necessity to draft detailed implementing regulations. These then had to be modified to protect British and Canadian access to American scrap while excluding the Japanese. At that point Secretary of State Hull thought it prudent to postpone temporarily further discussion.

On September 13 the president issued a proclamation requiring the obtaining of a federal license to export any equipment that could be used either to make plane engines or to process aviation fuel. Roosevelt attempted to impose an information embargo as well by prohibiting the sending abroad (without license) of any plans not "available to the general public" that showed how to construct equipment to refine petroleum. A similar prohibition was applied to "descriptive or technical information" not available to the general public which set "forth the design or construction of aircraft or aircraft engines."[38]

Both the president and government spokesmen defended the order on grounds of meeting the nation's defense needs. The Japanese government promptly protested but to no avail. Since Roosevelt's pro–British convictions were obvious, reporters concluded that the measure was not intended to apply to Great Britain. Application to countries in South America seemed unlikely because of the administration's continuing encouragement to them to join "in a program of rearmament of hemispheric defense." By this process of elimination, a reporter concluded, "it appeared that the new order ... is aimed almost exclusively at Japan, the only other major market for aviation equipment and special gasoline whose lines of communication have not been severed by the European war."[39]

Japanese Pro-Axis Tilt and Occupation of Northern Indochina Encourages an Intensification of American Trade Restrictions

With the occupation of the northern part of what is today Vietnam on September 23, 1940, Hull dropped his rearguard opposition to eliminating scrap exports to Japan. Although the occupation provided the immediate excuse and justification, the total ban represented a policy that had already been much debated and would already have been in place without Hull's continuing skepticism.

In one sense the delay had proved useful. If this measure had been put in place at an earlier date, the American government would have been confronted with the very real dilemma of what further action to take to express its displeasure at the most recent territorial expansion. A divided executive branch had adopted the total scrap prohibition only after vigorous internal debate and prolonged division. To have been forced to face yet another round of internal confrontation would only have damaged administration morale and delayed the adoption of any definitive reaction. Because of past delays, the government had in existence a viable policy, ready at hand, by which to show its intense displeasure without having to resort to even more extremely controversial measures.

In mid–January of the following year, a business correspondent reviewed the success of the measure and noted how additional limitations had made the impact even greater:

> Shipments of scrap steel, pig iron and steel ingots to Japan fell in November to nominal proportions—4,700 tons, as against 162,000 in October. A scrap embargo had supposedly been put into effect last Summer, but affected only the No. 1 or top grade. Consequently, Japanese purchases not only were not reduced, they were actually expanded sharply in anticipation of more drastic action by the United States.
>
> On October 16, however, the ban was extended to all types of scrap, November being the first full month in which it was effective. On December 31 it was further extended to cover steel ingots and virtually all other iron and steel products, which will preclude a possible shift of Japanese purchases to formerly non-embargoed steel products.[40]

Only a few days after the move into northern Vietnam, the Tripartite Pact was signed between Germany, Italy, and Japan. According to its provisions, if the United States undertook military action against any of the signatories, all three were obligated to oppose her. It was a psychological warfare measure intended to place maximum pressure upon the United States to remain outside the existing conflicts and to impose the greatest potential risks if it elected not to do so.

It should be stressed that this treaty, according to the actual wording of its terms, was a defensive alliance. It only guaranteed intervention if one of the three powers was the target of assault. It provided no pledge of intervention if a signatory were the *initiator* of the conflict, but such intervention was surely intended by the Nazi regime when it negotiated the pact. Since the Russo-German conflict fell outside the terms of the agreement, however, Japan was fully justified when it declined to become militarily involved, no matter how much it irritated its German colleagues.

Since the United States was the obvious (though unnamed) target of the Tripartite Pact, it further angered American opponents of the three signatories. At the very time those opposed to escalating the war of nerves with Japan direly needed some token of peaceful intentions, the signing of the covenant escalated the hostility level.

At the cabinet meeting of September 27, Secretary of the Navy Frank Knox in effect called for striking at the economic Achilles heel of the

Japanese: he proposed lowering to a mere 67 octane the permitted octane level of exports. Hull managed to postpone action, however.[41]

Assistant Secretary of State Breckinridge Long expressed deep worry in his diary entry of September 28, 1940, that the United States was locked in a cycle of action and counteraction that would result in a war before the United States was ready to fight. Others might look at Hull's efforts to delay drastic action; Long pointed to the actions he had approved:

> Cordell had his way. The Morgenthau activity in re: China vs. Russia is out and we have a direct loan to China—twenty-five million. The next day we announced an embargo on scrap iron and steel. Each measure directed against Japan. The next day, which was yesterday, Japan signed the axis with Germany and Italy, warning us. And so we go—more and more—farther and farther along the road to war. But we are not ready to fight any war now—to say nothing of a war on two oceans at once—and that is what the Berlin-Rome-Tokyo agreement means. Nor will we be ready to fight any war for eighteen months in the future.[42]

This was not quite as tit-for-tat as the chronology would indicate since each measure had been "in the works" for a period prior to its announcement. Yet the quick succession of measures, one after another, certainly encouraged such a public perception, and unquestionably, each was a reaction to the general hostility of the other side even if not, strictly speaking, a reaction to what had most recently been done.

The August 1940 issue of *Amerasia* had carried a historical justification for trade limitation in an article entitled: "A Bit of American History—[A] Successful Embargo Against Japan in 1918." It began by stressing the relative weakness of Japan as a protection against any serious retaliatory action: "Advocates of the embargo have repeatedly pointed out that if Japan, with large-scale American aid, is unable to conquer a country far weaker than herself, she is not likely to challenge a strong power like the United States once that aid has been removed."[43] The article also reviewed a 1918 case of economic arm-twisting in which the United States threatened to ban cotton exports to Japan and silk imports from it. This resulted in the Japanese reversing their military policy in Siberia in accordance with American demands. After reciting the details of the case, the article's author conceded:

> The situation today is, of course, very different from that of the autumn of 1918. Japan is a far stronger military power and her ruling class, both military and civilian, are thoroughly committed to a program of forceful expansion on the continent. Moreover, Japanese confidence and morale have been strengthened by the successes of her fellow-aggressors in Europe.
>
> But the United States, too, is far stronger than in 1918 and, which is even more important, Japan is today far more dependent upon American supplies for the continued functioning of her war industries. She no longer has alternative sources from which to secure sufficient quantities of iron and steel products, machine tools, oil, etc. In half a dozen key commodities, Japan is dependent upon the United States for the greater portion of her imports.[44]

At the October 4 cabinet meeting, Secretary of War Henry I. Stimson used this article to reinforce the proembargo case. He circulated copies of the article to all participants as evidence that the policy was both feasible and enjoyed the probability of accomplishing its goal.

In spite of such pressure, Hull was able to limit action to the calling up of military reserves and the strengthening of the fleet at Pearl Harbor. The strongest cabinet hawks of the day (Knox, Stimson, Ickes, and Morgenthau) failed in their efforts to push through stronger action. They were also unsuccessful in their pleas for saber rattling via special navy maneuvers carried out in Pacific waters.[45]

Hull's continued opposition was strictly utilitarian; despite the fervent pleas of their proponents, he didn't believe that the suggested measures were adequate to force a Japanese policy reversal. Hence they were doomed to failure. On the other hand, measures that *were* strong enough to accomplish their goal would likely result in war. In such a no-win situation, he preferred caution to bravado.

Although Hull generally kept his tongue under tight control, his personal anger was great at Japanese adventurism on the Asian continent. He provided some indication of the depth of his irritation during an October 1940 discussion with the Japanese ambassador. The ambassador protested the American scrap embargo as both a violation of Japan's rights and an unfriendly act. Hull immediately pointed out that Japan was acting in the same way it complained of: "Apparently the theory of the Japanese Government is for all other nations to acquiesce cheerfully in all injuries inflicted upon their citizens by the Japanese policy of force and conquest, accompanied by every sort of violence, unless they are to run the risk of being guilty of an unfriendly act."[46]

During early October, Roosevelt considered an extremely explosive set of options to deal with the Japanese. The commander-in-chief of the U.S. fleet, J. O. Richardson, briefed the commander-in-chief of the Asiatic fleet as to what was under consideration:

> During the recent visit of the Commander-in-Chief, U.S. Fleet, to Washington and on October 10, the Secretary [of the Navy] told the Commander-in-Chief that the President was considering, in connection with possible retaliatory measures taken by Japan against Great Britain upon opening of the Burma Road, the following:
> (a) Reinforcement of the Asiatic Fleet, as a peacetime move.
> (b) Declaring a complete embargo on shipments to and from Japan.
> (c) Attempting to stop *all* [Richardson's emphasis] trade between Japan and the Americas. To accomplish this latter measure, he proposed establishment of patrol lines of light forces from Honolulu westward to the Philippines and a second line roughly from Samoa to Singapore, "in support of" the first line.[47]

Admiral Richardson noted that he informed the secretary of the navy of "the impracticability of this and other suggestions." In response to such recommendations, Richardson submitted his own proposals to interdict Japanese–western hemisphere trading. In his attached list of "assumptions" on which his own scenario was based, he included a blunt warning of the possible consequences of adopting such a forceful policy: "The United States is prepared to accept war if the measures taken cause Japan to declare war."[48]

The president backed off from these extreme actions. Even so, before the year came to a close, zinc, copper, and nickel were added to the list of items for which the Japanese had to obtain specific licenses for each and every shipment. Hull continued to slow down the expansion of the restricted and banned lists out of fear that the Japanese might be incited to an even more expansionist policy than in the past.

NOTES

Praise for the Moral Embargo and Pleas for Firmer Action

1. "Shall We Embargo Japan?" *Christian Century*, 28 February 1940, 270–71.
2. Ibid., 271.
3. United Press, "Oil Supply Near Exhaustion, Expert Says; Shipments to Warring Nations Recounted," *New York Times*, 18 January 1940, 11. The headline was misleading. Pemberton testified that there was an eight-year known reserve, but that improvements in drilling plus the discovery of new fields would remedy the situation.
4. Kenneth L. Austin, "U.S. Export Policy Called Confusing," *New York Times*, 4 August 1940, III-1.
5. Hanson W. Baldwin, *World War One* (New York: Grove, 1962), 156–58, provides comparative losses for the nations involved in the war.
6. Walter H. Judd, "Let's Stop Arming Japan!" *Reader's Digest*, February 1940, 41–44.
7. "Shall We Embargo Japan?" 270.
8. Letter of Hugh Vernon White, "Embargoes and War," *Christian Century*, 13 March 1940, 356. Our interpretation of the reference to the "majority in the American churches" as meaning the "majority of leaders" would seem to be confirmed by White's later admission that he is discussing the topic within that context of "the Christian leaders who are urging the embargo."
9. Jonathan G. Utley, *Going to War with Japan, 1937–1941* (Knoxville: University of Tennessee Press, 1985), 93–95, provides a description of how these restrictions gained legal sanction. Also see 93–118 for a detailing of the ongoing policital strife that divided the administration as to what further trade limitations, if any, should be adopted. Unless specifically noted, all other references to "Utley" refer to this work.
10. This does not mean, of course, that they endorsed the war making potential of the legislation.
11. Jonathan G. Utley, *Going to War with Japan*, p. 95.

The Growing Pressure for Petroleum Export Limitations

12. Sumner Welles, *Seven Decisions That Changed History* (New York: Harper & Bros., 1950, 1951), 33.

13. The official government definition of prohibited petroleum referred to "high octane gasolines, hydrocarbons, and hydrocarbon mixtures (including crude oils) boiling between 75 degrees and 350 degrees F. which with the addition of tetraethyl lead up to a total content of 3 cc per gallon will exceed 87 octane number of the Astm Knock test method" (as quoted in "Embargo on Exports of Gasoline Still Holds," *New York Times*, 29 August 1940, 29). Presumably "87" was a typographical error by the newspaper since the cutoff began at that point rather than at any figure that "exceed[ed]" it. The original definition had been so broadly worded that 90% of all exports would have been eliminated, far beyond anything then acceptable to the president. By early August a more restricted definition had been adopted that restored the intent of targeting aviation-quality fuel. (For a discussion of this, see Jonathan C. Utley, "Upstairs, Downstairs at Foggy Bottom: Oil Exports and Japan, 1940–1941," *Prologue: The Journal of the National Archives* 8 (Spring 1976): 17–28, especially 19–21.

14. W. N. Medlicott, *The Economic Blockade*, 2 vols., vol. 7 and 8 of the *History of the Second World War*, United Kingdom Civil Series, edited by W. Keith Hancock (London: H.M.S.O., 1952; revised edition including confidential source references, London: H.M.S.O./Nendeln, Liechtenstein: Kraus Reprint, 1978), 1:480.

15. Bertram D. Hulen, "Washington Gets Tokyo Complaint," *New York Times*, 4 August 1940, 19.

16. Except for the percentages quoted by the reporter in the Hulen article above, all percentages are calculated from the data he summarizes from the government report, as are the statistics in Table 2.1.

17. For text of the prohibition, see Medlicott, *Economic Blockade*, 1:479.

18. [Henry Morgenthau, Jr.], Internal Security Subcommittee of the Committee on the Judiciary, United States Senate, *Morgenthau Diary (China)* (Washington, D.C.: U.S. Government Printing Office, 1965), 1:194. The original diaries consist of hundreds of volumes of letters, memorandums, reports, etc.; those editing this volume selected those materials most related to China. Hence they include a number of documents related to Japan as well. All citations given as coming from the *Diary* refer to volume 1 of this government document.

19. Quoted by James H. Herzog, in "Influence of the United States Navy in the Embargo of Oil to Japan, 1940–1941," *Pacific Historical Review* 35 (August 1966): 320.

20. "Weighs Tightening Gasoline Embargo," *New York Times*, 8 September 1940, 24.

21. "Japan Still Gets Gasoline from U.S." *New York Times*, 9 October 1940, 6.

22. Utley, *Going to War*, 100.

23. Waldo Heinrichs, *Threshold of War: Franklin D. Roosevelt and American Entry into World War II* (New York: Oxford University Press, 1988), 133.

24. Herzog, "Influence of U.S. Navy," 323.

25. Ibid.

26. "Embargo with Loopholes," *Nation*, 10 August 1940, 105.

27. I. F. Stone, "Oil Is Still Neutral," *Nation*, 1 March 1941, 231.

28. For the figures from which the percentages are computed, see "Table 25. World Tanker Fleet, by Countries, June 30, 1939," as compiled by the "U.S. Maritime Commission, from Lloyd's Register," reprinted in Leonard M. Fanning, *American Oil Operations Abroad* (New York: McGraw-Hill, 1947), 234.

29. Irvin H. Anderson, Jr., *The Standard-Vacuum Oil Company and United States East Asian Policy, 1933–1941* (Princeton: Princeton University Press, 1975), 155. The

"Stavac" referred to in extract on page 33 alludes to the oil company discussed in this volume.

30. "An End to Appeasing Japan?" editorial, *Roanoke* (Virginia) *World-News* as reprinted in the *Richmond* (Virginia) *Times Dispatch*, 27 July 1941, IV-6. The article lists the names of recent vessels carrying oil from the United States and provides further information about a few of them.

31. *On the Treadmill to Pearl Harbor: The Memoirs of Admiral James D. Richardson* (Washington, D.C.: U.S. Government Printing Office, 1973), 389.

Increasing Support for Scrap Export Limitations

32. U.S. Department of Commerce, *Economic Review of Foreign Countries: 1939 and Early 1940*, Economic Series No. 9 (Washington: U.S. Government Printing Office, 1941), 312.

33. Ibid., 312–13.

34. For Tower and his efforts in behalf of limiting scrap exports, see Utley, *Going to War*, 106–7.

35. W. N. Medlicott, *Economic Blockade*, 1:479.

36. Ibid, 1:479–80.

37. Kenneth L. Austin, "U.S. Export Policy Called Confusing," *New York Times*, 4 August 1940, III-1.

38. Charles Hurd, "Aircraft Embargo Adds More Items," *New York Times*, 4 September 1940, 8.

39. Ibid.

Japanese Pro-Axis Tilt and Occupation of Northern Indochina Encourage Intensification of American Trade Restrictions

40. Winthrop W. Case, "Demands of War Shown in Exports," *New York Times*, 19 January 1941, III-1.

41. Utley, *Going to War*, 108.

42. *The War Diary of Breckinridge Long: Selections from the Years 1939–1944*, ed. Fred L. Israel (Lincoln: University of Nebraska Press, 1966), 132.

43. The *Morgenthau Diary*, 235–38, contains the complete text; in the unedited diaries, it is on 319:1–4.

44. *Morgenthau Diary*, 238.

45. Utley, *Going to War*, 108–9, provides a discussion of the meeting.

46. Ibid., 109.

47. Photographic reproduction in *Pearl Harbor Attack: Hearings Before the Joint Committee on the Investigation of the Pearl Harbor Attack* (Washington: U.S. Government Printing Office, 1946), 14/1006). The other government investigations we cite in this volume were reprinted as part of the joint congressional committee's report. The specific investigation cited from is indicated in the body of the text except when documents rather than testimony is referred to. The entire thirty-nine volumes are abbreviated as *PHA* (Pearl Harbor Attack), followed by the volume number, slash, and page number(s). The page numbers do not continue in consecutive order throughout the set; hence the volume number is essential.

48. *PHA* 14/1012.

Chapter 3
BUILDUP TO CONFRONTATION: JANUARY TO JULY 1941

Hidden Petroleum Export Curbs

In January, two major exporters of petroleum to Japan, Stanvac and Shell, were contacted by Japanese officials and offered the opportunity to increase substantially the volume of oil they were shipping. Not wishing to run afoul of American policy, these companies contacted Dr. Stanley K. Hornbeck, a State Department expert on Far Eastern affairs. Hornbeck sounded out other government officials to discuss what position they should take on the proposal. After hearing their suggestions, Hornbeck recommended to the companies that since they had traditionally sought Japanese permission for such an expansion of their market, that they should accept the offer and then conveniently find it impossible to lay their hands on the tankers to meet their commitment. This way the end result would be the same, but the United States government would be spared the need to take formal prohibitive action and the companies would be protected from Japanese retaliation on their foreign investments.[1]

During sessions with Stanvac and Shell executives, Dr. Hornbeck discovered that in a desperate effort to increase the volume of production reaching it, Japan was routinely putting fuel in metal drums to be stored aboard regular freighters. On February 4, President Roosevelt issued a proclamation that applied the export license requirement to sending metal containers abroad. As written, the proclamation could have been interpreted to prohibit exporting even empty canisters of any size that had the capacity to contain oil. On February 13, the administrator of export control issued a modification of the requirement that limited its application to containers with a capacity of five gallons or more. It was truthfully (though disingenuously) stressed that this was not an embargo on petroleum products but only on the containers used to ship such products.[2] On a more credible level, this new limitation fit in well with existing self-protective restrictions. These were steel products and the navy was genuinely concerned to assure itself of ample supplies of storage drums in case war broke out. These military attitudes reinforced the policy direction Hornbeck already wished to pursue.

During this period, it became increasingly obvious that the American government could not indefinitely endure such massive exports of petroleum as were currently occurring. Self-defense prudence combined with political considerations and anti–Japanese commitments to make serious action inevitable. From July 1940 through March 1941, four million gallons had left the United States and licenses had been issued for another five million that had not yet been shipped. Licenses were under consideration for an additional two million gallons. These eleven million American gallons represented more than double the shipments of any previous year.[3] Even the most sympathetic official (and there weren't that many) would have been hard pushed to justify the continuance of such large amounts.

Among government bureaucrats, major policy changes are rarely adopted with any great speed. In this case, though, the administrator of export control and the State Department agreed together surprisingly quickly to ban the issuance of any new export licenses until a revised oil policy could be adopted. To avoid any public controversy, this March 6, 1941, decision was not announced to the media. Within a month, general agreement had been reached that exports should be limited to allegedly "normal" levels (those of 1936 and before). The loophole that permitted 86 octane gas to be exported was eliminated by reducing the permissible octane level. The official announcement of these changes was postponed indefinitely to avoid complicating negotiations between Shell, Stanvac, and Japan.

The decision to limit shipments further represented official policy; the *appearance* was that nothing was being done and the *reality* was total prohibition. As Anderson points out, "Since shipments continued for the time being under previously validated licenses, the action caused little comment, but as matters turned out (except for two minor special cases) the Department actually issued no new licenses for gasoline, lubricating oil, or crude to Japan in the five months preceding the de facto embargo."[4] By discreetly declining to issue any new licenses, the government had actually turned off the spigot. The public was unaware of this, and many people were outraged at the amount of continued shippage to a potentially dangerous Oriental power.

Even petroleum industry officials were unaware of the full scope of the new policy. Indeed, administration comments to them were somewhat misleading. On July 17, two Standard-Vacuum Oil Company executives met with members of the State Department to discuss Japan's ongoing pressure to increase shipments. According to the department's summary:

> Mr. Parker and Mr. May were informed that, although they could not use such information vis-a-vis the Japanese, no licenses had in fact been issued for some

months for the exportation to Japan or occupied China of gasoline of an 86 octane rating. This information seemed to be good news to Mr. Parker and Mr. May. They asked, however, whether unused licenses issued several months ago would be revoked. They were told that they could be given no assurances in this respect.[5]

The specification of 86 octane shipments was misleading in light of the fact that no petroleum of any octane had been granted an export license. The silence in regard to existing approved licenses would suggest that at least some members of the State Department were inclined not only to issue no new ones but also to revoke those remaining unused. The freeze on assets that occurred less than two weeks afterwards effectively did exactly that.

Although petroleum represented the highest visibility export, the government remained concerned about other resources that would be needed if a full-scale world war terminated existing world trade. Hence during the early months of 1941, there was a slow expansion of the list of items for which export licenses were required. On February 3, copper, zinc, nickel, bronze, and brass were among the items added to the list. On March 10, newly added products included carbon black, titanium, and petroleum coke. On March 24, lead and jute were among the products joined to the growing list. On April 15, the list grew by another fifty-one items.[6]

Requiring a license did not necessarily mean that trade in a given product would be either banned or even severely restricted. In these early months of the year, the actual impact was hard even for the British to determine. As a later authority on the subject notes:

> There seemed to be considerable administrative confusion at this time in the State Department, so that it was not easy for the embassy to find out how far the restriction of exports was enforced. In a survey of the system made in the middle of March the Ministry concluded that, for nearly all items apart from those which were licensed freely, no licenses were granted for Japan; in a number of cases, however, licenses could be granted if the political sections of the State Department pressed for them, and there was no information as to how far this happened in practice.... This still did not mean, however, that the United States Government was deliberately using the system for pressure on Japan; the great majority of items were either not produced in the United States or were in short supply there, and supply considerations almost certainly still dominated the administration.[7]

Part of the confusion was surely caused by the fact that the administration was deeply divided as to how pronounced and how explicit an anti–Japanese policy it should embrace. In addition, the more hawkish policies were not always the official ones of a given government agency. We have already seen how the State Department was adopting an actual embargo on petroleum while officially only regulating the shipments. Some in the State Department were probably unaware of what was actually going on and those in the know would only risk the continuation of their end run on the official position if they were to acknowledge it openly.

If these measures were brought to public attention, it was quite possible for more drastic ones to be repudiated openly by the White House. In the middle of June, Harold Ickes was temporarily able to prevent the shipment of some two thousand barrels of lubricating oil to Japan on the grounds of a potential shortage in this country the following year. Roosevelt had a fit over this because Ickes had done it unilaterally, without the concurrence of the State Department.[8] Roosevelt warned him both personally[9] and in writing[10] that because of the foreign policy implications, there must be no repetition of the incident unless first approved by the State Department or by Roosevelt personally.

The State Department was quite willing to meet Ickes part way, and on June 20, Dean Acheson showed him the proposed text of a new policy that would require special export licenses for any future shipments. Ickes promptly embraced the proposal, and the president signed it. Indeed, the president even went a step further and made the permissive ban called for by the measure an obligatory one for East Coast exports.[11]

Another area of concern for the administration lay in the potential use of the Philippines to obtain supplies that were limited or prohibited when coming from the continental United States. This was something that could indeed be resolved since the Philippines was not scheduled to receive its independence for several years. From January to April 1941, exports from the Philippines of hemp, manganese, copper, iron ore, chromite, and coconut oil reached unprecedented heights, and it was feared that Japan would transship much of this on to Germany.[12] On May 29, President Roosevelt signed legislation to regulate the volume of exports to Japan from that territory.[13] He also issued a proclamation the same day prohibiting strategic materials from being transshipped from the forty-eight continental States to Japan via the Philippines.[14]

Warned in advance that the United States was about to require export licenses for defense-related goods, the president of the Philippines, Manuel Quezon, ordered the immediate implementation of the above legislation the same day the American president signed it.[15] The Japanese Foreign Office promptly let it be known unofficially that it regarded these actions "as part of United States economic pressure on the Axis Powers, although the reason given by Washington was the necessity of conserving materials vital to the Philippines."[16]

The role that the Philippines would play in any Pacific war also concerned Washington. Ongoing contingency plans assumed that the Philippines would be quickly lost if attacked. As the result of military consultations with Britain during the first three months of the year, the American military produced a new war plan, Rainbow 5. Adopted in May 1941, this plan still assumed the fall of the Philippines. In July, however, this plan was modified to assume a vigorous defense of the islands and a determined effort to prevent them from being seized.[17]

In spite of efforts to accelerate the buildup of military forces in the Philippines, only so much could be accomplished with the available resources. In July 1941, the target date of December was set for being able to withstand an attack. By September this target date had slipped to a February–April 1942 time frame.[18] Throughout the fall and into late November 1941, top military officials urged a cautious Far East policy that would allow them time to complete these preparations.[19]

Even without the completion of a Philippine defensive-offensive military complex, the Japanese faced a disintegrating situation that had the potential for economic collapse, a situation that only required the avoidance of any act that would so prick their pride that Japan would feel obligated to strike out to maintain national self-respect. At least such a scenario was well-known within the administration. A State Department economic analysis of May 1941 noted that even without further trade restrictions, Japan faced an economic judgment day which seemed inescapable:

> The essential fact remains that Japan lacks essential raw materials to support either her manufacturing trade or a major war effort. To procure them she must have foreign exchange. If the present unfavorable trade balance is not radically adjusted it appears that complete exhaustion of all assets capable of being converted into foreign exchange to balance the debit in international payments will occur in the near future (some say by the end of 1941). This will result in the stoppage in the inflow of a considerable part of the raw materials which are vital to the organic well-being of Japan, and her ability to wage war will be seriously curtailed.[20]

Immediately after stressing Japan's long-range danger, the study emphasized that America—acting alone—could inflict a more immediate disaster:

> No other country even approaches the United States in its importance to Japan both as a source of raw materials and as a market for exports. From the point of view of the Japanese, discontinuance of this trade with the United States would be catastrophic. In other words, the United States is today in a position to wreck completely the economic structure of the Japanese Empire.[21]

The British Shipping Crunch: Justification and Excuse

During the first year of war in Europe, about a thousand merchant vessels were lost. Even under the most optimistic scenario, British shipyards could not replace even a third of that number.[22] On the western side of the Atlantic, discreet steps were taken to alleviate the situation. The chairman of the American Maritime Commission later noted that "During

1940, a number of obsolete or idle American flag ships were transferred to foreign registry to aid Great Britain and her Allies in meeting transportation demands and maintaining supplies."[23] In order that this not hinder America's own increased demand for freighter capacity, "Vessels were shifted from the intercoastal trade to strengthen our foreign lines which were hauling essential commodities homeward."[24] To further relieve the pressure, a British shipbuilding mission arrived in the United States in October 1940. It promptly contracted for the construction of sixty merchant vessels in American ports.[25]

As an industrialized island nation, Great Britain was vitally dependent upon the supplies these vessels brought from abroad. Since petroleum was vital to the operation of its industries (not to mention its defensive and offensive military capacity), the merchant fleet shrinkage hurt even worse when the loss of tankers was involved.

During the fall of 1940, Britain began to be impeded seriously by tanker shortages. As a close student of the subject has observed, actual losses to enemy fire played a secondary role: of all the tankers Britain had in her service in July only ten percent had been lost by the end of the year.[26] On the other hand, available vessels were typically traveling between destinations that resulted in prolonged voyages, thereby reducing the number available at any given moment for the North Atlantic trade.[27] Long-delayed maintenance finally began to catch up with a vengeance. "During the last three months of 1940 between seventy and eighty tankers were reported out of action in Britain waiting for equipment to be fitted or for repairs which would take more than seven days. In February 1941 a million deadweight tons of tanker tonnage was thus immobilized."[28]

As 1940 came to an end and the new year began, British authorities attempted to deal with the problem by rescheduling the destinations of many of the available tankers, thereby boosting the supply of oil available to the endangered British Isles. Tankers stationed in the Indian Ocean were transferred to the Atlantic. A more efficient usage of Atlantic shipping was implemented: instead of having vessels carry oil all the way from the Caribbean, shorter runs from the Caribbean to northeastern United States ports and from there to Britain by different vessels kept individual tankers at sea a shorter period of time and permitted a quicker round trip than if any one vessel had to uninterruptedly carry out the entire transit by itself. Where possible, American vessels were utilized for the Caribbean-Northeastern leg, thereby allowing British vessels to make the much shorter (and quicker) crossing across the Atlantic. Efforts to obtain foreign-owned tankers met with greater success. Vigorous measures were taken to minimize the turning around time for vessels in domestic or foreign ports. Greater efficiency in such matters produced a net increase in the volume of oil that could be shipped at any given moment.[29]

By February 1941, the British authorities faced the future with considerable confidence. They believed that they had at last gotten all the elements in their supply system working effectively and efficiently. Optimistic predictions quickly became unglued, however, as bad weather, human fatigue after long voyages and prolonged periods at sea, and plain bad luck undermined the assumptions on which the rosy predictions had been based.[30] The Germans quickly turned this embarrassing situation into borderline catastrophe as substantially more British tankers were sunk than had been expected: "Between January and March, thirteen tankers were sent to the bottom by German surface ships alone. March was a particularly bad month, with nearly as much British-controlled tonnage lost as in the whole of the first nine months of the war. April was nearly as bad, with losses around Greece and Crete added to the heavy toll in the North Atlantic."[31]

In January 1941 the British sent another shipbuilding mission to the United States to extend the efforts already made. The visibility and prestige of the British endeavor was upgraded in early March when Sir Arthur Salter was sent to head the program. By this point, British supply efforts were at crisis stage. Although the Americans quickly agreed to increase the number of new tankers being constructed, this would only provide long-term relief and would do nothing to solve the short-term dilemma.[32] In order to ensure that the president was fully aware of Britain's desperate situation, Sir Salter briefed Harry Hopkins in detail: even assuming that the British tanker capacity remained stable (i.e., that replacements were available for all losses), there remained an urgent need to increase fleet capacity by a minimum of seventy-five additional tankers. Sir Salter urged that they be provided on the basis of approximately twenty a month.[33]

Although it was clear that the British situation required as much assistance as feasible in replacing her tanker and her other merchantman losses, there was considerable tension between the goals of helping the British and providing for America's own oceanic transportation requirements. Speaking of this early spring period, one individual deeply involved in the problem later wrote, "Besides new tonnage and any older vessels which could be acquired, the British were getting what American shipping men claimed was more than their share of cargo lent or leased to Britain."[34] Even the pro–English writer of these lines could not help protesting to Roosevelt in April, "If we do not watch our step, we shall find the White House on route to England with the Washington Monument as a steering oar."[35] Roosevelt's response, in essence, was that however large the short-term sacrifice might be, it would help prevent the deeper tragedy of an Axis victory.[36]

In late May it became clear that the most Britain could hope to secure in the way of newly built tankers would be about twenty-one vessels, and these would not become available till close to year's end.[37] This was crushing news for the British, especially when combined with the inescapable pressure caused by the effort to destroy the German invasion of Crete. That daring airborne operation was countered by a British land buildup that was reinforced by naval operations both before and after the initial assault.

British merchantman capacity was pushed to the breaking point by this latest expansion of the conflict, and without constant resupply the military action would of necessity grind to a halt. President Roosevelt personally called the chairman of the American Maritime Commission and requested that he "assign" a number of United States-flagged civilian vessels to the British to assist them in the Mediterranean.

The chairman was very reluctant to do so, stating, "The action would be illegal, Mr. President." Would his opinion be different if the attorney general officially advised him that the proposal *was* legal? "Yes, sir!" was the immediate response, and the next morning the requested endorsement was provided him. Thus legally protected, the chairman vigorously pressured American firms to charter their available shipping to what was nicknamed the "Red Sea project." The American firms (intentionally or otherwise) used the opportunity for a "royal" price gouging.[38]

The Neutrality Act still prevented U.S.-flagged vessels from entering ports in wartime Britain, and this affected tanker capacity. In response to the latest crisis, the United States quickly moved to taking sole responsibility for the shuttle of fuel from the Gulf Coast and the Caribbean to the Atlantic Northeast, and this policy allowed British craft to be concentrated on carrying the precious fuel to Great Britain itself.[39] Even the financial costs of the intra-east coast shuttle were assumed by the United States:

> The first tanker in the American-organised Shuttle set sail on 21st May. By the middle of July 1941 there were forty-three United States-flag tankers—roughly 11 percent of the whole United States-flag commercial tanker fleet—involved in the Shuttle operation. Most discharged at New York, although transit storage was also rented at Baltimore and Philadelphia. The entire cost, including the hire of the storage—as well as the dollar cost of the original Shuttle operation which the British had organised for themselves in January—was born [sic] by the American government.[40]

American-chartered foreign vessels were not subject to the same destination limitations as those imposed upon American-owned tankers. Hence to meet the still perilous situation, efforts were made to tap this additional resource more fully. The Norwegian government had been refusing to permit the use of its ships currently involved in western hemispheric trade to be used for voyages to wartime Britian. The professed reason was worry that the United States would be offended by any such decision. In early May, the American government made plain not only that it would not be offended, but that it expected such vessels to be used in a way that would do the most good for the war effort. By the end of the month, the Norwegian government removed all restrictions that had previously hindered the use of its vessels.[41]

May also saw the British petroleum reserves drop below the minimum safety level. In late June, the United States petroleum coordinator assumed all responsibility for tanker distribution of oil needed in the western hemisphere, permitting additional foreign tankers to be shifted to the United States–Great Britain trade. On July 11, the same official "requested" that all American charterers of foreign-flag tankers permit their vessels to be used in a similar capacity where and when needed. The situation had sufficiently changed that he was able to "request" that twenty-six Panamanian-flag fuelers (owned by United States corporations) also be utilized to supply Britain. Although such actions were officially only requests, it was no secret that the American Maritime Commission had full legal authority to requisition the vessels if it so desired. Full cooperation quickly ensued.[42]

During this period of late summer, oil supplies on the East Coast dropped and demand quickly surpassed availability in the Northeast. This naturally outraged many Americans, especially when juxtaposed in their minds with the very visible and very large continuing exports to Japan. It was annoying enough to many that an aggressor nation was being so abundantly supplied; it added a substantial element of indignation when peacetime American consumers were simultaneously denied their hard-earned leisure. Although Japan took the blame, other causes played the dominant role, including the fact that distribution capacity was markedly inferior to actual production. Sensitive to the charge that the East Coast was suffering a petroleum shortage because supplies were being sent to Japan, a spokesman for the petroleum industry on the West Coast attempted to reassure the public on July 24. He pointed out that America's production was quite adequate to meet total demand and that what was being sent to Japan in no way compromised that ability. Nor had East Coast problems been created by Japan's use of American tankers since for an unstated period of time, no oil had been moved by that means.[43]

Most Americans seem to have overlooked or been unaware of such facts. Great responsibility, even less recognized by the public, also had to be borne by the United States' policy decision to put supply of the British above domestic supply in the East. A careful student of Britain's wartime petroleum needs has noted, "The diversion of so many American vessels into the Shuttle [i.e., of oil to northeastern ports for transshipment] as well as into other western hemisphere trades [i.e., to take the place of Norwegian and Panamanian shipment being used to carry oil to Britain] led to petroleum shortages in the northeastern states."[44]

The general Atlantic situation and the need to assist the British provided the excuse the American government needed to disavow any blatantly anti–Japanese bias to its limitations upon Japan's access to petroleum. However much the Japanese might be indignant because of the implications of such restrictions upon their own access to resources, the argument enjoyed a certain inherent credibility. During the spring, all oil shipments to Japan from the East Coast and the Caribbean were openly prohibited by the United States. American officialdom carefully stressed its pro–British intent rather than its anti–Japanese impact.

Behind the scenes, government pressure attempted to deny usage of tankers from other American ports as well. About the beginning of the year, the normal fee for chartering a Pacific coast tanker to go to Japan would have been in the range of five to six dollars per ton. With the limited supply of tankers still available to her, Japan found herself faced with rapidly escalating costs. These soared as high as $20 a ton, with an insurance surcharge of $3 a ton per round trip. These rates were sufficiently high to encourage an end run around American policy in order to secure greater profits. This was accomplished by transferring vessels to Panamanian registry. On February 2, it was reported that three American tankers had recently been made available to Japan by this method.[45]

Unofficial American opposition slowly eroded this loophole. The American Maritime Commission announced on June 14 that, with one exception involving a contract written well before that date, no American flag vessels were currently transporting petroleum to Japan. It indicated that American-controlled vessels under Panamanian registry were also no longer involved in such voyages.[46] So effective were the efforts to limit Japanese access to foreign flag vessels that a reporter could comment in early August that "all movements" had been "in Japanese ships for several months."[47]

Japanese Provocation in Southeast Asia

During July, the Japanese government took three major steps that encouraged the United States to make its preexisting unofficial petroleum embargo official and to extend it to all other areas of trade as well. The least alarming step occurred when Japan ordered all merchantmen flying its flag to leave the Atlantic and to return to the Pacific. Because it would have been difficult (if not impossible) to carry out this step after the outbreak of hostilities, this action provided a significant indication of how seriously Nippon viewed the war danger. On the other hand, American and British pressure had so reduced Japanese access to North and South American goods that a partial or complete return to Pacific waters made considerable sense on its own merits.

More ominously, Japan called up reservists to duty, some one million men in all. This was a natural step to provide a reservoir of physically able and (at least theoretically) well-trained manpower for a nation seriously contemplating imminent military action.

Most ominous was the Japanese occupation (over the protests of Vichy France) of the southern half of French Indochina. The northern half of this colony (later broken into Vietnam, Cambodia, and Laos) had been occupied a year earlier. The United States had made plain its displeasure at this earlier action and was intensely annoyed when Japanese imperialists seized the other half.

Actions of a moderate nature to indicate American opposition would have been perfectly natural and appropriate. But why did so many Americans (especially in the political leadership) believe it necessary to go so far as to inflict a total trade cutoff, with all the grave dangers it imposed?

On the psychological plane, the "Munich syndrome" had made all too clear the potentially disastrous consequences of letting hard-line dictatorships get their way. It was not so much that the betrayal of Czechoslovakia had occurred; it was that she had been cold-bloodly sacrificed and Germany had still continued her policy of expansionism. The Western powers had been played for fools, and when they belatedly recognized it, public attitudes hardened. What had previously been dismissed as sensible power politics was transformed into what it always had been, shameful betrayal. When general war broke out in 1939, millions of Americans became convinced that giving in to militaristic hooliganism at the price of sacrificing minor or secondary powers not only was inherently immoral but only postponed the ultimate day of personal involvement in curbing the aggressor. If a policy of "weakness" had not saved the peace in Europe, why should Americans feel it would work any better in the Far East? To fully understand American impatience at a conciliatory policy toward Japan, one must remember the failure of that approach in Europe.

On the other hand, however repugnant the aggressor powers were, did this justify the expenditure of vast fortunes and thousands of American lives to force them to free their forcefully acquired empires? To the cautious, this question could be answered in the affirmative only if American interests were so obviously and dangerously threatened as to impel a military response. To the isolationist, the international situation was far more ambiguous and less clear-cut. Furthermore, in the minds of many, the United States had been conned by British propaganda and American arms merchants into intervention less than twenty-five years before. The danger of the current situation was further downplayed as it was viewed through the lenses of these past resentments.

Those convinced that strong actions were necessary held an image of a Japan far more radical than a traditional aggressor. Some saw it moving more or less hand-in-hand with Nazi Germany to carve up the world between them; the Tripartite Pact was seen as evidence of this intention. Some individuals even looked upon Japan as a virtual puppet of Germany, although it was highly unlikely that an intensely race-conscious Japan was about to permit a "white" nation like Germany to inflict such a fate upon it.

Others saw Japan as psychologically unable to back off from a continued course of expansionism. Shortly before the embargo was announced, the *Washington Post* editorialized on this theme and presented it as proof that strong "economic and financial" retaliation was now unquestionably essential:

> At the moment Japan is unprepared to launch an attack either on Siberia or the Dutch East-Indies. But the occupation of Indo-China will make it easier for her to embark on the latter objective when and if the situation develops in Tokyo's favor. *That she will move then can be taken for granted. Like Hitler, Japan cannot stop.* She must move on from aggression to aggression, from conquest to conquest. Indo-China happens to be along the line of least resistance. However, its tremendous importance as a way station on the road to greater objectives cannot be minimized. That is why the United States cannot afford to let the Japanese occupation of Indo-China go uncontested. [emphasis added][48]

The *Los Angeles Times* editorialized in a similar vein only two days later: "Because its plain purpose is that of *further* aggression against English and English-protected interests, it plumps Japan into the till now eschewed role of a full war partner of the Axis" (emphasis added).[49]

In early July 1941, the American decryption service "Magic" intercepted a diplomatic communiqué summarizing a July 2 imperial conference and informing its recipients of future policy:

> In order to guarantee the security and preservation of the nation, the Imperial Government will carry on with all necessary diplomatic negotiations concerning the southern regions.... In case diplomatic negotiations break down, preparations for a war with England and America will also be carried forward. First of all, the plans which have been made with regard to French Indochina ... will be followed through in order to consolidate our position in the southern lands.[50]

High American officials read this as a definitive policy change that foreshadowed an expansion of a potentially threatening size into British and even American territorial possessions. These Americans read this communiqué as establishing a definitive and irrevocable policy for (presumably) vast expansion into European-American holdings in the Far East. With considerable justice, this has been called "a historic mistake."[51] They read correctly what was said; what was overlooked was the background against which the message had been sent:

> The Foreign Ministry's smooth resume of the conference naturally gave no hint of the abiding divisions between advocates of the northern and southern strategies, within and between the Army and the Navy, and between the armed services and

the government, over peace and war. It was merely reporting the latest round in an intractable debate which both sides assumed would go on for a long time yet. There was no need to record all the well-worn arguments, even more familiar to Japanese diplomats than to the Americans who themselves had heard them times out of number from orthodox as well as clandestine sources. Indeed, Washington itself might well have come round to a more relaxed assessment of the text in due course—but for the Japanese ultimatum in the middle of the month to Vichy France.[52]

Although there had been many harsh words between Japan and the United States, the message of early July spoke of negotiations at the same time as it spoke of expansionism. The crunch point would have been when negotiations were unable to obtain what Japan desired and even demanded. Then the twin policies of expansion and negotiation would have become irreconcilable and a definitive choice would have become necessary. As of July, that point had not yet been reached, at least so far as negotiations with the major Western powers were concerned. Negotiation with Vichy needed to be little more than ultimatum since France possessed precious little with which to resist. In regard to any further expansion into southern Asia, a very different situation would exist.

Although it was quite possible to take that final step into war with the United States, psychologically it was a major hurdle and the continued negotiations with America attempted to postpone it as long as possible, until a military option had to be exercised if it were to be used at all. The insistence of the Japanese government that at least a narrow option for peace be kept open bears witness to the existence of a will for peace as well as one for war. As late as October, Admiral Matome Ugaki (the combined fleet's chief of staff, serving under Admiral Yamamoto) wrote of the latent unwillingness to enter such a war:

> When we think about it, arms are the most serious matter for the state. This is especially true this time, because the situation is quite unlike the Russo-Japanese War. Since we have long followed the principal policy of avoiding trouble with the United States and not fighting with her, it won't be easy to reverse this policy. Certain steps will be necessary to get there, and I think the process by which matters are moving toward that end has already been appearing.[53]

Although the American government may well have suspected Japan had broader territorial ambitions, an expansion into the remainder of Indochina was about to occur. Everything else might well be speculation; but that was grim reality. The presidential cabinet met beforehand to discuss possible responses to what was about to occur. Roosevelt promptly announced that he did not desire any total embargo lest the Japanese feel themselves compelled to seize the Netherlands East Indies for the oil they could obtain from that source. Morgenthau recommended that the United States officially reduce the exportable level of refined petroleum from 87 to 67 octane. Representing the State Department, Sumner Welles concurred with this suggestion, which seemed to overcome Roosevelt's initial reluctance. (The fact that a far more comprehensive suspension of exportation was already a fact indicates that this was another case where one part of government did not know what another part was doing. In light of the intense discussion about how far to proceed with the new, "stronger" measures one may reasonably assume that the very lack of widespread knowledge made such measures possible.)

Dean Acheson, an assistant secretary of state, was assigned the responsibility for drafting the actual policy papers that would formalize the cabinet's consensus. Another meeting was held to consider what he had prepared, but Roosevelt remained troubled over the possible Japanese reaction. When the Indochinese expansion was actually carried out, the president believed it was essential to respond with far more than mere verbal condemnation. In spite of his reservations, he agreed to a public announcement of strong American retaliatory measures.

The statement released to the public left (as we will later notice) a generally discounted loophole in its restrictions. It should be stressed at this point, however, that much of the administration did, indeed, anticipate substantially less than a total and permanent cessation of trade; the threat of a total cessation would be there, but not the reality.

For example, the top echelon of America's military understood the new policy to require only a temporary termination of commerce, with the door to renewed trade being reopened as time went by. Hence on July 25, 1941, the following telegram was sent to provide advance warning of the new policy:

> This is a joint dispatch from the CNO [Chief of Naval Operations] and the Chief of US Army X Appropriate adees [?] deliver copies to Commanding Generals Hawaii Philippines and Caribbean Defense Command and to General Chaney in London X You are advised that at 1400 GCT July twenty-sixth United States will impose economic sanctions against Japan X It is expected these sanctions will embargo all trade between Japan and the United States subject to modification through a licensing system for certain material X It is anticipated that export licenses will be granted for certain grades of petroleum products cotton and possibly some other materials and that import licenses may be granted for raw silk X Japanese assets and funds in the United States will be frozen except that they may be moved if licenses are granted for such movement X It is not repeat not expected that Japanese merchant vessels in United States ports will be seized at this time X United States flag merchant vessels will not at present be ordered to depart from or not to enter ports controlled by Japan X CNO and COS do not anticipate immediate hostile reaction by Japan through the use of military means but you are furnished this information in order that you may take appropriate precautionary measures against possible eventualities....[54]

Even before the public announcement of the Japanese takeover of southern Indochina, there were widespread rumors that some type of major move was in the works and discussion of how the United States should react. Senator James M. Mead of New York used the reports to push for further restrictions on oil exports. He noted that Japan had recently received 400,000 barrels of petroleum from the United States at the same time that East Coast supplies were falling short of meeting public demands. Senator Tom Conally of Texas attended a White House meeting on the possible coming crisis and afterwards attempted to throw cold water on such talk of a petroleum cutoff: If it were implemented, he stressed Japan would certainly invade the Netherlands East Indies.[55]

On the twenty-third, the Vichy government in France announced that in principle an agreement had been reached to cede major rights throughout Indochina to the Japanese. Although faced with private American government opposition as well as public indignation, the top Japanese diplomats publicly expressed hopefulness that better days lay in the future. The Japanese ambassador to the United States, Kichisaburo Nomura, stressed his "hope" that "the feeling between our two nations will become better and better." He played down the danger in the current international situation: "I have read in the newspapers about difficulties, but I think it will depend on how things develop."[56]

The British government let it be known that it was quite willing to follow an American lead in clamping down a total boycott. Not only would Britain do so, but it would also utilize its considerable influence to ensure that the dominions followed suit. One reporter noted that the British believed that such an "embargo would have an eventual devastating effect on [the] Japanese economy."[57]

On the twenty-fourth, the American president addressed a group of civilian defense volunteers to encourage them in their work. Among other matters, Roosevelt discussed the administration's rationale for having permitted petroleum exports for such a long period. The press interpreted the remarks as laying the groundwork for a reversal of past policy. The *New York Times* noted that "it was considered significant" to listening reporters that in the speech the president "employed the past tense" in justifying the policy.[58]

Across the continent, the *Los Angeles Times* headlined its report: "U.S. DENOUNCES JAPAN AGGRESSION / HINTS OIL ALREADY REFUSED TOKYO / APPEASEMENT NOW BELIEVED AT END." The accompanying article spoke of the president giving a "veiled hint" of a petroleum cutoff and stated that there had been "a strong implication" that the "appeasement policy has been scrapped."[59]

The *Washington Post* drew a similar conclusion in its coverage.[60] At the beginning of the report, the correspondent asserted that "President Roosevelt plainly indicated ... that he is about ready to cut off Japan's supply of American oil." Six paragraphs later, the correspondent backed off a little. He noted that the discussion had been "entirely in the past tense," which led "to [the] belief among some that the United States was now ready to shut off the stream of oil that is vital to fuel the Japanese military forces." The hedging was likely to be overlooked by the casual reader both in light of the earlier positive assertion and in light of the fact that the accompanying headline interpreted the remarks in a similar vein, as a forerunner of future policy.

NOTES

Hidden Petroleum Export Curbs

1. See the discussion in Irvin H. Anderson, Jr., *The Standard-Vacuum Oil Company and United States East Asian Policy, 1933-1941* (Princeton: Princeton University Press, 1975), 160.
2. Associated Press, "Containers for Oil Under Export Ban," *New York Times*, 13 February 1941, 12.
3. Anderson, *Standard Vacuum Oil Company*, 165.
4. Ibid.
5. "Memorandum of Conversation, Division of Far Eastern Affairs, July 17, 1941," State Department document 894.24/1569, page 3, "Records of the U.S. Department of State Relating to the Internal Affairs of Japan, 1940-1944—Decimal File 894."
6. W. N. Medlicott, *The Economic Blockade*, 2 vols., vols. 7 and 8 of the *History of the Second World War*, United Kingdom Civil Series, ed. W. Keith Hancock (London: H.M.S.O., 1952; reprint, Nendeln, Liechtenstein: Kraus, 1978), 1:497-98.
7. Ibid., 1:498.
8. Ickes' side of the controversy appears in Harold L. Ickes, *The Secret Diary of Harold L. Ickes*, vol. 3, *The Lowering Clouds, 1939-1941* (New York: Simon and Schuster, 1954), 543-48, 552-60.
9. Ibid., 545.
10. Ibid., 553, 559.
11. Ibid., 547.
12. United Press, "Action Taken Within an Hour," *New York Times*, 30 May 1941, 4.
13. "Manila Clamps Down on Exports; Control Act Stops Japanese Ships," *New York Times*, 30 May 1941, 1.
14. "President Proclaims New Curb," *New York Times*, 30 May 1940, 4.
15. "Manila Clamps Down on Exports," 1, 6.
16. "Pressure on Axis Seen in Tokyo," *New York Times*, 30 May 1941, 6.
17. Lester H. Brune, "Considerations of Force in Cordell Hull's Diplomacy, July 26 to November 26, 1941," *Diplomatic History* 2 (Winter 1978): 394-95.
18. Ibid., 396, n. 21.
19. Ibid., 400.
20. "Japan: Economic Estimate, May 27, 1941," State Department Document 894.50/154, page 61, "Records of the U.S. Department of State Relating to the Internal Affairs of Japan, 1940-1944—Decimal File 894."
21. Ibid.

The British Shipping Crunch: Justification and Excuse

22. Emory S. Land, *Winning the War with Ships* (New York: Robert M. McBride, 1958), 21.
23. Ibid.
24. Ibid., 22.
25. Ibid., 23–24, 29.
26. D. J. Payton-Smith, *Oil: A Study of War-Time Policy and Administration* (London: H.M.S.O., 1971), 158.
27. Ibid.,
28. Ibid., 159.
29. Ibid., 161–62, provides a description of these measures.
30. Ibid., 178.
31. Ibid.
32. Ibid., 198.
33. Ibid., 199.
34. Land, *Winning the War*, 30.
35. For text of letter from E. S. Land to FDR, dated 14 April 1941, see Land, *Winning the War*, 30–31.
36. Ibid.
37. Payton-Smith, *Oil*, 199.
38. Land, *Winning the War*, 31–32, recounts the incident and notes his role in the effort to recover the exorbitant charges. Some firms cooperated in the effort but most did not. The courts ultimately ruled that since the firms were officially working for the "British" the American government had no authority to compel such repayments.
39. Payton-Smith, *Oil*, 199.
40. Ibid., 200.
41. Ibid.
42. Ibid., 201–02.
43. "News on Oil Exports Hailed," *Los Angeles Times*, 25 July 1941, 6.
44. Payton-Smith, *Oil*, 202.
45. J. H. Carmical reported on these dodges in "Japan Increases Petroleum Stock," *New York Times*, 2 February 1941, III-1.
46. "Denies U.S. Tankers Carry Oil to Japan," *New York Times*, 15 June 1941, 3. A July State Department study referred to this report, "On June 14, 1941, the Maritime Commission announced that, with the solitary exception of one ship under foreign registry which was then completing its voyage, no American-owned or American-controlled tankers were engaged in trade to Japan or had been so engaged for the past six months" ("Oil Shipments to Japan: A Survey of This Government's Policy, July 31, 1941," State Department document 894.24/1587, page 21, "Records of the U.S. State Department Relating to the Internal Affairs of Japan, 1940–1944—Decimal File 894."
47. "Japan Is Likely to Get Crude Oil under New Ban, Exporters Say," *New York Times*, 2 August 1941, 5. See notes 43 and 46 above on this theme of limitation on exports.

Japanese Provocation in Southeast Asia

48. "Japan Invites Reprisals," *Washington Post*, 25 July 1941, 8.
49. "Talking Turkey to Tokyo," *Los Angeles Times*, 27 July 1941, II-4.
50. Dan van der Vat, *The Pacific Campaign: World War II, the U.S.–Japanese Naval War, 1941–1945* (New York: Simon and Schuster, 1991), 71.
51. Ibid., 17.

52. Ibid., 72.
53. Admiral Matome Ugaki, *Fading Victory: The Diary of Admiral Matome Ugaki*, trans. Masataka Chiya, ed. Donald M. Goldstein and Katherine V. Dillon (Pittsburgh, Penn.: University of Pittsburgh Press, 1991), 8.
54. Joint Committee on the Investigation of the Pearl Harbor Attack, *Pearl Harbor Attack: Hearings Before the Joint Committee on the Investigation of the Pearl Harbor Attack* (Washington, D.C.: U.S. Government Printing Office, 1946), 14/1327.
55. Bertram D. Hulen, "U.S. Is Cautious on Pacific Peril," *New York Times*, 24 July 1941, 6.
56. Ibid.
57. Robert P. Post, "British Ready to Back U.S. to Hilt in Any Action Taken Against Japan," *New York Times*, 25 July 1941, 4.
58. Bertram D. Hulen, "Roosevelt Hints at Oil Curb on Japan," *New York Times*, 25 July 1941, 1.
59. Warren B. Francis, *Los Angeles Times*, 25 July 1941, 1.
60. George Bookman, "Roosevelt Hints Oil Embargo as Welles Says Japan Menaces Philippines with New Bases," *Washington Post*, 25 July 1941, 1.

Chapter 4

AN APPEARANCE OF TOTALITY: THE EMBARGO BECOMES OFFICIAL, JULY 1941

The Announcement and the Impression It Left

An unofficial embargo of all new petroleum exports had been going on for months. The president's willingness to support an official embargo (howbeit as a temporary policy) bestowed upon it an authority that it had not enjoyed in the past. Indeed, the determination to go beyond this oil embargo to a general termination of the economic relationship (again on a temporary basis) marked a modest hardening of Roosevelt's position. Previously, his rage at Japanese expansionism had been counterbalanced with great caution. Now, for the first time, he was willing to endorse publicly a policy that had at least the appearance of being a complete reversal of past American behavior.

Few Americans were aware of just how much trade had already been reined in. Even many top officials were unaware of how widespread the restrictions had become. To hard-liners in that group, the presidential restraint was appalling. At the cabinet meeting on the Thursday immediately following the Japanese takeover in southern Indochina, the president made it clear that behind the rhetoric of firmness there was to be only a gradual tightening of trade with Japan. A disgruntled Harold Ickes recorded in his diary:

> Notwithstanding that Japan was boldly making this hostile move, the President on Thursday was still unwilling to draw the noose tight. He thought that it might be better to slip the noose around Japan's neck and give it a jerk now and then. Naturally I am in favor of a complete job as quickly as possible. The effect of the freezing order is to require an export license before any goods can be shipped to Japan but the President indicated that we would still continue to ship oil and gasoline. This will be fooling the country again as we fooled it about a year ago.[1]

Much of the credit (or blame) for the new policy becoming a permanent one lies in how it was announced to the public. It was presented as

The Embargo Becomes Official: July 1941

permanent rather than temporary, and it was presented as being such a strongly affirmative action that any retreat would easily be perceived as a cowardly backdown. The enthusiastic reception the policy gained gave Roosevelt every reason to allow the appearance to become the actual reality. Likewise, those supporting radical anti–Japanese steps were encouraged by both the public response and Roosevelt's wavering to persevere in the unofficial trade restrictions they had been able to adopt. The presidential indecision gave an aura of presidential endorsement and permanency to their strong-arm policies, policies which Roosevelt was inclined toward in the first place.

On July 25, 1941, the administration issued a statement announcing the government's response to the latest expansion of the Japanese empire into southeastern Indochina:

> In view of the unlimited national emergency declared by the President, he has today issued an Executive Order freezing Japanese assets in the United States in the same manner in which assets of various European countries were frozen on June 14, 1941. This measure, in effect, brings all financial and import and export trade transactions in which Japanese interests are involved under the control of the government, and imposes criminal penalties for violation of the order.
>
> The Executive Order, just as the order of June 14, 1941, is designed among other things to prevent the use of the financial facilities of the United States and trade between Japan and the United States in ways harmful to national defense and American interests, to prevent the liquidation in the United States of assets obtained by duress or conquest and to curb subversive activities in the United States.
>
> At the specific request of Generalissimo Chiang Kai-shek, and for the purpose of helping the Chinese Government, the President has, at the same time, extended the freezing control to Chinese assets in the United States. The administration of the licensing system with respect to Chinese assets will be conducted with a view to strengthening the foreign trade and exchange position of the Chinese Government. The inclusion of China in the Executive Order, in accordance with the wishes of the Chinese Government, is a continuation of this government's policy of assisting China.[2]

The announcement carried with it two important innovations in American Far Eastern policy: a total asset freeze combined with a complete trade termination. The two were interlocked, the first being an easy means of accomplishing the second. In a July 26 dispatch, the Associated Press concisely explained how the freezing order could easily be used as an indirect method of cutting off petroleum exports:

> The freezing order means simply that Japan cannot liquidate any of her American assets without first obtaining a license from the Treasury permitting her to do so. Hence, oil shipments to Japan, which have been considerable in the past, could be stopped by simply refusing to issue a license for the conversion of assets into cash when the purpose was the purchase of oil. The same technique could be applied to any commodity.[3]

The asset freeze imposed American control over all of Japan's $131 million in funds held in American banks. This action resulted from at least three motives. The most obvious was the one already stressed, the ease with which it could be used to grind trade to a halt: if goods could not be paid for, there was no way the sellers would send them out of the country. Furthermore, if an export license were somehow granted, a separate set of officials would control granting permission to pay for the goods. If either approval process were controlled by those opposed to resuming exportation, supplies sent abroad could at least be reduced to a minimum if not totally terminated. The fact that the administration had not yet reached a full consensus made this a potentially vital choke point for the maximalist approach. The number of such choke points was increased even further in future weeks, as will be seen later.

In a broader context than the desire to punish Japan for its expansionism, the American government was seriously concerned that Japanese funds might be used to finance fifth-column-style activities inside the United States. The use of those of a similar ethnic heritage was an obvious concern, especially in Hawaii and in California. At least superficially Japan was a firm supporter of the other Tripartite Pact signatories. Since the funds of Germany and Italy had been frozen in mid–June, there was the possibility that these powers would funnel their money through Japanese fronts into spying or sabotage.

A third factor lay in pure economic retaliation. Such severe exchange controls were being imposed upon American banks operating in Japan that they were in danger of being driven out of business. If nothing else, the freeze might at least produce a negotiated end to such harassment.

A perhaps unanticipated bonus to the freeze was its impact upon Japanese trade with other hemispheric countries; most of its commerce with Central and South America was effectively eliminated by the decision to freeze all funds. Japan had commonly used United States banking institutions to handle payments for such transactions,[4] and the effective prohibition of the use of U.S. banks crippled this potential alternative source of supplies.

The extension of the restrictions to China may at first seem rather odd. However, because of Japanese influence in the large areas of China that it occupied (and, presumably, among collaborators outside those regions), Japan had the potential of using China as a conduit around the trade restrictions. The application of controls to China minimized the danger.

The Chinese Embassy in Washington pointed to the fact that the Japanese were believed to control large Chinese currency accounts in such occupied cities as Shanghai even though theoretically the money was controlled by Chinese nationals.[5] Immediately, the Treasury Department authorized the suspension of the asset freeze so long as any purchases were either approved by the Nationalist government of China or conducted through the government-controlled Central Bank of China.[6] Neither of these would, of course, be willing to provide the necessary credentials to those suspected of serious economic collaboration.

Until now, China had leaked like a sieve due to widespread corruption. In September 1941, an American publication with special interest in the Far East published a lengthy article detailing the pervasiveness of smuggling. "Large-scale contraband organizations, soldiers, corrupt revenue guards, peasants, fishermen, peddlers and loafers living in convenient areas turn many a profitable penny at the game."[7] Although both sides had officially regulated (and limited) cross-border trade, these agreements represented little more than a piece of paper.[8] Both sides took ample advantage of the opportunity to turn an illicit profit. "On some fronts, Chinese and Japanese purchasing agencies on either side of the lines compete lustily in the buying up of supplies, and military movements themselves are adapted to the exigencies of production, payment and delivery."[9]

Although these problems continued to exist, this description was already somewhat dated by the time it appeared in print. Human rapacity could never make the frontier greed-proof, but the new restrictions did much to rein in the worst extremes. The English-language Tokyo publication *Japan Times and Advertiser* gave vent in mid-September to its intense resentment over the success of such measures. It noted that to import through Shanghai, goods had to be paid for in either dollars or sterling, thereby necessitating that yen be exchanged for one of these two foreign currencies. Western banks based in Shanghai refused to grant their preferential exchange rate to anyone not approved by the Chinese Currency Stabilization Fund (CCSF). To obtain the approval of the director of the CCSF required that one be acceptable to the Nationalist Chinese government. Indignantly (and with surprising candor) the *Japan Times and Advertiser* reported:

> Other trade is to be strangled. "Legitimate" trade is being interpreted according to the design of the freezing order. Any open or covert Japanese or Nanking Chinese trade is denied facilities. There are some funds available in the "black market" but these are being systematically attacked by the Fund bankers in order to get all exchange in their hands.
>
> Due to this systematic freezing and privileged trade Shanghai imports have been drastically reduced. Heaviest sufferers are the Chinese themselves. But as their difficulties are intended to react upon Japanese and Nanking Chinese interests, the Fund is obviously a weapon of offense.[10]

The Common Perception: A Total and Complete Embargo

It is appropriate to examine the asset freeze first not only because it was the "clout" used to eliminate trade but also because it tends to be overlooked in the discussion of these events. To the public at large, it was more of an academic matter than anything else. Their minds were focused upon the cutoff of trade, an action that was commonly taken to be both total and (barring a dramatic reversal of Japanese policy) permanent. Although we have seen that Roosevelt himself anticipated considerable leniency in implementing the policy, there was absolutely nothing in the administration's announcement to suggest this would occur. The impression that was conveyed (intentionally or otherwise) was that the new course would be the government's continuing policy. Even the possibility of negotiations that might produce a less restrictive embargo was not mentioned in the announcement given to the press.

The American public wanted stern action. The announcement was in full accord with that preference, and there was nothing added by authoritative sources to limit the initial interpretation. As Anderson rightly comments, "The public remained under the impression that all trade with Japan had ended."[11] The public perception, of course, worked in favor of those officials who wanted to maintain just such a total prohibition. And it must be remembered that even though Roosevelt had decided to oppose such extreme measures, he had done so on the grounds of prudence rather than principle. Hence he would not be adverse to being pressured into a more militant policy than he had endorsed.

Some specific examples of how the decision was reported to the public are of interest. The *New York Times* presented the embargo announced on July 26, 1941, as if it were designed to be both total and permanent: "President Roosevelt tonight froze all Japanese assets in the United States, thus virtually severing trade ties with the empire and dealing it the most drastic blow short of actual war."[12] A concise front-page summary of the day's events carried the same implication:

> The United States and Great Britain dealt Japan a severe blow overnight by parallel action freezing Japanese assets.
> President Roosevelt issued a freezing order last night that spelled an end to shipments of American petroleum and to Japan's great silk market in this country.[13]

The Associated Press was more restrained, leaving the degree of trade limitation open to question:

> President Roosevelt struck back last night against Japan for her push in French Indo-China by clamping a sweeping control over all economic intercourse between the United States and Japan, including cash, oil, ships, silk and other assets.
> At the same time, at the request of China, he tied up Chinese assets in this country so that no one but the beleaguered government of Generalissimo Chiang Kai-shek can use them.
> Hereafter a Treasury license will be needed to take any Japanese assets outside the country or to send anything to Japan. This meant, according to a Treasury

The Embargo Becomes Official: July 1941

spokesman, that oil can be kept from Japan's war machine by refusal of or even failure to act upon requests for permission to ship oil.

Whether such an embargo actually would be clamped down, however, remained to be seen. The asset "freezing" order put the Treasury in a position to turn the economic screws on Japan. Just how hard they will be applied may depend, to some extent, on future events in the Far East.[14]

Such "ifs" and "buts" were effectively diluted (if not entirely blotted out) when such reports appeared in papers like the *Richmond* (Virginia) *Times Dispatch* over a headline reading: "Japanese Assets in U.S. Frozen by Roosevelt; Britain and Canada Join in Vast Economic War." The accompanying smaller heads read: "China Funds Are Tied Up for Safety / Trade Moves Expected Later." The additional front-page article, "U.S.-British Blockade Seen Choking Japan," further reinforced the interpretation that whatever official restraint might be found in the words used, the real decision was to persevere with severe restrictions.[15]

The same newspaper interpreted the action editorially in the way its headlines had suggested: "President Roosevelt's order freezing all Japanese assets in the United States, is expected virtually to suspend all trade between the country and Japan, including petroleum shipments to that country's war machine. ... It seems highly probable, then, that nearly all commerce between the two countries will cease in the near future."[16]

Other papers were sometimes more effective in perceiving the calculated ambiguity in the government policy. The front-page headline of the *Los Angeles Times* on July 26, 1941, announced: "U.S., Britain Freeze Japan Assets in Retaliation for Indo-China Move / Action May Cut Off Oil for Nippon's War Use / President's Order Puts Treasury in Position to Turn Economic Screws on Tokyo, / But Extent of Application Expected to Depend on Future Events in Indo-China and Dutch East Indies."[17]

Although at first that West Coast publication was wary that the latest steps would turn out to be a pseudo-blow at Japan's economic interests,[18] within a few days it was editorializing with far greater confidence that the trade ban had come to stay. Although Japan would indeed seize more properties and funds than the Western powers could take in tit-for-tat retaliatory "freezings," the trade cessation was viewed as far more harmful to the Japanese side than to the West. Indeed, on August 1 the paper viewed with apparent satisfaction the fact that the ultimate result would be nothing short of nightmarish for both the Japanese military and civilian economy:

> The worst that Japan can do to us is not much more than a fleabite. But the worst that we and the other countries which are following our lead can do to Japan, if circumstances force it, could easily mean industrial and commercial extinction to the Island Empire....
>
> If Japan's imports, latterly mostly war materials, are literally life to her military

establishment, her exports are equally vital to her domestic existence. If both are cut off or even largely reduced, she will quickly find herself in a bad way, since her reserve stocks are low and neither new sources of supply nor new customers for her goods can be soon developed. If she loses her trade with the United States, the British group of nations and the Netherlands possessions, her small and dwindling commerce with the Latin Americas will be virtually all that remains. Reports from Washington of prospective action by several South American republics indicate that even this may disappear too.[19]

The *Washington Post*'s headline also conveyed the element of uncertainty intended in the administration's policy by its inclusion of the word "if": "U.S. and Britain 'Freeze' Japanese Trade / Dutch Joint Move to Cut Nippon's Lifeline If She Persists in Aggression." The introductory paragraph also suggested the preliminary nature of the decision by noting that the Western powers were "threatening the Tokyo government with the loss of the greater part of its foreign trade" rather than by asserting that such an embargo was now an accomplished fact.[20] Would the typical reader have caught the hedging or missed it by concentrating on the central point, the establishment of an embargo?

The point obviously should have been clear by the fifth paragraph, where the writer effectively brought out the ambiguity in what had been announced: "Neither the United States, nor the other cooperating governments, indicated whether Japan would lose all its foreign trade with the antiaxis coalition, but President Roosevelt and his British and Dutch allies had assumed power to choke off that vital trade at a moment's notice."[21] If subscribers followed the text into its continuation several pages later, even the most superficial readers among them would have realized that only a limited policy had actually been pledged, although a comprehensive cutoff was threatened:

> How soon actual blows that might cripple the empire economically would be launched was a matter of speculation, but officials intimated that for the time being Japan would be on probation and would not feel the full effect of the new restrictions if she follows a moderate course. The machinery had been created, however, for invoking overnight the full economic power of the United States against the empires.[22]

The coverage by the two national news weeklies left the impression of decisive restrictive action by the American government. The first *Newsweek* to appear after the announcement referred to it as a declaration of "virtual economic war on Japan"[23] and a "virtual economic blockade of Japan by the United States and Great Britain."[24] In spite of such rhetoric, the magazine did acknowledge the existence of a loophole by which greater trade might be allowed if Japan decided to alter its policies.[25]

While the lead articles in *Time* stressed the seriousness and war potential of the American actions, the reader had to plunge deep into the issue

The Embargo Becomes Official: July 1941

before discovering any emphasis on the possibility that the embargo might not be as comprehensive as most Americans thought. In a perceptive half-column discussion, the magazine pointed out that "There were plenty of official loopholes in the freezing order through which trade could be carried on."[26]

Even so, word had been leaked to *Time* that the licensing system was nothing but a polite facade behind which to eliminate all exports. As the issue immediately after the embargo noted, "Hints came down that the license business at the Treasury would be as indefatigably polite as Japanese statesmanship, but also just as reluctant to right wrongs." A sample of such icy politeness had already occurred during July. Ten freighters from Japan were repeatedly denied permission to enter the Panama Canal from the Caribbean. As they sat there in the stifling summer heat, vessels from other nations were permitted entrance. The American War Department piously insisted that necessary repairs were being carried out. Giving up hope, all ten vessels were forced to sail around Cape Horn, the long way home.[27]

American officials fudged their comments as to exactly what they intended to do to implement the president's orders. The acting secretary of the Treasury, Edward H. Foley, Jr., stressed that an interdepartmental committee would make the decision on issuing treasury licenses that would permit frozen funds to be utilized. The furthest he would go on August 25 was to comment that the actions "necessarily will have a restraining effect on trade," though he would not specify how much.[28]

At a press conference on the same day, both Foley and Dean Acheson (not only an assistant secretary of state but also a member of the licensing committee) refused to commit themselves as to how frequently licenses would be issued to permit exports to Japan. Acheson protested against labeling the American policy one of "embargo."[29] In private, however, he was a fervent advocate of extreme trade termination actions, so much so that one careful student of the bureaucratic wars over the matter singles him out as bearing the primary responsibility for preventing the reinauguration of trade.[30]

When Sumner Welles, under-secretary of state, was interviewed the morning of August 26, he avoided committing himself to any opinion about how total the cutoff of petroleum would be. A reporter who interviewed him deduced, on the basis of unnamed authorities, "that licenses may be granted at the rate of one out of every three applications." This would reveal how seriously the United States took Japan's recent expansion into southern Indochina and at the same time lessen the danger that the Japanese would retaliate by igniting a bigger war to gain the oil they needed.[31] Rather than being reassured by Welles' public vagueness, however, officials in Japan became even more worried.[32]

On August 28, top officials continued their policy of intentional vagueness. George Bookman of the *Washington Post* staff reported that "Officials in Washington professed not to know whether the freezing order will be administered as a complete embargo against Japan, or will be somewhat relaxed depending upon the course that Nippon pursues." Bookman added, "It was said that only the President himself knows how much force will be behind the economic punch that the United States has now readied itself to deliver to Japan."[33]

On the following day, the *Wall Street Journal* indicated its own inability to come up with any definitive answer. Government sources were hinting at only modest curbs but were avoiding any clear commitment. Hence the *Journal* could only speak in terms of what the government might do: "apply only mild pressure while Japan 'behaves.'"[34]

Even the president himself was careful not to commit himself to any specifics. At a press conference on August 29, Roosevelt was repeatedly pressed as to how and to what degree the new trade limitations would be enforced. With equal persistence he turned aside all inquiries on the grounds that it was not yet the proper time to discuss such matters publicly.[35]

The initial British interpretation of the two governments' policy was that it involved moderate restrictions. The Monday after the trade freeze was announced, an unidentified British correspondent reported to London that even though a total elimination of trade had been authorized, "unless the Japanese make it impossible, it is likely that licenses will be granted by both Britain and America to enable a certain amount of trade to continue. How much, it is too soon to say." Barter deals (such as cotton for Japanese silk and canned salmon) were viewed as possibilities. "American supplies of oil to Japan may not be reduced much immediately, and assurance of full backing would be needed by the Netherlands East Indies if they were to refuse to supply, say, oil to Japan."[36] The *Wall Street Journal* picked up speculation in London that "substantial oil exports to Japan" were likely to continue at least "temporarily";[37] United Press in London simultaneously reported such speculation.[38] With the United States publicly hedging as to how thorough the embargo would be, British economic warfare officials quickly retreated into an equal vagueness about the toughness of their own government's policy.[39]

If one were so inclined, one could find in the president's preembargo remarks the hint of considerable restraint lying behind the bold White House announcement. Writing the day after the trade freeze was made public, Hallet Abend used the president's earlier civilian defense speech as evidence that any reduction of petroleum exports would fall well short of being total: "In view of President Roosevelt's statement of last Thursday to the effect that if a complete embargo on oil sales to Japan had been instituted 'then you would have war,' it is doubted if sales will be entirely prohibited." Even so, the headline above the analysis predicted a hefty two-thirds cut, a prediction oddly omitted from the text itself.[40]

At the beginning of August, unidentified businessmen (only vaguely referred to as "exporters," and that in the headline) predicted that the new government approach would still permit oil to flow to Japan. Although Japan would have to pay cash and transport the fuel exclusively in its own vessels, such items as crude oil were expected to be exempted from any continuing trade ban.[41] It is unknown whether these businessmen had any grounds on which to base this speculation or whether they were floating it as a trial balloon in the hope of obtaining a positive reaction.

Massive American Support for the Action

There was widespread public support for the embargo measures, which were perceived to be draconian. Although FDR's European strategy was bitterly protested throughout 1940 and 1941, there was what *Time* magazine labeled an "unusual unanimity [of] the press and the public" in support of the embargo. Part of this attitude, the magazine suggested, arose from Americans' confidence that "the U.S. can probably lick the Japanese." A war would primarily be a naval one and Americans were "surer of its powerful navy than of its half-equipped Army."[42]

The British ambassador evaluated public reaction in the same way. In his annual "Political Review for 1941," he observed, "The imposition of these measures received almost universal approval in the United States, and it was shown once more that the Isolationists were, in the main, only Isolationists in respect of Europe."[43]

As the ambassador observed, even isolationists—so bitterly opposed to Roosevelt's confrontational policy in the Atlantic—tended to be firm backers of "standing up" to Japan. Burton K. Wheeler, who had so often dipped his tongue in acid when describing (and opposing) Roosevelt's pro-intervention policies in Europe, quickly endorsed the new step. "I think the President did the right thing. You may say for me that I agree with him—for the first time."[44]

The *Washington Post* cited this example as evidence of just how widespread was support for the action: "The Japanese Government will now have realized that by severing trade with Japan, the Roosevelt Administration could have done nothing more calculated to win the approval of the American people. Even Senator Wheeler has joined in the applause."[45] But not indefinitely, for within a month Wheeler was beginning to have second thoughts.[46]

At least in the case of some of the other isolationists, the passage of time did nothing to weaken their hawkish sentiments. In the middle of October, Senator Norris of Nebraska went so far as to remark that he was "not so sure that war with Japan would be a bad thing for us." The navy had assured him that "they could sink the Japanese fleet within two weeks." He conceded that this prediction "may be a little optimistic." American action would be centered not on military targets in particular but on the massive destruction of Japan's urban centers. "A Navy man told me that our bombers could set the whole island ablaze in one night, because Japanese cities are built of wood and are just so much tinder."[47]

A cautious German policy was guaranteed at least a decent degree of regional support; not so temperance in regard to Japan. A *New York Times* editorial of July 29, 1941, probably summed up the underlying attitude of the vast majority of East Coasters when it linked regional oil shortages and the continued large supply being sent to Japan: "It was disagreeable enough to supply Japan out of our abundance. It is intolerable that we should supply her out of our scarcity."[48] A July 31 decision to impose a 7 P.M. curfew on gas sales on the East Coast did nothing to alleviate such hostility.[49]

Those in the Pacific Northwest had been pressuring for strong action long before the administration embraced it. One of the more temperate protests came from Monroe Sweetland, secretary of a major isolationist group in Oregon. Less than a week before the embargo announcement, he observed, "There is no reason why our logging railroads should furnish bullets for the Japanese militarists."[50]

The executive committee of the America First Committee's New York branch was one of the few groups to lodge a public protest against the new course.[51] Their vehemence might have attracted considerable attention in regard to an European issue, but it attracted little notice in regard to Japan and appears to have found few if any imitators.

The intensity of American hostility to further trade with Japan—petroleum shipments in particular—was so pervasive that defying the public mood would risk vehement outrage. Although prior to this time, the oil dealers were willing to bear much of the heat for continuing exports to Japan, the sentiment in the nation was now so uniformly hostile that they wanted explicit government sanction before proceeding any further. A July 30 meeting between officials of the Standard-Vacuum Oil Company and the State Department made this particularly clear:

> Mr. Walden said that in his opinion public criticism of oil shipments to Japan is so great that his Company cannot accept the responsibility for making such sales without the approval of this Government. He said that in the past he had been willing to deal on an informal basis but that he thinks he should get some definite approval in writing at the present time.... Mr. Walder said that he will not give his representatives in the Indies instructions to apply for export permits unless he first receives formal approval by the United States government for the transfer of exchange.[52]

The Embargo Becomes Official: July 1941

The war danger was clearly acknowledged by the press, as some of the previous citations have indicated. In the following months, this natural linkage of embargo and war was dropped: war was discussed as the result if negotiations were unsuccessful, not if the embargo itself were maintained. Most seem to have regarded war as an acceptable risk or were so angered at the Japanese that they almost didn't care: they just wanted it done and over with. On the other hand, at this early stage there were also some who acknowledged the danger of a boycott-produced war but were convinced that the military balance had already so shifted as to rule out aggressive Japanese retaliation. One such eastern newspaper conceded that international conflict represented a real possibility but went on to downgrade the danger drastically:

> Hitherto the assumption has been that if shipments of oil, rubber, tin and other supplies were cut off from Japan, the Japanese would have attacked the Dutch East Indies. They may do so now. It happens, however, that during the past year Japan has grown weaker rather than stronger because of the debilitating effects of the prolonged China war, while the defense of the Dutch East Indies have been considerably built up. The same is true of Singapore, which now has a sizable garrison and a fair-sized air force. Moreover, the policy of parallel action now being pursued in the Far East by the United States, Great Britain and the Dutch East Indies means a move to the south by Japan would probably mean war against three nations, and not merely a segment of one nation.[53]

Closely tied in with this attitude was the hope that rational dollar-and-cents calculations would overrule any temptation to seek out a military solution. If Japan was to be hurt as badly as this boycott seemed certain to injure it, was there any rational course except a negotiated backing away from foreign adventurism? In late August, Max Hill of the Associated Press filed a report from Tokyo expressing hope that despite "the cloak of pessimism," reality would win out. He stressed that sympathetic as leading Nipponese officials were to the military community, they were even more committed to the "economic welfare of Japan. That, say observers, is above all other considerations."[54]

The war potential did not in any way undermine general American support for the embargo. The only reservation concerned the danger that the boycott would not live up to the comprehensiveness that was expected. I. F. Stone, for example, pointed out that past presidential actions had not been nearly as restrictive as the accompanying rhetoric had first indicated. Stone warned that Americans had to be on the alert lest that happen once again.[55]

Another skeptic was Eliot Janeway. Although he was happy that oil had finally been cut off, as late as an October magazine article (presumably written in mid or late August), he expressed concern that "the State Department could without much emotional difficulty act as a slot machine, automatically emitting licenses to each Japanese applicant" for exports.[56] The following month he reacted with horror that Japanese-American negotiations might result in the removal of the boycott without a Japanese withdrawal from her conquest.[57]

Roosevelt's constant dilemma in regard to Europe was that he was always ahead of much of public opinion in pressing for a stronger and more overt commitment to British victory. Powerful anti-intervention groups and major newspapers were prepared to go to the mat to oppose much of this policy. But when it came to Japan, such groups' very silence or low-key opposition removed all domestic obstacles to the administration yielding to its own preferences and the demands of its vocal hard-liners.

International Support for the Action

The United States did not stand alone for long in its imposition of an asset freeze and the cutoff of trade that inevitably accompanied it. Only a few hours later Canada became the first nation to announce publicly a similar step.[58] Her prime minister, W. L. MacKenzie, informed the public that "the necessary steps have been taken to prevent the withdrawal of assets in Canada belonging to residents of Japan."[59] He added that "no financial transactions affecting residents of Japan can be undertaken without specific permission of the Foreign Exchange Control Board."[60]

Four hours later Great Britain went on the record as backing the move.[61] Informed British sources stressed that their nation's actions were "exactly parallel" to those of the United States.[62] Unidentified "informed sources" pointed out that the British trade freeze was unique in its long history. They were quoted as saying that it was the only time Britain had ever taken such an action against "a country which neither is a declared enemy nor occupied [by] or controlled by a declared enemy."[63]

The Foreign Office official announcement informed citizens that "Treasury directions have been given bankers under Defense [Finance] Regulation 2A prohibiting as of today the carrying out of orders affecting Japanese balances, gold and securities in the United Kingdom without license from the Treasury." The seriousness of this action was reinforced by its comment that "Corresponding action is being arranged in other parts of the empire."[64] The head of the British Foreign Office, Sir Alexander Cadogan, had already been attempting to rally support for a Commonwealth-wide boycott. In his diary entry of July 24, 1941, this exasperated official wrote: "These stupid Dominions of course get cold feet, and don't want to freeze Japanese assets without an assurance of support from [the] U.S. They must know that they can't get this."[65] Presumably worried over a policy that would place a disproportionate amount of immediate danger

The Embargo Becomes Official: July 1941

upon Far Eastern Commonwealth nations and colonies, once the United States had publicly committed itself to the new course, the dominions still quickly agreed to take the risk.

Later the same day Hong Kong froze Japanese funds,[66] as did Singapore on behalf of the Straits Settlements.[67] South Africa, Burma, and the Federated Malay States affirmed a similar policy.[68] Both Britain[69] and her dominion compatriots who joined in the freeze quickly announced that they were terminating their respective trade agreements with Japan.[70] Officials of the British government informed the press that they had received a positive response on trade termination from all members of the British Commonwealth.[71] New Zealand officially embraced the new policy on July 28.[72] Walter Nash, the finance minister, explicitly linked the trade freeze and Japan's actions in Indochina: "Our case is just, our policy clear. It is against aggression, whatever its form or from wherever it comes."[73]

Australia's reaction was more ambiguous. The day Britain endorsed the freeze policy, the Australian prime minister, Robert G. Menzies, asserted that the Japanese funds had already been effectively frozen and therefore nothing more needed to be done by his country.[74] Even so, his government also informed the public that it was reviewing what additional steps might be appropriate.[75] Well-placed British spokesmen implied the same day Australia's backing for the new policy.[76] On July 28, Japanese funds were officially frozen, an action which suggests that the prime minister had been exaggerating considerably in his earlier assertion that such curbs were already in force.[77]

Although Australia's substantial trade ties with Japan had previously made it cautious in its public rhetoric and restrictions on Japan, there was also an acute awareness of Australia's exposed military position. With much of the Australian army engaged in the Middle East, the Japanese might well take advantage of Britain's inability to field a major military force to protect the Commonwealth nations in Asia.[78] Hence Australia sought to assure itself of American support if a worst case scenario were to develop. Without such guarantees, there was a natural reluctance to adopt any strong policy that might provoke military countermeasures. Although explicit commitments could not be obtained, the British reassured the Australians that there was an implicit certainty of American backing if war were to break out. The secretary of state for dominion affairs of the United Kingdom wrote the Australian war cabinet on July 25:

> In our view, the United States Government will be compelled to support us if need arises. It is clear that if the Japanese are provoked to extreme measures, it will be as a result of the dramatic effect of the action taken by the United States and not of our own cooperation therein. Both by reason of the general policy of the United States toward us, and their special interest in the Far East, we do not believe that they would find it possible not to give us their full support.[79]

By the 28th, all reservations had been shelved and Australia had publicly embraced the potentially dangerous new policy. Menzies vowed to maintain the embargo and spoke of it as being a direct outgrowth of Japan's move into Indochina.[80]

A Tokyo-based correspondent observed in an August 2 dispatch that "the whole British Empire is now lined up with the United States in economic warfare against Japan."[81]

When the trade freeze was first announced, the Netherlands government in exile at first declined to act. Yet in the very act of postponing a decision, it implied that this would only be a temporary policy: "In connection with the British and American action, the Netherlands government in London is in consultation with authorities in Batavia [Dutch East Indies] with regard to measures to be taken in view of the situation that has arisen as a result of Japan's encroachment upon Indo-China."[82]

The temporary respite ended on July 28 when the Dutch had the Netherlands East Indies suspend its most recent trade pact with Japan. Under that agreement, exports of petroleum to Japan had tripled,[83] and its shipments of rubber, tin, and especially petroleum, had made Japan the Indies' third largest customer.[84] The chief Dutch negotiator with the Japanese, H. J. van Mook, exaggerated only modestly when he wrote a few years later that "The American and British embargoes [on petroleum] would remain without effect unless the Netherlands Indies joined in."[85]

Presumably because of its exposed position and minimal defenses, the Netherlands East Indies conspicuously did not announce the trade freeze in terms that would suggest it was a response to Japanese aggression. It was couched as a necessary response to the Anglo-American freeze of Japanese assets, which placed the Dutch in a position of being unable to receive payment for their products.[86] In order to guarantee that the prohibitions were not circumvented via petroleum shipments to Manchukuo and Japanese-occupied sections of China, special licenses were to be required in the future.[87]

The Dutch Indies held out the possibility of future barter deals if the vexatious question of guaranteeing payments could somehow be worked out.[88] In the meantime, a permit system for exports was implemented. The main Dutch economic negotiator with Japan, H. J. van Mook, conceded that even this, by itself, "should limit the trade."[89] The Dutch-language press saw this approach as one of moderation that allowed both the east and west to back down if Japan's policy should change.[90]

On July 29 the Dutch representative in Washington, Dr. Alexander Loudon, discussed the international situation with Acting Secretary of State Sumner Welles. Afterwards as he left the State Department, he attempted to discourage the Japanese from overt intervention in the Netherlands East Indies: "All measures have been taken for some time and can be put into effect immediately to insure the complete destruction of the oil fields and refineries. There will be no hesitation in making capital destruction of the oil industry in the islands if we are forced to do so."[91] He insisted that "These plants won't be merely disabled. They will be effectively destroyed."[92]

It appeared that the threat was for real. An August 9 dispatch from Java reported that, literally, "the petroleum industry of the Netherlands East Indies is resting on a keg of dynamite." It would be a mere "one hour job" to thoroughly devastate the oil fields. The carrying out of the task could be performed by Europeans and Americans working for the industry assisted by "just a few" of the local inhabitants.[93]

NOTES

The Announcement and the Impression It Left

1. Harold L. Ickes, *The Secret Diary of Harold L. Ickes*, vol. 3, *Lowering Clouds, 1939-1941* (New York: Simon and Schuster, 1954), 588.

2. For the full text, see "222. Statement Issued by the White House on July 26, 1941," Department of State, *Peace and War: United States Foreign Policy, 1931-1941* (Washington, D.C.: U.S. Government Printing Office, 1943), 704-05. Among the newspapers that reprinted the entire announcement were the *New York Times* ("Freezing Statement's Text," 26 July 1941, 5) and the *Los Angeles Times* (Associated Press, "Text of President's Asset Freezing Order," 26 July 1941, 5).

3. "New Economic Blows Against Japan Loom," *Los Angeles Times*, 27 July 1941, I-2.

4. Charles E. Egan, "Much Latin Trade Is Lost by Japan," *New York Times*, 29 July 1941, 23.

5. George Bookman, "U.S. and Britain 'Freeze' Japanese Trade," *Washington Post*, 26 July 1941, 1, 6.

6. Ibid., 6.

7. I. Epstein, "Japanese Goods in Free China," *Asia* 41, no. 9 (September 1941): 502.

8. Ibid.

9. Ibid., 505.

10. "Aggressive Finance: Blocking Shanghai's Trade," *Japanese Times and Advertiser*, 13 September 1941 (evening edition), 1.

The Common Perception: A Total and Complete Embargo

11. Irvin H. Anderson, Jr., *The Standard-Vacuum Oil Company and United States East Asian Policy, 1933-1941* (Princeton: Princeton University Press, 1975), 176.

12. John H. Crider, "U.S. and Britain Freeze Japanese Assets: Oil Shipments and Silk Imports Halted," *New York Times*, 26 July 1941, 1.

13. "The International Situation," *New York Times*, 26 July 1941, 1.

14. "Japanese Assets in U.S. Frozen by Roosevelt: Britain and Canada Join in Vast Economic War," *Richmond Times Dispatch*, 26 July 1941, 1.

15. In addition to various references provided in the current chapter, one should

also examine the chapter on the American government's recognition that the embargo could easily lead to war. Citations discussed in that context also reveal that Americans, even when recognizing the theoretical possibility that the embargo might not be rigidly adhered to, wanted it to be sternly enforced and, perhaps for that very reason, believed that it would be.

16. "The End of Trade with Japan?" *Richmond Times Dispatch*, 27 July 1941, IV-6.
17. *Los Angeles Times*, 26 July 1941, 1.
18. "Talking Turkey to Tokyo" (editorial), *Los Angeles Times*, 27 July 1941, II-4.
19. "A War Japan Can Never Win" (editorial), *Los Angeles Times*, 1 August 1941, II-4.
20. George Bookman, "U.S. and Britain 'Freeze' Japanese Trade," *Los Angeles Times*, 26 July 1941, 1.
21. Ibid.
22. Continuation of the above article (note 20) under the heading "U.S. Freezes Japan Assets Here," 6.
23. "Showdown in Pacific Hastened by Firm Stand of Democracies," *Newsweek*, 4 August 1941, 11.
24. Ibid., 12.
25. Ibid., 13.
26. "Loaded Gun," *Time*, 4 August 1941, 61.
27. "The Last Step Taken," *Time*, 4 August 1941, 11.
28. Associated Press, "Japanese Assets in U.S. Frozen by Roosevelt," *Richmond Times Dispatch*, 26 July 1941, 1.
29. "Japanese Trade Needs Licenses," *New York Times*, 26 July 1941, 4.
30. Jonathan D. Utley, *Going to War with Japan, 1937–1941* (Knoxville, Tenn.: University of Knoxville Press, 1985), 180, sees the situation as one in which subordinate bureaucrats successfully imposed upon the government a far more militant policy than that demanded by the president. Utley contends that though war might have erupted anyway, less severe actions would at least have postponed the conflict till the following year. This would have found the United States in a far stronger position to wage a two-front war and Japan with a substantially weaker offensive capacity. This picture of a covert overthrow of official policy is true as far as it goes. However, in all fairness, the press coverage of the trade freeze reveals that Americans eagerly embraced it. Having popular support for a change even among activists opposed to a European war and being personally and thoroughly disgruntled by the ongoing Japanese foreign policy adventurism, the hidden policymakers were advocating a stance that Roosevelt would have preferred if it had not been for reasons of prudence. One should remember his advocacy several years earlier of a naval blockade (not a mere boycott) of Japan.
31. Hallet Abend, "Two-Thirds Cut Due in Oil Sales," *New York Times*, 27 July 1941, I-14.
32. Otto D. Tolischus, "Japan Smolders Over Oil Threat," *New York Times*, 30 July 1941, 4.
33. George Bookman, "40 Japanese Ships Hovering Off Coast Get U.S. Clearance," *Washington Post*, 29 July 1941, 1.
34. "Japan Ships Can Clear U.S. Report," *Wall Street Journal*, 29 July 1941, 1. This is discussed in more detail later in the same issue (page 2) under the title "Further Sanctions Against Japan Depend on Moves by That Country."
35. George Bookman, "...Indies to Destroy Oil if Invaded / President Implies Japan in Plot to Split Democracies," *Washington Post*, 30 July 1941, 1, 2.
36. "A Total Weapon Against Japan," *Times* (London), 29 July 1941, 5.
37. "Japan Ships Can Clear U.S.," *Wall Street Journal*, 29 July 1941, 1.

38. "Anti-Japanese Action," *Wall Street Journal*, 29 July 1941, 2.
39. Associated Press, "'Reflect While Time,' Eden Warns Japan," *Washington Post*, 31 July 1941, 2.
40. Abend, "Two-Thirds Cut Due in Oil Sales," I-14.
41. "Japan Is Likely to Get Crude Oil Under New Ban, Exporters Say," *New York Times*, 2 August 1941, 5.

Massive American Support for the Action

42. *Time*, 4 August 1941.
43. [Lord Halifax, a.k.a. Edward Frederick Lindley Wood], *Confidential Dispatches: Analyses of America by the British Ambassador, 1939–1945* (Evanston, Ill.: New University Press, 1974), 33.
44. Summary of the public reasoning and the quotation from Wheeler found in "The Last Step Taken," *Washington Post*, 4 August 1941, 12. It is also quoted by the United press, "'First Time': Wheeler Praises Roosevelt on Japan," *Washington Post*, 26 July 1941, 2. At the very time of the embargo announcement, the senator and the president were engaged in an ongoing verbal slugfest over administration policy toward Europe ("'Wheeler Goes Too Far,' Says Roosevelt," *Washington Post*, 26 July 1941, 1, 2).
45. "End of a Road," *Washington Post*, B-6.
46. As to the possibility of war in the Orient, Wheeler charged in late August that "there are some within the Administration who apparently have been anxious for war for some time." Such a conflict would only serve to protect the empire of Great Britain and would be of no real benefit to the United States, Wheeler believed. "Japan is one of our best customers, for cotton and petroleum and we are one of her best customers," he reminded his listeners. "There is no reason why we should not live in peace with them." (Quoted in "War on Japan Would Be Folly, Wheeler Says," *Washington Post*, 28 August 1941, 3.)
47. Associated Press, "Norris Warns of War in Pacific at Any Time," *Washington Post*, 15 October 1941, 3.
48. "Japan and the West," *New York Times*, July 29, 1941, 14.
49. "7 P.M. Curfew on Gasoline Sales to Be Imposed on Eastern Seaboard," *New York Times*, 1 August 1941, 1.
50. Richard L. Neuberger, "Northwest Backs Ban on Oil to Japan," *New York Times*, 22 June 1941, IV-5.
51. The committee protested against the rationale which lay behind the trade freeze in a telegram it sent to Sumner Welles. Welles had vigorously condemned the Japanese for obtaining new bases in Indochina and believed that something had to be done to demonstrate American disapproval. The America First Committee felt compelled to rebuke this "new and dangerous doctrine that if a foreign power acquires bases of another foreign power this may be construed as an attack on our country and treated accordingly. Your proposition is obviously one of international anarchy." If the United States had the right to abort Japan's gaining of bases in Indochina, why didn't Japan have the same veto right over the United States obtaining foreign bases in such South American nations as Brazil? (Quoted by the Associated Press, "Denunciation of Japan by U.S. Called 'Anarchy'," *Washington Post*, 27 July 1941, A-9.
52. "Memorandum of Conversation, July 30, 1941," State Department document 894.24/1566, pages 1–2.
53. "Dutch Follow Suit," *Washington Post*, 29 July 1941, 10.
54. "Hope for Better Relations with U.S. Visible in Japan," *Washington Post*, 29 August 1941, 3.
55. "Oil on the Pacific," *Nation*, 9 August 1941, 109.

56. "The Economic Warfare Front," *Asia* 41, no. 10 (October 1941): 528.
57. "Appeasement as Usual," *Asia* 41, no. 11 (November 1941): 596.

International Support for the Action

58. Associated Press, "Japanese Assets in U.S. Frozen by Roosevelt; Britain and Canada Join in Vast Economic War," *Richmond Times Dispatch*, 26 July 1941, 1.
59. Associated Press, "Canada Joins in Order," *Richmond Times Dispatch*, 26 July 1941, 2. Identical report carried under the heading "Ottawa Order Includes China," *New York Times*, 26 July 1941, 5.
60. Associated Press, "'Necessary Steps' Taken by Canada," *Los Angeles Times*, 26 July 1941, 5.
61. Associated Press, "Japanese Assets in U.S. Frozen," 1.
62. Associated Press, "Nippon Assets Also Frozen by Britain," *Richmond Times Dispatch*, 26 July 1941, 2.
63. Associated Press, "British Freezing Held First of Kind," *Los Angeles Times*, 26 July 1941, 5.
64. For the text of the announcement, see United Press, "Drastic Pressure Expected," *New York Times*, 26 July 1941, 5; "Japanese Assets in Britain: Official Statement," [London] *Times*, 26 July 1941, 4; and Associated Press, "British Freezing Held First of Kind," *Los Angeles Times*, 26 July 1941, 5.
65. Sir Alexander Cadogan, *The Diaries of Sir Alexander Cadogan, 1938–1945*, ed. Fred L. Israel (Lincoln: University of Nebraska Press, 1966), 394.
66. Associated Press, "Hong Kong Steps into Line," *New York Times*, 27 July 1941, I-13.
67. Associated Press, "Singapore Follows London Step," *New York Times*, 27 July 1941, I-13.
68. United Press, "Far East Posts Strengthened," *New York Times*, 27 July 1941, I-13. For Malaya, also see Associated Press, "Malaya Halts Tokyo Business," *New York Times*, 29 July 1941, 4, and for Singapore, "Japanese Ship Off Singapore," *New York Times*, 29 July 1941, 4.
69. David Anderson, "British Denounce Japanese Pacts," *New York Times*, 27 July 1941, I-13.
70. United Press, "Far East Posts Strengthened," *New York Times*, 27 July 1941, I-13.
71. Unidentified source, inserted into an Associated Press dispatch, "Quick Moves Take Tokio [sic] by Surprise," *Richmond Times Dispatch*, 24 July 1941, I-1.
72. "New Zealand Orders Freezing," *New York Times*, 29 July 1941, 4.
73. Quoted by Associated Press, "New Zealand Acts with Other Nations," *Los Angeles Times*, 29 July 1941, I-5.
74. United Press, "Australia Explains Position," *New York Times*, 27 July 1941, I-13.
75. Unidentified source, inserted into the Associated Press filing, "Quick Moves Take Tokio [sic] by Surprise," I-1. The government announced that it was "taking all steps which consultations suggest to be necessary for the protection of Australia's interests affected by Japan's move to the South" (quoted by Associated Press, "Tokyo Stocks Drop in Panic," *Los Angeles Times*, 27 July 1941, I-1).
76. This was done by pointing out that all the Commonwealth nations had been consulted and concurred in the boycott (Associated Press, "Tokyo Stocks Drop in Panic," *Los Angeles Times*, 27 July 1941, I-1).
77. "Australia Blocks Credits," *New York Times*, 29 July 1941, 4.
78. On both the economic ties and suspicions of Japanese intentions, see Trevor

The Embargo Becomes Official: July 1941

R. Reese, *Australia, New Zealand and the United States: A Survey of International Relations, 1941-1968* (London: Oxford University Press, 1969), 7. On Australia's substantial military commitments to the Atlantic, anti–German war also see P. H. Partride, "Depression and War, 1929-1950," in *Australia: A Social and Political History*, ed. Gordon Greenwood (Sydney: Angus and Robertson, 1955; reprint 1969), 374-75.

79. Roger J. Bell, *Unequal Allies: Australian-American Relations and the Pacific War* [Melbourne]: (Melbourne University Press, 1977), 21-22. Two other quotations on the British recognition of the war-making potential of the embargo can be found on 21. For a discussion of Australia's efforts to cooperate with the United States on such matters and to assure itself of support in case of crisis, see 20-34.

80. Associated Press, "Australia Will Stand Firm Beside U.S., Menzies Says," *Los Angeles Times*, 29 July 1941, I-5.

81. Otto D. Tolischus, "More Assets Are Frozen," *New York Times*, 3 August 1941, I-22. The article title refers to the Japanese counterfreezing of assets of those nations who had done the same to them.

82. Associated Press, "Nippon Assets Also Frozen by Britain," *Richmond Times Dispatch*, 26 July 1941, 2.

83. International News Service, "...Dutch Cancel Tokyo Oil Rights / Netherlands Indies Scraps Treaty, Puts All Nipponese Trade on a License Basis," *Washington Post*, 29 July 1941, 1.

84. Associated Press, "Dutch Indies to Curb All Trade with Japan," *Richmond Times Dispatch*, 29 July 1941, 1.

85. H. J. van Mook, *The Netherlands Indies and Japan: Their Relations, 1940-1941* (London: George Allen & Unwin, 1944), 103. This volume provides a concise summary of the Japanese-Indies negotiations during the two years prior to Pearl Harbor. For a brief American summary of these negotiations, see "Political Estimate, August 20, 1941," State Department document 894.00/1132, page 36.

86. Associated Press, "Dutch Indies to Curb All Trade," 1.

87. International News Service, "Dutch Cancel Tokyo Oil Rights," 1.

88. Ibid.

89. "...Dutch to Limit Oil to Japan / Batavia Risks War," *New York Times*, 29 July 1941, 1.

90. Ibid.

91. Associated Press, "Dutch Ready to Destroy Oil," *Los Angeles Times*, 30 July 1941, 1.

92. "Envoy Says Dutch Will Wreck Wells," *New York Times*, 30 July 1941, 4. This was no new threat. In the summer of 1940, it was "generally believed that the producing oil wells have been mined and would be promptly destroyed in case of a Japanese attack" (Robert Emerson, "The Dutch East Indies Adrift," *Foreign Affairs* 18 [July 1940]: 738.

93. Belman Morin, Associated Press, "Dutch Indies Develop Plan to Destroy Oil If Invaded," *Los Angeles Times*, 10 August 1941, 41, II-5.

Chapter 5

GAMBLING ON ECONOMIC STRANGULATION: APPEARANCE BECOMES REALITY, AUGUST TO DECEMBER 1941

The Choke Points for Trade Multiply as Government Policy Firms into Total Prohibition

On August 1, the White House issued another Janus-type statement that moved a major step toward a permanent banning of all petroleum exports yet was worded in such a way that the action was still not definitive in nature and did not necessarily have to go much beyond what had already been publicly revealed:

> It was announced today that the President has directed the administrator of export control to initiate further regulation in respect to the export of petroleum products in the interest of national defense.
>
> The action will have two immediate effects. It will prohibit the exportation of motor fuels and oils suitable for use in aircraft and of certain raw stocks from which such products are derived to destinations other than the Western Hemisphere, the British Empire and the unoccupied territories of other countries engaged in resisting aggression.
>
> It will also limit the exportation of other petroleum products, except to the destinations referred to above, to usual or pre-war quantities and provide for the pro-rata issuance of licenses on that basis.[1]

From the Japanese standpoint, the clearest and strongest negative indication conveyed by the White House was its reference to "the pro rata issuance of licenses." In effect, this would seem to mean that petroleum Japan had already paid for but which had not yet left the country would be charged against the new quotas.[2] Yet the Americans had always been insistent upon fairness in international dealings, and a reasonable case could be made that to charge past sales against future quotas was inherently unfair. There was at least room for hope that the Americans would compromise when faced with the question.

The statement that the U.S. would "prohibit the exportation of motor fuels and oils suitable for use in aircraft and of certain raw stocks from which such products are derived" implied that something drastically new was about to occur. The announcement referred to the "immediate effects" that would be the result, seemingly implying that products previously allowable had now been banned. Yet the banning of aviation-quality fuel had been the official stance of the U.S. government since the previous year. Hence the Japanese would have to seek out what was genuinely new in all this and what was intended by the Roosevelt administration strictly for domestic political consumption, to give the illusion of action when there was none. Or was it all or mainly political posturing with few genuine long-term repercussions? For one thing, the statement referred to "certain raw stocks" from which petroleum could be made. Would "certain" be interpreted to include virtually all sources or would it carry its more natural, more limited meaning?

Furthermore, the use of the words "usual or pre-war quantities" concerning "other petroleum products" indicated that in regard to this category of unidentified nature and size, there would be something (substantially?) short of total cessation. The wording permitted considerable leeway in just how severe the new restrictions would be. It really came down to what official policy the administration finally established or, failing that, to the decisions of those with administrative responsibilities over such matters. Ominously, key officials indicated that the benchmark year would be 1936. Based upon that year's level of exports, "a cut of at least one-half in oil exports to Japan seemed to be indicated," noted one reporter.[3]

Headlines such as "President Cuts Off Oil to Japan"[4] clearly overstated the case, but they were reasonably deduced from the official statement if one were battling a deadline and had to go by immediate appearances. A close reading indicated a more flexible policy. It is likely that these contradictory messages were intended by the White House. On the one hand, Roosevelt wanted to convey the appearance of stern determination to the public and to Japan. On the other hand, he did not want to seem so stern that negotiations were doomed. The calculated ambiguity permitted the Japanese camel to keep its nose within the American trade tent and to retain the hope that eventually it might be permitted to crawl all the way back in.

Most Americans probably viewed this latest edict (and the decision the same day to reserve all silk for U.S. military usage) as primarily a public affirmation of what had been logically implied a week earlier in the freeze on Japanese assets. One astute reporter noted that "The two orders taken together only can be interpreted as meaning that America has abandoned completely a policy of trying to appease Japan."[5] Buried in one United Press dispatch of August 1 was an acknowledgment of the damage that would come from a total rupture of the oil trade: "For years Japan has been purchasing its major oil supplies here and experts assert that without them Nipponese industry may grind to a halt."[6]

At least one United Press report of the day combined the two actions with Roosevelt's civilian defense speech to support the conclusion that "Washington believes war in the Pacific is near." This was published in at least one Western newspaper under the subheading, "War in Pacific Believed Near."[7] Others treated the war danger with greater reserve. United Press correspondent Miles W. Vaughn, for instance, noted that though the day's "developments lead the American people nearer to war," this was not to say that war was "certain" to occur "immediately."[8]

On August 1 the State Department issued a statement that it had "revoked today all valid licenses authorizing the exportation of petroleum products" to all countries except those in North America, the British Empire, "and the unoccupied territories and other countries resisting aggression." Rejected applicants were told that they could resubmit their requests and that they would be "promptly considered in accordance with the policy set forth in the statement issued by the President today concerning the exportation of petroleum products."[9]

We have stressed that the various announcements of that day did not have to result in the extreme consequences that they appeared to require. Whether we brand this intentional duplicity or the result of internal division, the ambiguity in American policy continued to exist. Members of the administration were fully aware of the fact that even the August 1 restrictions left room for at least limited exports. Ickes' diary entry of Sunday, August 3, implies that Dean Acheson had played a major role in pushing through the newest restrictions (note the reference to "in great triumph"):

> Dean Acheson telephoned me in great triumph on Friday morning. The President had just signed certain orders greatly restricting the flow of oil and gasoline between the United States and Japan. He was particularly glad to relate that all high octane gas had been barred as well as crude oil from which high octane gasoline could be made.
>
> Hereafter no oil will be permitted to be sent to Japan that could be used in airplanes even if tetraethyl lead were applied. No crude oil at all can be imported for Japan from our Pacific Coast. Only low-grade crudes from the Gulf of Mexico and low-grade gasoline may be exported under the new regulations, and the quantities of these that may be exported are only about twenty-five percent of what has been going recently.
>
> If these regulations remain in force, and I now believe that they will, we will be laying a heavy hand upon the whole Japanese economy. However, I wish that petroleum had been cut off altogether.[10]

As if to guarantee maximum possible confusion (or to minimize the danger of effective pressure being brought to bear if there were only one stumbling block), decision making over exportation of petroleum and other products was divided among five separate bodies. Only if a proposed shipment could safely pass all five hurdles would anything be sent to Japan.

    1. An export license had to be obtained from the Department of State.
    2. To obtain that license, the request would have to meet standards set by the administrator of export control (who was only partially answerable to State Department policy).
    3. The Treasury Department had to issue an exchange permit so that the frozen Japanese funds could be utilized.
    4. To obtain that permit, the request would have to fall within the guidelines issued by the Interdepartmental Foreign Funds Control Committee.
    5. Approval was also required from the Economic Defense Board, chaired by the vice president. (It had the vaguely defined agenda of guaranteeing the economic security of the United States.)[11]

A few determined parties in one or more of these "choke points" could guarantee that the petroleum embargo became and stayed what the public perceived it to be, total and permanent. And that is exactly what occurred. Although these officials might be rebuked for zeal beyond their bureaucratic rank, such an approach did match the one that the United States had *appeared* to adopt on July 26.

If the American government refused to commit itself unequivocally to an absolute application of its trade cutoff during these early weeks of the trade freeze, the actual degree of intended strictness perplexed the British and the Dutch, who desired to make their policies match those of the United States. In these intergovernment discussions, the U.S. participants indicated the likelihood of flexibility while actually implementing a comprehensive ban. As an early student of the impact of economic measures during the war noted, in early August "while Acheson still spent a good deal of time discussing with [Noel F.] Hall [of the British Embassy] and the Dutch representatives details of quantities and qualities of goods to go to Japan, he and his associates were already administering the freezing order in ways which made these discussions abortive."[12]

As the tightening-up process was carried out during August, the secretary of state was preoccupied with proposed new initiatives for dealing with Japan. He left the administration of the freeze to Acheson, who represented the State Department on the Foreign Funds Control Committee. Here Acheson pressed his long-standing, hard-line inclinations to force as complete a ban on trade as feasible. This produced some backlash within the department itself. The Far Eastern Division protested that Acheson was exceeding his authority by refusing to approve the expenditure of any Japanese funds for exports; the protest did not alter his position in the least.[13] By the time Hull became fully aware of what had transpired, the de facto policy had taken on a life of its own. To change it would aggravate China and could easily be perceived by Japanese militarists as vindication for refusing to yield to American pressure.[14]

On August 7, *New York Times* reported: "Although the United States technically did not cut off crude oil shipments to Japan but announced that these would be restricted to a pre-war level, no crude oil is moving from this country to Japan, official agencies reported today." The obvious question would be, "Why not?" For one thing, the State Department had received no export license requests from the Japanese. The choke point of the Treasury had not been surmounted: "while requests for release of some funds that would make possible Japanese purchase of American crude oil had been received, none had been granted."[15]

The mid-August case of the *Nitiel Maru* provides a useful example of how the existence of multiple choke points acted to minimize the possibility that any fuel would actually be exported. When the Japanese-owned vessel arrived in Los Angeles Harbor, it was viewed as a test case by West Coasters as to how rigorously the embargo would be enforced. According to a press report of the following day, the Japanese were seeking "a cargo of Diesel low-grade oil."[16] A second tanker, the *Otowasan Maru*, arrived a few days afterwards. Both sought to fill their respective holds with some 75,000 barrels of diesel oil[17] and both departed empty less than ten days later.[18] Although they had received the necessary export licenses, they had been unable to obtain a release of the necessary funds from the Treasury Department. Once again, the choke point was the Treasury.

This represented a continuing pattern for the limited number of requests that were able to pass the first hurdle of obtaining an export license from a reluctant State Department. In October one paper reported that "A few Japanese tankers have licenses, but have been unable to obtain the funds for completing the purchases, while it is doubtful that more export licenses will be granted for such shipments."[19] Hence the Treasury continued its totally obstructionist approach. Since only a few export licenses had been issued, the State Department had not been much more flexible. Furthermore, that minor degree of cooperation was about to end; and this was clearly a grim situation from the Japanese viewpoint.

Regardless of which specific choke point was utilized to destroy a specific exportation request, the result was the same: the petroleum did not move. On August 20, government officials revealed that since the July 26 asset freeze, only one shipment had been made and according to the press report, "that was only to enable a ship to return to her home port."[20] On the 24th, another correspondent noted that because of the multinational petroleum embargo, "the movement of foreign-produced oil to Japan [has] virtually stopped."[21] A story datelined from Washington on August 30 noted that "Officials said today that no oil has been shipped to Japan since the issuance of the President's new restriction orders" at the beginning of the month.[22]

The United States government remained officially coy about exactly what degree and kind of future trade would be permitted. It soon became clear that even under an optimistic scenario, some type of political reconciliation would have to occur first. On August 30, the Japanese newspaper agency Domei reported from Washington the latest speculation from "well-informed sources." According to Domei, it was still uncertain what degree of trade would eventually be permitted. The agency pointed out that although Roosevelt had indicated a willingness to permit "usual or prewar quantities" of petroleum to be exported, the interpretation of this phrase was producing a goodly amount of intra-administration squabbling. Some wanted to go so far as to define the expression in terms of the volume sold "before the Manchurian Incident in 1932, thus drastically reducing amounts permittable for export to Japan."[23]

A creative bureaucracy multiplied the obstacles to prevent the resumption of even a modest trade. One method utilized was to reject any large export license request while refusing to say what size request would be granted. For example, the effort of the Japanese to secure licenses to export four million dollars worth of American cotton had gained low-level approval but was rejected by Sumner Welles. Welles insisted that such licenses should be granted only in much smaller amounts, but never informed the Japanese of the actual cutoff point. After all, "if they applied for more modest quantities, they would discover the quota limit slowly by a building-up process."[24] Any government would, of course, find such mickey mouse techniques embarrassing, if not unbearably humiliating; this was especially true for the "face conscious" Japanese. The positive side of this policy would be that American officials could piously note that they could hardly take responsibility for denying applications when the applications had not been filed.

Another fruitful method for not permitting exportation was to wrangle over how it would be paid for. Just before the asset freeze went into effect some two million dollars had been withdrawn by the Yokohama Specie Bank. Hence, United States officials argued, the impounded funds that remained in American banks did not need to be used; the Japanese could simply transfer the two million dollars back into the United States in order to finance approved, low-quality petroleum exports. The Japanese protested that these were navy funds and not under the control of the central government. The Americans countered with the suggestion that the Japanese utilize funds they had in banks in South America. The Japanese replied with an unofficial suggestion of a barter deal: silk for cotton and oil. The U.S. was not receptive.[25]

And just in case the Japanese government was able to convince a reluctant navy to release its two million dollars, a further wrinkle was added. The money had been received in ten thousand dollar bills, and the United States had decided to withdraw these from circulation to protect against them being used as kidnapping ransoms. So the Japanese could not redeposit the bills, but unless they redeposited the money, there would be no trade permitted.[26] No refusal to permit trade, just the setting of conditions to make it impossible.

In mid-September, rumors began to surface that it had definitely been decided to cut off all petroleum supplies. In early October reports circulated that the British, Americans, and Dutch had agreed to go beyond this and eliminate all exports of all types.[27] Although government officials were not willing to be so explicit on a for-attribution-basis, in private, they were more candid. An internal memorandum from the Division of Far Eastern Affairs of the Department of State noted on September 24 that no change in the total ban on petroleum was anticipated:

> Under procedure and practice now in effect in the United States, no exports to Japan of petroleum products and of cotton are taking place. it is believed advisable to have this situation continue, but not to tell the Japanese that exports of all petroleum products and of all cotton to Japan have been prohibited. It is therefore suggested that the British and the Dutch might be told that with regard to petroleum products and cotton no exportation from the United States to Japan is now taking place and that if there is any change in that situation we shall expect to inform them in advance of the changes to be made.[28]

Oddly enough, as late as the third week in September, Dean Acheson could write to the secretary of state that the British and Dutch had imposed more explicitly prohibitory regulations than had the United States. "Our own policy, owing in part to the dual control which we exercise over trade with Japan through export control and financial control, is obscure and not fully developed." (The trade issue was not a peripheral one; it was a central issue in the relationship of the Western powers and Japan. Hence the cynic is surely justified in wondering how two months could have gone by without a definitive policy being drafted unless there had been intentional foot dragging that guaranteed a full trade freeze without the burden of officially adopting one.) Officially the policy remained vague and imprecise. The reality was far stronger: "In so far as the actual treatment of trade with Japan is concerned, as distinguished from the policy decisions, the situation is about the same in all three countries. Trade is virtually at a standstill."[29]

Comparison of policies between Britain and the United States provides useful information in regard to both nations as well as several members of the British Commonwealth. The practice of the United States in regard to the use of blocked (frozen) accounts remained carefully uncommitted: "Frozen funds may not be used for payments for exports until cash and Japanese balances in Latin America have been used up. *If* cash and balances in Latin America are used up, under present policy determinations the use of blocked funds would then *presumably* be permissible for the payment of such exports as might be permitted" (emphasis added).[30]

As to petroleum, Acheson's analysis noted, it had been decided that only "certain types of crude petroleum and lower grade petroleum products" could be sent to Japan from the continental forty-eight states. These were subject to quotas, some of which were restrictive and others not. On the other hand, these quotas "are being reconsidered." This was the theory, but the practice was clearly different: "Factual situation at present: As a result of the conditions imposed under the export control and financial control, no exports of petroleum products to Japan have taken place. Three export licenses have been granted, to a value of $178,000, but exports have not been permitted in view of the inability of the Japanese to arrange satisfactory methods of payment."[31]

A monthly figure of $600,000 worth of cotton exports had been authorized. That was the theory. The reality was, "None has been exported since the freezing orders became effective, owing to the shipping and payments situations."[32]

Canada continued to participate fully in the embargo. "Trade with Japan is at a standstill."[33]

> Exports had been restricted, prior to freezing, to products not useful from a military viewpoint and only one small cargo of wood products and paper ($19,000 in value) has left since freezing.
> All exports to Japan are subject to export licenses. The only licenses outstanding at the time of the freezing order, for 7,000 tons of wheat, have been recalled. Licenses are being granted only for the personal effects of persons returning to Japan.[34]

In Australia, the Japanese were also up against a total ban on commerce: "Trade with Japan is at a standstill. One vessel has come to Australia since the freezing order. It was permitted to discharge its cargo and take on a cargo of wool of equal value. Apparently the wool had been purchased prior to the freezing order, although this is not entirely clear."[35]

As to India, Acheson continued, "Aside from exports of coir and cotton, trade is at a standstill. Exports of cotton covered by pre-freezing confirmed credits are being permitted within the limits of the 1940 level. These credits are now practically exhausted."[36]

In the British Empire, the only major "hole" through which any real trade still flowed to Japan was Malaya. Malaya continued to export iron ore and manganese.[37]

Oddly enough, the *New York Times* inserted a supplementary paragraph into a dispatch from Tokyo in mid-October taking umbrage at those who called the Western policy an "all-out" embargo: "There has been no confirmation from Washington or elsewhere of an 'all-out' embargo against Japan, although it was indicated several weeks ago that the Japanese no longer were able to import oil from the United States and the Tokyo newspaper *Miyako* recently complained that Japan had not been able to import 'a drop' of gasoline in two months."[38]

If such an extensive stoppage is not an "all-out" embargo, what additional steps would be required to make it one? Even Secretary of State Hull piously proclaimed in October, in the words of one report, that "he knew nothing of a purported agreement under which the United States, Great Britain and the Netherlands Indies" would not send any future "oil to Japan."[39] Doubtlessly, a man with the skill of Hull worded his remarks in such a way that they were within the letter of the truth, there being no formal, written treaty agreeing to the course being undertaken. But such diplomatic niceties did not hide the fact that there was a clear understanding of the general policy that would be followed.

A Secondary Challenge: The Call-up of the Philippine Militia

Although we briefly discussed the extension of the American embargo to the Philippines and the attending military buildup, certain aspects of the latter decision deserve additional emphasis because it represented a further intensification of American-Japanese tensions.

On the day the embargo went into effect, July 26, 1941, the United States engaged in a piece of widely publicized saber rattling virtually in the Japanese backyard. Invoking the authority of the Philippine Independence Act, President Roosevelt issued an order saying, "I . . . call and order into the service of the armed forces of the United States for the period of the existing emergency . . . all of the organized military forces of the Commonwealth of the Philippines."[40] This gravely expanded the military obligations of America thousands of miles further westward. Retired General Douglas MacArthur was recalled to active duty and given command of American forces in the Far East.[41]

The United States considered the Japanese expansion into the southern half of Indochina as a security threat to the Philippines. The upgrading of naval operations out of the islands could result in either offensive or defensive actions. Since by their very design and nature, bombers are designed for offensive operations, the steady influx of B17s could not so easily be interpreted in a benign fashion. If the Russians could be convinced to permit the use of their Siberian bases for "round robin" shuttle bombing, the effectiveness of the B17s would be further magnified. Hence, to the wary Japanese, the American actions transformed the Philippines into an unquestionably offensive dagger aimed right at the heart of Japan.

Assuming that the situation had to end in military conflict, the decision may well have been a wise one; without such an assumption the action was far more subject to challenge. And even if one accepts the decision, such forward basing required the postponing of open conflict until the buildup reached its height. The total embargo, in effect, imposed rigid time limits that kept this goal from being met.

Furthermore, coming so quickly upon the heels of the asset freeze, the Philippine actions vastly increased the difficulty of carrying out the original presidential desire to hold the boycott to a minimum. It upped the psychological ante on both sides.

The mustering of the Philippine militia into federal service implied the possibility of strenuous action to enforce the embargo militarily. As one account noted, "This action strengthens the possibility of a blockade."[42] That such an outcome may have been toyed with in some quarters may be hinted at by other evidence as well. An official in London (described as "a qualified informant") was quoted on August 9 as asserting that the embargo was "merely the first step in a policy toward Japan which is to grow increasingly tougher." And what might these stronger measures be? (One obvious one would be a blockade. After all, Washington had played around with the idea in 1938.) The informant, however, refused to engage in speculation: "What the next steps will be naturally must remain secret. Naturally you don't show your hand to the other fellow."[43]

If the beefing up of the Philippines posed a threat to Japan, it also posed a threat to the American military's capacity to fulfill its assigned duties under contingency war plans. However impressive the Philippine action appeared in the headlines, it created explicit new responsibilities that could prove difficult to meet. As the chief intelligence officer for the Pacific fleet wrote many years later:

> This signaled the beginnings of a major reinforcement of our military strength in the Philippines as a strategic barrier to deter a Japanese southward move to grab the oil reserves of the Dutch East Indies.
>
> It was a move that reversed the strategic doctrines of both the Rainbow 5 war plan and a twenty-year-old policy *not* to make any major commitment of American forces west of Hawaii. As far as the Pacific Fleet was concerned, the Cavite base outside Manila did not have adequate repair facilities or fuel reserves to act as a forward base. So General MacArthur would be faced with defending the Philippines with untrained troops at the end of an exposed and insufficient ocean supply line.
>
> It was a military commitment that neither the army nor our already overstretched fleet at Hawaii could fulfill. Within four short months the Japanese would prove the point. . . .
>
> Against the advice of the navy department, a presidential decision had been made to shift our front line of defense five thousand miles westward across the reaches of the Pacific Ocean. This decision invited all the risks attendant on launching a military buildup on the front doorstep of an adversary's intended domain.[44]

The Possibility of an End Run on U.S. Restrictions Via South America

Japan's desire to diversify its markets and be less dependent upon the United States was an obvious motivating factor in its efforts to expand trade with South America. Due to trade limitations in 1940 and early 1941, Japan was provided further incentive for efforts in this direction. According to a State Department evaluation of mid-August, these efforts had met with little success:

> But Japan's interest in Latin America was and is, chiefly economic. Japan has launched a concerted drive to expand and increase its Latin American trade, primarily, to counteract the importance that its trade with the United States holds in its national economy. To date this Japanese policy has made but little headway, first, because of a prevailing fear of Japanese penetration in many countries of Latin America, and secondly, because of difficulties in balancing its trade with countries which do not produce the raw materials urgently needed in Japan.
>
> Japan desires cotton, oil, and scrap iron, formerly exported in large quantities from the United States, and in return wants markets for its own products. In spite of currency and other difficulties such as a lack of demand for Japanese products, Japan has negotiated trade agreements with Argentina, Chile, Colombia, Venezuela, Paraguay and Mexico during the past year. The meager returns from this drive from Latin American markets may readily be seen from the fact that today Japan enjoys only 3 percent of the aggregate trade volume of the Latin American countries.[45]

The South American countries went along with the cutoff of trade with minimal domestic protest and retribution from Japan. In early September, Ambassador Grew in Tokyo contacted the various Latin American diplomatic representatives in that capital to probe their governments' reactions to the stricter measures:

> The Embassy's informants gave the impression that they are not unduly perturbed at the prospect of Japan's cutting off trade with their countries. They state that although Japan is still continuing to send ships to the West Coast of South America their numbers have been considerably curtailed during the last two months and they explain that this lack of shipping together with [North] American purchases of raw materials and the Latin-American countries own restrictions on exports outside of the American Continent have already greatly decreased trade with Japan which in any event was never very large. In the case of Peru in particular the stoppage of the exports of Japanese textiles is rather welcome as those exports had previously seriously competed with Peruvian textile industries.[46]

Two other factors played a major role in denying Japan any major access to South American markets. Most of its business in that region was actually paid for through United States banks. Hence the trade freeze had an inevitable spillover effect south of the border. Furthermore, in addition to its increased South American trade, the United States was energetically negotiating formal trade agreements under which it would become the sole recipient of any locally produced "strategic raw materials."[47] In light of the lack of products desired by South America, Japan's trade expansion efforts were probably doomed to failure. These various additional hindrances, guaranteed their failure.

The Minimal Impact of the Embargo on the United States Itself

Even as late as early September the United States government was officially speaking of the embargo in terms of potentiality rather than actuality. In releasing a study of the United States Tariff Commission, the government stressed "the problems which would be created *if* a complete stoppage of imports from Japan should occur" (emphasis added).[48] The term *problems* substantially exaggerated the reality. As the study's statistics make plain (Table 5.1), the only serious import problem the United States would face would be the replacement of the silk normally received from Japan:

> Present users of silk hosiery would be the principal consumer interests affected. For at least a limited time, aggregate consumption of full-fashioned hosiery would have to be sharply reduced. However, after necessary readjustments were made by the hosiery industry and by the suppliers of yarn (which would probably require a year or so) domestic production of hosiery of fibers other than silk would probably be sufficient to supply the great bulk of the country's requirements.[49]

There would also be some military impact since parachutes were made of silk.[50] On the other hand, sufficient supplies were already held by the American government to manufacture "about one-half million parachutes."[51]

Other sources make it plain that there were individual (as contrasted to national) hardships in the United States. When all civilian use of silk was finally terminated at midnight on the evening of August 2, some 175,000 workers in silk mills were temporarily put out of work.[52] Many of these workers were quickly shifted to work on government contracts (for military parachutes and powder bags), and others were recalled as various synthetics took the place of silk. So far as the consuming public at large went, the main impact was the elimination of silk hosiery. One contemporary headline summed it up well: "Curb on Japan to Affect Many of the Little Things in U.S. Life."[53] A nuisance such losses might be, but in no sense a catastrophe.

From the import side of matters, this was as close as possible to a perfect situation: minimum impact upon the American side and the maximum impact upon the Japanese. A somewhat similar situation existed with respect to the impact of the termination of trade upon American exports. Just as the United States would suffer little damage from an elimination of Japanese imports, it would also suffer only modest harm due to the loss of the Japanese export market. The most obvious negative factor would come from the monetary losses suffered by the elimination of petroleum exports. From the Japanese standpoint, the reliance upon American petroleum was horrendous. From the American side, however, the reliance upon Japan as

Table 5.1. United States Imports for Consumption from Japan, by Principal Commodity Groups, 1940 and January–May 1940 and 1941

Commodity group	Value* (1,000 dollars)			Proportion of total value of imports from Japan (Percent)		
	1940	January–May 1940	January–May 1941	1940	January–May 1940	January–May 1941
Silk and silk products	106,588	36,526	34,538	67.9	63.6	65.8
Fish and fish products	8,776	4,990	1,533	5.6	8.7	2.9
Cotton goods	6,452	2,498	3,206	4.1	4.3	6.1
Chemicals and industrial oils	3,475	1,807	1,176	2.2	3.1	2.3
China, porcelain, and earthenware	3,461	1,164	985	2.2	2.0	1.9
Teas	3,190	708	718	2.0	1.2	1.4
Pedaline braid and unfinished paper hat bodies	1,506	872	794	1.0	1.5	1.5
Canned fruits	1,185	109	387	.8	.2	.7
Rayon staple fiber	1,033	501	487	.7	.9	.9
Vegetables, sauces, and other food preparations	941	387	302	.6	.7	.6
Electric lamps	924	258	163	.6	.4	.3
Mink furs	898	506	917	.6	.9	1.7
Lily bulbs	845	30	35	.5	.1	.1
Pearls, cultured, and solid imitation	585	218	418	.4	.4	.8
Slide fasteners	526	205	196	.3	.4	.4
Bristles	515	274	256	.3	.5	.5
Bamboo sticks	355	140	168	.2	.2	.3
Miscellaneous pyroxylin articles	287	111	50	.2	.2	.1
Paper manufacturers, n.s.p.f.	266	91	83	.2	.2	.2
Pearl shells	171	133	216	.1	.2	.4
Total imports enumerated above	141,979	51,528	46,628	90.5	89.7	88.9
All others†	14,954	5,912	5,833	9.5	10.3	11.1
Total	156,933	57,440	52,461	100.0	100.0	100.0

*The values given do not necessarily show the values of total imports from Japan within each of the classes indicated; instead, they show the total of only the imports which are separately listed in the appendix table. For example, the value of all fish and fish products from Japan was in excess of $8,776,000 in 1940, but that sum represents the total value of those fish and fish products which are separately analyzed in this report. †Includes imports valued at about $8,000 in 1940 of optical lenses, unmanufactured mica, and platinum grains, nuggets, sponge, and scrap, which classes are designated as "critical" or "strategic" materials. No other materials, except silk, which were designated by the Army and Navy Munitions Board as "critical" or "strategic," were imported from Japan in 1940. *Source:* U.S. Tariff Commission, *United States Imports from Japan* (1941), Table 1.

Economic Strangulation: August to December 1941

Table 5.2. Worldwide United States Domestic Petroleum Exports, by Principal Commodities, in Specified Years, 1931 to 1942

(In Thousands of Barrels)

Commodity	1931	1933	1937	1939	1940	1941	1942
Crude petroleum	25,535	36,584	67,127	72,064	51,495	34,484	35,560
Gasoline and naphtha*	43,838	27,710	35,879	42,189	22,748	24,238	33,026
Kerosene	12,534	8,764	8,664	7,994	3,139	2,991	2,499
Distillate fuel oil	26,588	10,232	29,011	30,618	17,565	14,934	20,230
Residual fuel oil†		8,223	12,810	14,972	11,880	10,330	8,590
Lubricating oil	8,049	8,147	10,838	11,766	10,332	9,394	7.974
Total	116,544	99,660	164,329	179,603	117,159	96,371	107,879

*Includes antiknock compounds, mineral spirits, and solvents; also natural gasoline. †Does not include fuel oil for bunkers of vessels engaged in foreign trade, totaling between 33 million and 37 million barrels in most prewar years.

Source: U.S. Tariff Commission, *Petroleum* (1946), Table 20 (1943, 1944 omitted).

a market was not nearly as significant. In 1939 Japan received 15.6% of all petroleum products the United States exported and in 1940 it received 19.6% (see Tables 5.2 and 5.3).[54] This placed exports to Japan second in volume only to the amounts transported across the border into Canada. In 1941 Japan dropped back to third place, falling behind both Canada and Britain because of the midyear ban. If the exports had continued unabated, it is likely that the gallonage received by both Japan and Britain would have been almost identical.

Although this makes a paper case for damage to the U.S. economy, it must be remembered that at least on the East Coast substantial cutbacks in petroleum consumption were made in August. Hence petroleum denied to Japan would not be lost to the marketplace but eventually rechanneled to American civilian customers and the growing American military market. Once again we find the United States having little in the way of dollar and cents reasons to avoid continuing the asset freeze and trade ban: it inflicted minimal damage stateside and maximum damage on the Japanese.

After providing an Associated Press summary of the Tariff Commission report, the *Wall Street Journal* presented its own analysis of the impact of the import/export trade cutoff on one particular aspect of Nippon's economy: "Japan is slipping fast from a dominant position in the world textile field. ... Japan can no longer be considered a world factor in apparel wool consumption, and is directly faced with the loss of major influence in synthetic textile trade. Inability to obtain supplies of raw materials can be directly, and almost solely, blamed."[55]

Table 5.3. Petroleum and Principal Liquid
Products: United States Domestic Exports by
Principal Markets, in Specified Years, 1931 to 1942

Country	1931	1933	1937	1939	1940	1941	1942
	Quantity (1,000 barrels)						
Japan	10,909	10,175	28,378	27,995	22,912	12,195	—
Canada	24,517	22,711	31,662	32,975	34,191	31,390	39,329
France	9,069	15,977	13,846	18,046	6,453	—	—
United Kingdom	19,258	11,870	12,562	18,466	12,600	25,212	44,110
Netherlands West Indies	2,177	2,437	11,051	10,549	3,112	576	557
Germany*	4,035	2,853	6,635	5,882	—	—	—
Italy	1,271	1,111	6,328	7,355	2,128	†	†
Netherlands	3,964	2,703	6,819	6,392	887	†	—
Sweden	1,882	1,186	2,794	6,066	813	341	660
Belgium	2,826	2,643	5,172	3,592	410	†	—
Spain	1,550	1,174	1,294	4,217	4,454	1,628	107
All other	35,086	24,820	37,788	38,068	29,199	25,029	23,116
Total	116,544	99,660	164,329	179,603	117,159	96,371	107,879
	Percent of total quantity						
Japan	9.4	10.2	17.3	15.6	19.6	12.6	—
Canada	21.0	22.8	19.3	18.4	29.2	32.6	36.5
France	7.8	16.0	8.4	10.0	5.5	—	—
United Kingdom	16.5	11.9	7.6	10.3	10.8	26.2	40.9
Netherlands West Indies	1.9	2.4	6.7	5.9	2.6	.6	.5
Germany*	3.5	2.9	4.0	3.3	—	—	—
Italy	1.1	1.1	3.9	4.1	1.8	§	§
Netherlands	3.4	2.7	4.2	3.5	.8	§	—
Sweden	1.6	1.2	1.7	3.4	.7	.3	.6
Belgium	2.4	2.7	3.1	2.0	.3	§	—
Spain	1.3	1.2	.8	2.3	3.8	1.7	.1
All other	30.1	24.9	23.0	21.2	24.9	26.0	21.4
Total	100.0	100.0	100.0	100.0	100.0	100.0	100.0

*Includes Austria in 1938–44. †Less than 500. §Less than 0.05 percent.
Source: U.S. Tariff Commission, Petroleum (1946), Table 21 (1943, 1944 omitted).

NOTES

The Choke Points for Trade Multiply as Government Policy Firms into Total Prohibition

1. Quoted in the following press accounts: Associated Press, "Oil Exports to Japan Are Slashed," *Richmond Times Dispatch*, 2 August 1941, 3; United Press, "President Bans Oil for Japan," *Los Angeles Times*, 2 August 1941, I-6; George Bookman, "U.S. Bans Plane Fuel to Japan . . . / Sale to Nippon of Oil Is Put on Ration Basis of Half 1940's," *Washington Post*, 2 August 1941, 1.
2. Bookman, "U.S. Bans Plane Fuel to Japan," 1.
3. Ibid.
4. *Los Angeles Times*, 2 August 1941, I-1.
5. United Press, "President Cuts Off Oil to Japan, Freezes All Silk Stocks in U.S.," *Los Angeles Times*, 2 August 1941, I-1.
6. "President Bans Oil for Japan," *Los Angeles Times*, 2 August 1941, I-6.
7. United Press, "President Cuts Off Oil to Japan," I-1.
8. "Tangles of East Asia Situation and Repercussions Analyzed," *Los Angeles Times*, 2 August 1941, I-5.
9. John H. Crider, "Aviation Fuel Barred to Japan as Roosevelt Order Curbs Exports," *New York Times*, 2 August 1941, 1.
10. Harold L. Ickes, *The Secret Diary of Harold L. Ickes*, vol. 3, *The Lowering Clouds, 1939–1941* (New York: Simon and Schuster, 1954), 591–92.
11. The five points are my own summary. On July 31, the president announced the creation of the Economic Defense Board. To be chaired by Vice President Wallace, the board was to be composed of himself and five additional top government officials (or their representatives): the attorney general, the secretary of state, the secretary of commerce, the secretary of the treasury, and the secretary of agriculture. Although it was not explicitly spelled out in the published order creating the board, "reliable quarters" told the press that among its duties would be "handling the frozen assets of the Axis powers" and "watching export controls designed to keep essential war goods from reaching the Axis nations" (Associated Press, "Super War Board Named for Economic Battle on Axis," *Los Angeles Times*, 1 August 1941, I-6).
12. W. N. Medlicott, *The Economic Blockade*, 2 vols., vols. 7 and 8 of the *History of the Second World War*, United Kingdom Civil Series, ed. W. Keith Hancock (London: H.M.S.O., 1952), 2:115.
13. Jonathan C. Utley, "Upstairs, Downstairs at Foggy Bottom: Oil Exports and Japan, 1940–1941," *Prologue: The Journal of the National Archives* 8 (Spring 1976): 26.
14. Ibid., 26–27.
15. Frank L. Kluckhohn, "U.S. and Britain Warn Japan on Thailand," *New York Times*, 7 August 1941, 1.
16. "Japan Tanker Waits for Oil," *Los Angeles Times*, 6 August 1941.
17. "Two Tankers Prepare to Sail for Japan without Cargoes," *Los Angeles Times*, 14 August 1941, I-1. The 6 August article (footnote 16) indicated that the *Nitiel Maru* was the first to test the embargo; hence our deduction that the *Otowasan Maru* arrived a few days later.
18. "Two Tankers Prepare to Sail," I-1. Also see "Last Japan Ship Leaves Sans Oil," *Los Angeles Times*, 15 August 1941, I-7. Since the last ship referred to in the article was identified as the *Nitiel Maru*, this implies that the *Otowasan Maru* had left slightly earlier. On their departure and the problems associated with attempting to obtain a load of fuel, also see Associated Press, "Japanese Load U.S. Oil," *New York Times*,

13 August 1941, 6, and United Press, "Tankers Clear for Japan," *New York Times*, 13 August 1941, 6.

19. "Agitation in Tokyo Held Unimpressive," *New York Times*, 10 October 1941, 8.
20. "Oil Shipments to Japan Cease," *New York Times*, 21 August 1941, 10.
21. J. H. Carmical, "Japanese Oil Seen as Key to Policy," *New York Times*, 24 August 1941, III-1.
22. Bertram D. Hulen, "Hull Minimizes Talk with Japan," *New York Times*, 31 August 1941, 14. Hulen observed: "Such shipments ceased August 2."
23. Domei, "Added Restrictions on U.S. Oil Exports for Japan Studied," *Japan Times and Advertiser* (morning edition), 1 September 1941, 1.
24. Medlicott, *Economic Blockade*, 2:115.
25. Ibid., 115–16.
26. Ibid., 116.
27. Otto D. Tolischus, "Japanese Profess Unconcern on Oil," *New York Times*, 10 October 1941, 8.
28. "Department of State, Division of Far Eastern Affairs, September 24, 1941"; attached to State Department document 894.24/1749.
29. "Trade with Japan," dated 22 September 1941; State Department document 894.24/1750. An attached "Restrictions on Japanese Trade and Payments in the British Empire" carries the same date and identification number.
30. "Restrictions on Japanese Trade," 2.
31. Ibid., 3.
32. Ibid., 4.
33. Ibid., 7.
34. Ibid., 7–8.
35. Ibid., 8.
36. Ibid., 9.
37. Ibid., 1.
38. Inserted by an unidentified author into an article by Otto D. Tolischus, "Japanese Profess Unconcern on Oil," *New York Times*, 10 October 1941, 8.
39. "Agitation in Tokyo Held Unimpressive," *New York Times*, 10 October 1941, 8.

A Secondary Challenge: The Call-up of the Philippine Militia

40. For entire text, see "Roosevelt Order on Army," *New York Times*, 27 July 1941, I-13.
41. For the complete text of General Marshall's notification to MacArthur and MacArthur's response, see George C. Marshall, *The Papers of George Catlett Marshall*, vol. 2, *We Cannot Delay, July 1, 1939–December 6, 1941*, ed. Larry I. Bland (Baltimore: Johns Hopkins University Press, 1986), 577.
42. John H. Crider, "Roosevelt Puts Filipino Forces in U.S. Army," *New York Times*, 27 July 1941, I-1.
43. Associated Press, "'Tough' Curbs on Japanese Are Discussed / U.S.-British Sanctions Merely a Beginning," *Richmond Times Dispatch*, 10 August 1941, I-6.
44. Edwin L. Layton, with Roger Pineau and John Costello, *"And I Was There": Pearl Harbor and Midway—Breaking the Secrets* (New York: William Morrow, 1985), 121–22.

The Possibility of an End Run on U.S. Restrictions Via South America

45. "Japan Political Estimate, August 20, 1941," State Department document 894.00/1132, 34.

46. Telegram from Grew to State Department, September 6, 1941; State Department document 894.24/1582, 1–2.

47. Ernest K. Lindley, "On Capitol Hill," *Richmond Times Dispatch*, 30 July 1941, 9.

The Minimal Impact of the Embargo on the United States Itself

48. Press release dated September 10, 1941; United States Tariff Commission, *United States Imports from Japan and Their Relation to the Defense Program and to the Economy of the Country* (Washington, D.C.: U.S. Government Printing Office, 1941). Press release bound with book.

49. U.S. Tariff Commission, *United States Imports from Japan*, 22; For a detailed discussion, see 159–79.

50. Ibid., 159.

51. Ibid., 161.

52. Alfred Friendly, "OPM Order to Shut Silk Mills . . . / Army to Need All Silk Stocks; 175,000 Face Loss of Work," *Washington Post*, 2 August 1941, 1.

53. International News Service, *Washington Post*, 27 July 1941, A-4.

54. U.S. Tariff Commission, *Petroleum*, War Changes in Industry Series, Report No. 17 (Washington: U.S. Government Printing Office, 1946).

55. "Stoppage of Japan Imports Will Have Only Slight Effect on U.S. Economy," *Wall Street Journal*, 10 September 1941, 4.

Chapter 6

IMPACT OF THE 1940 EMBARGO MEASURES ON JAPAN

Any serious limitations on trade or the obtaining of essential foreign resources inevitably produced an awkward situation for Japan both commercially and militarily. As one prominent historian of warfare has noted, "From the first, the position of Japan has been one of extreme strategic fragility, because her economic potential was approximately only 10 percent of that of the United States, and her acreage of arable land no more than 3 percent, yet it had to support a population over half as large."[1] With the one exception of sugar (imported mainly out of Taiwan), Japan could satisfy most of its food requirements in the decade prior to the Pacific war.[2] There were two areas, however, where this basic self-sufficiency could be quickly eroded. There was substantial reliance upon imported fertilizer (about 30 percent in the typical year of 1936)[3] and between 20 and 25 percent of Japan's rice came from abroad.[4] If the Western powers could interdict those supplies (easier said than done in the first years of the war), Japan's food supply would dramatically deteriorate.

Industrially, Japan was weak when contrasted with its potential American foe. Both steel capacity[5] and coal production[6] were only a meager 13 percent (approximately) of that of the United States. During the war, munitions production never exceeded 10 percent of that in the United States.[7]

In spite of this economic weakness, Japan possessed a large army and a first-class fleet. Although striking at the economic Achilles heel of Japan was naturally appealing in light of its economy's comparative weakness, it only made sense if one were genuinely ready to negotiate a mutually acceptable compromise (which meant leaving Japan a good part of its empire) or it one were willing to risk the military retaliation that Japan's world-class military was quite capable of inflicting. As Cordell Hull points out below (and has already been noted in previous chapters), the danger of war occurring had led to an ongoing go-slow attitude in the highest echelons of the government. Hence we would expect the early measures of 1940 to have had an impact but not the kind of decisive one that could have pushed Japan over the edge into overt hostilities.

In evaluating the results of the 1940 embargo measures, it is useful to extend the studied period into the spring or early summer of the following year because the impact being commented upon by various public sources in 1941 resulted, in the main, from the earlier trade limitations. In retrospect, Cordell Hull was convinced that the 1940 actions had forced the Japanese to be more cautious in undertaking further expansionism in Asia:

> Japan knew that our economic pressure was growing. By the beginning of 1941, shipments to her from the United States of iron, steel, most other important metals, high-octane gasoline, and plants for producing it had virtually ceased. We still permitted shipments of petroleum lest Japan use such an embargo as an excuse for taking over the oil production of the Netherlands East Indies. . . .
> What Japan did not know was whether and in what circumstances we would use force. Isolationist sentiment in the United States was still strong, as the Lend-Lease debate in Congress showed. But she also saw that the Administration was acting with determination, and that an increasing number of Americans were coming to realize the dangers threatening us in both the Atlantic and the Pacific.[8]

Critics of the relative mildness of American sanctions during this period stressed the failure of the limitations to inflict the degree of economic punishment that they wished to see. As Edwin L. James wrote in the fall of 1941 (in the context of warning of possible loopholes in the new "total" boycott), "It is recalled by some critics that when Washington cut off scrap iron from Japan, it put no limitation [at first] on pig iron, and when it halted pig iron, it left free the shipment of ingots and finished steel." Nor did the banning of aviation gas amount to a knockout punch. "Last year's oil curb," James argued, "did not seriously hurt the Japanese, for, if so, there would have been no call for a new order" prohibiting exports in the summer of 1941.[9]

The *New York Times* editorially criticized the actions as inadequate extensions of the "moral embargo" begun several years earlier:

> The arrival of Japanese warships off the coast of Indo-China should mark the end of an American policy in the Far East. This policy is the "moral embargo" which we first employed in 1937, concurrently with the League of Nations, and then developed independently in 1938. The "moral embargo" has always been a halfway measure. It was intended to warn Japan of our disapproval of her aggressive action, but it was never strict enough to cripple seriously her war machine.
> Under this policy we shut off the shipment to Japan of airplanes, aviation gasoline and certain types of iron and steel scrap. But we did not shut off shipments of low-grade gasoline, petroleum, various types of steel and iron, copper, cotton and ferroalloys, all of which were indispensable to Japan's war effort.[10]

Although the restrictions fell well short of representing the fatal weapon such opinions makers sought, they did impose considerable difficulties upon the Japanese economy. In January of 1941, the *New York Times*

Table 6.1. Japanese Reliance Upon American Scrap Metal (As a Percentage of Her Total Requirements)

Year	Percentage
1931	16.2%
1932	29.3%
1933	54.1%
1934	82.3%
1935	66.1%
1936	70.0%
1937	70.0%
1938	55.3%
1939 (estimated)	approx. 75.0%

Source: Converted into chart form from percentages in "Steel Scrap Moves in New Channels," *New York Times*, 4 August 1940, III-1.

noted that specific data on the impact of the embargo were unavailable though "commentaries that have appeared in recent months in various economic writings in Japan" did indicate that "production has been slowed up considerably." The only specific number the *Times* provided was in regard to the steel industry. "Japanese open hearths, which formerly used a large proportion of scrap metal, have switched to 70 percent pig iron and 30 percent scrap, with a drop in output to 30 percent of capacity."[11]

In March 1941, the United States Commerce Department released a survey of the economic effects of the Japanese conflict with China. With a war-related budget in 1940 seven times the size of the budget of the "peace year" of 1936-1937, the conflict was putting immense strains upon Japan. The economic limitations imposed by the Western powers had added to the damage. Trade with the United States had been "materially" reduced, while that with the Soviet Union had increased only marginally. "Trade with the British Empire," the press summary noted, "continued important, despite its dwindling volume and restrictions on exports to Japan from Canada, Australia, and India."[12]

A Commerce Department report issued two months later summed up Japan's industrial problems in March. "Industrial production," it noted, "has been generally lagging as a result of such restrictive factors as acute shortages of raw materials and labor." Even when Japan could obtain the external supplies it sought, its maximum utilization of these resources was hindered by a lack of freighters and tankers.[13]

When the Commerce Department released intentional trade figures for May 1941, trade with Japan had dropped to $6,621,000, less than half the figure for the same month in 1940. Indeed, it was the lowest monthly dollar amount of exports to that nation since 1933. The Associated Press added, "How much of this decline was due to curtailed shipments of oil, metals, machinery and other war materials could not be learned, however,

Table 6.2. Iron and Steel Export from the U.S. to Japan (In Tons)

Year	Tons
1935	1,065,143
1936	1,009,767
1937	1,872,646
1938	1,365,721
1939	2,024,264
1940	958,778
1941*	289
1941†	495

*Actual (January–July). †Hypothetical (seven-month figure projected for entire calendar year).
Source: U.S. Department of Commerce annual compilations *Foreign Commerce and Navigation of the United States*.

because the department recently stopped publication of such figures."[14] Since the Japanese obviously knew how much they were purchasing, the main purposes of this prohibition were probably twofold: it eased Japanese pride by not publicly revealing how hard certain restrictions were hurting and it protected the administration from criticism concerning those items it continued to export which some Americans fervently wished to see halted (such as all petroleum).

An internal State Department analysis of late May attempted to explain how Japan had been able to cope successfully with the existing pressures:

> There are, however, increasing signs of economic strain in Japan. In spite of the fact that war has brought a temporary prosperity, manufacture is booming (where raw materials are obtainable), and there is no great unemployment problem, wages have not increased in proportion and the people are carrying a heavy burden. Japan is facing inflation, a lack of foreign credits; the only reason that there has not been a complete disruption of her domestic financial organization may be found in internal governmental control, heavy taxation, and the increasing savings accounts built up by the people.[15]

Just after the comprehensive embargo was imposed in 1941, the Associated Press looked retroactively at what had already been accomplished by selective trade limitation: "Not long ago Japan was the United States' fourth best foreign customer. In 1940 she purchased American goods to the extent of $227,200,000. Since then her purchases have undergone a fairly continuous decline."[16]

Restrictions on scrap metal exports were especially injurious to Japanese industry. Depending upon the year under consideration (see Table 6.1), Japan typically relied on the United States for between half and three-quarters of all its scrap. Table 6.2 documents how Japanese scrap

Table 6.3. Japanese Aviation Motor Fuel
Imports from the U.S. (In 42-Gallon Barrels)

Year	Aviation	Other	Total
1939	562,223	635,499	1,197,722
1940	527,451	2,624,342	3,151,793
1941*	581,379	1,643,411	2,224,790

*7 months (January–July)
Source: U.S. Department of Commerce annual compilations, *Foreign Commerce and Navigation of the United States.*
In 1939 and 1941 the term "aviation" motor fuel was used, while the higher classification in 1940 was called "high grade." Prior to 1939 it was not listed as a separate category.

imports were reduced by more than half between 1939 and 1940 and were reduced to a pittance in 1941.

A *New York Times* article cited above noted in January 1941 that American restrictions had reduced steel production at open hearths to 30 percent of capacity.[17] In July, British economic warfare experts told the press that to replace banned scrap iron imports, Japan had been forced to dip into her reserve stockpile. They pointed out that Japan was especially vulnerable to any ban on actual iron ore importation: 73 percent of her supplies came from Britain and the United States, while an additional 21 percent was supplied by India.[18]

In his extensive study of Japan's prewar policy, Michael A. Barnhart argues that the restrictions imposed during this period had a great long-range significance:

> The American pressures of 1940 hurt the Japanese economy gravely. One can argue persuasively that those pressures were largely responsible for the inability of the Imperial economy to function effectively in the later years of the Pacific War, when the failures of earlier efforts to expand production and inadequacies in maintaining existing capital plant and transportation (especially seaborne) would become glaring.[19]

Hence if one views war as inevitable in the Pacific, the American actions served a very useful long-term purpose. On the other hand, if one believes that the war was avoidable, actions that ran the risk of seriously injuring Japan's economy must be evaluated as, at some point, crossing the line into overt encouragement of war. True, in the First World War era, economic pressure had forced Japan to retreat from empire building on the Asian mainland. On the other hand, Japan was now deeply entrenched in much of China and Indochina, and Japan possessed a major army and a world-class fleet. The efficiency of the first might legitimately be questioned and American pride downgraded the significance of the latter. But unless common prudence were to be laid aside totally, Japan's army and navy were substantial enough to dictate the greatest caution in the use of any economic blackjack.

The Washington administration was extremely divided as to how vigorously and how far to exercise this trade option. The most volatile area lay in petroleum restrictions. Although these restrictions hurt the civilian economy, they were a dagger at the heart of the Japanese military, for the navy in particular and to a lesser extent the army as well. Of special concern was the availability of aviation-grade oil. Here the United States (in 1940 and early 1941) did far less than it appeared to be doing and the restrictions it did enforce were effectively bent by Japanese enhancement of lower grades. Much depended upon how one defined aviation-quality fuel. Using the Commerce Department's definition, the export of aviation fuel went down only a modest 10% from 1939 to 1940 and the 1941 figure was actually an increase over the 1939 figure (see Table 6.3). Any restraint this may have encouraged was eliminated when in the summer of 1941 a truly total boycott appeared to be proclaimed and, within a matter of weeks, became the reality. It was hard enough for the Japanese military to ignore the plight of the homeland (whose defenders it claimed to be). The lack of petroleum was even more threatening when it endangered the military's own ability to protect the home islands adequately, not to mention the always tempting fantasy to engage in expanded empire building.

Although a firm beginning on trade limitation had been begun in 1940, it was far from an effort at a knockout punishment. Even so, it decisively warned the Japanese of how seriously the United States regarded their activities in that part of the world and created the precedents for even more comprehensive action during 1941.

NOTES

1. J. F. C. Fuller, *The Conduct of War, 1789–1961* (N.p.: Rutgers University Press, 1961; reprint, Minerva: n.d.), 297.
2. Jon Halliday, *A Political History of Japanese Capitalism* (New York: Pantheon, 1975), 131.
3. Ibid.
4. Ibid., 156.
5. Nobutake Ike, translator and editor, *Japan's Decision for War: Records of the 1941 Policy Conferences* Stanford, Calif.: Stanford University Press, 1967), 187. Also see Halliday, *Political History*, 156.
6. Halliday, *Political History*, 156.
7. Ibid.
8. Cordell Hull, *The Memoirs of Cordell Hull*, vol. 2 (New York: Macmillan, 1948), 983.
9. "Once Again We Tease Japan on Oil Supply," *New York Times*, 3 August 1941, E-3.

10. "America and Japan," *New York Times*, 25 July 1941, 14.
11. "Industry in Japan Seen Slowed Down," *New York Times*, 26 January 1941, III-3.
12. "U.S. Study Shows Burdens in Japan," *New York Times*, 23 March 1941, 7.
13. "Economic Tension in Japan Growing," *New York Times*, 4 May 1941, 30.
14. "U.S.-Japanese Trade Tumbles," *Los Angeles Times*, 26 July 1941, 11.
15. "Japan: Economic Estimate, May 27, 1941," State Department document 894.50/154, 61.
16. "New Economic Blows Against Japan Loom," *Los Angeles Times*, 27 July 1941, I-2.
17. "Industry in Japan Seen Slowed Down," III-3.
18. "Crippling of Japan in Six Months by British-U.S. Blockade Is Seen," *New York Times*, 26 July 1941, 1.
19. Michael A. Barnhart, *Japan Prepares for Total War: The Search for Economic Security, 1919–1941* (Ithaca, N.Y.: Cornell University Press, 1987), 196–97.

Chapter 7
IMPACT OF THE 1941 EMBARGO MEASURES ON JAPAN

Initial Estimates

While the idea of a total embargo was still being discussed as a possible option, British economic warfare experts spread the word that they were convinced that a full termination of trade would probably sink the Japanese economy within six months. The *New York Times* carried a front-page summary of the British conclusions,[1] and the first postembargo issue of *Time* magazine devoted considerable space to a discussion of the British reasoning.[2] The latter publication, just like the British, was careful to hedge by noting that "it *might* lay the Japanese low in six months" (emphasis added).[3] Taking over the line of reasoning used by those specialists, *Time* noted the heavy reliance upon foreign imports, which we have indicated in Table 7.1. In addition to the items summarized in that chart, copper and coal were sufficient only for normal "peacetime needs."[4] What *Time*'s authors did not mention is that in a wartime context (and Japan had been at war with China for years), the normal "need" level for any particular commodity had increased dramatically. Hence the impact of any thoroughgoing embargo would be even greater than under normal conditions.

Time noted that part of the justification Japan advanced for pushing its "new order" in the Far East was to secure self-sufficiency in the supply of such materials. The publication doubted, however, whether Japan possessed "the technological know-how" and "industrial machinery to exploit the Far East's resources in time to become a serious contender for international power." Indeed, to utilize the resources of the region effectively, the quick development of entire new industries would be required, plus a massive boost in the generation of electricity.[5] In other words, accomplished conquests and possible ones gave Japan the potential for self-sufficiency, but it would be extremely difficult for Japan to translate that into the reality.

Writing upon the basis of 1939 figures, *Newsweek* asserted in its first issue of August that a complete boycott would remove the 34 percent of

Table 7.1. Dependence of Japanese Economy on Foreign Imports

Commodity	Percentage Dependence
Petroleum	90%
Steel industry raw materials (pig iron, scrap, iron ore)	88%
Zinc	50⅛
Tin	80%
Cotton	100%
Wool	99%
Rubber	100%
"Important alloy metals" (nickel, manganese, chrome, tungsten, atimony)	almost 100%

Source: Converted into chart form from percentages provided by *Time*, 4 August 1941, 61–62.

Japanese imports that originated from the United States, the 4.2 percent that came from Canada, the 2.4 percent that arrived from Australia, and the tiny .8 percent shipped from Britain.[6] A few days earlier, when the trade freeze was first announced, a *New York Times* reporter filing from London estimated that "If in fact all British trade is cut off"—presumably meaning, in addition to American commerce—"she will lose almost three-quarters of her foreign trade."[7]

The (London) *Times'* diplomatic correspondent reported on the first Monday after the embargo announcement that 54.6 percent of Japan's imports in 1938 came from a combination of Britain, the British Empire, and the United States and that 35.7 percent of its exports went to those destinations. The most recent dramatic steps would "further diminish an already declining trade."[8]

The following day the same publication provided another analysis of the embargo's likely impact, noting that, unlike item-by-item restrictions, the new effort was far more wide reaching: "The new measures are more severe and they are comprehensive; instead of control of individual commodities they deal at one blow with the whole orbit of trade with Japan." If administered to the full degree permitted by the public announcements, the result would be "a killing stranglehold on her trade and sources of indispensable supplies." If this course were implemented, a grim future awaited the Oriental foe:

> Should the measures taken by the two sides [America and Britain] be applied in full and resolutely, on balance Japan will suffer, and suffer severely. As far as our trade with Japan goes, it may be uncomfortable for the Dominions, India, and the Colonies, but far from ruinous; whereas for Japan complete loss of oil, cotton, wool,

and other commodities would be *fatal in a year or so*. Her industries are largely dependent on imported raw materials, and on keeping open long ocean lanes of supply. She has been careful to keep secret the precise extent of her accumulated resources of vital raw materials, but, over the broad field of her manifold needs, her stocks might be made to eke out for a year or a year and a half. After that, in the absence of more successful conquest than the last few years have brought her, the prospect would be bleak [emphasis added].[9]

At the time the embargo was made public, top echelon American analysts concurred in that general time scenario. "High Government quarters," noted one contemporary report, "predicted the economic strangulation of Japan within a year on the premise that the democracies would continue their tightening economic blockade of the island empire." In this same context, an unidentified governmental Far East expert indicated that "Japan's economic structure could not stand for long under the burden of being cut off from trade with the United States, the British Empire and the Netherlands Colonial Empire."[10]

The same press report drew attention to the fact that others were convinced that the embargo would be devastating on an even quicker basis: "Some economists [unidentified] say that Japanese industry could be brought to its knees in a few months if British and American shipments of iron, scrap iron, pig iron, copper, nickel, aluminum, manganese, mercury, cotton and wool were stopped."[11]

As always, some commentators avoided committing themselves to any estimate of what damage might occur or how soon it might occur. Almost immediately after the announcement of the asset freeze, one lengthy analysis in the *Washington Post* suggested: "How Japan could stand up against this economic warfare remained to be seen." In spite of this uncertainty, there was no denying that Japan "has been vitally dependent on imports." After providing a lengthy rehash of an Associated Press report on Japan's lack of resources, the writer noted: "No country that presumes to call itself a 'power' is so lacking in vital materials as Japan."[12]

Even prior to the official announcement, there was speculation as to how far the United States would go in responding to Japan's Indochina move. The day before the announcement, the *New York Times* expressed concern about "any action in the Pacific which would interfere with our ability to help Britain destroy Hitler." Even so, the *Times* believed that if Japan were truly committed to major aggression, the United States should unleash its powerful economic club upon the Nipponese economy:

> We can shut off her supplies. More than a third of Japan's exports, beyond the "yen-bloc" area, go to the United States, and nearly three-quarters to American, British and Dutch territories; a complete embargo on these exports would cripple Japan's purchasing power throughout the world and shake her economy at home. Japan is equally vulnerable to pressure on her imports. Nearly half of the vital supplies she gets from outside the "yen-bloc" area come from the United States, and

nearly three-quarters from American, British and Dutch territory. Japan has made frantic efforts to achieve self-sufficiency, but she is still dependent on foreign sources for her raw materials—above all, for her oil and steel.[13]

A late August internal State Department document drew attention to the fact that in regard to "raw materials and finished products," in excess of "70 percent of Japan's gainful trade is done with America and Britain."[14] In a very real sense the situation was even worse than that percentage would indicate because "until the freezing order of this month, Japan depended" on the United States and Britain "for 77 percent of war materials."[15]

Later Contemporary Estimates

In an early September column, Ernest Lindley surveyed the three possible options open to Japan: prompt war, "a general settlement," or an indefinite delay. The last "is worth while only if the economic noose is untied so that waiting does not drain away Japanese strength." And how decisive a pressure was the embargo currently imposing? "The economic pressure applied by the Western nations is squeezing Japan and ultimately will strangle her."[16]

A *Washington Post* editorial on the fifth stressed that none of Japan's alternatives were desirable ones: "If she moves now she courts war, and war against an extremely formidable coalition; if she stands still she courts economic strangulation. An honorable retreat away from the disastrous course she has been taking might mean her salvation. Yet there is not a Japanese leader who dares sponsor such a retreat. It would mark him as a certain victim of Japan's patriotic assassins."[17]

In an interview the same month with Chiang Kai-shek, the Nationalist leader argued that the Japanese were now on the defensive. Although he overstated the significance of his own nation's contribution to that situation, he still gave abundant credit to the trade freeze:

> Two factors are largely responsible for the situation confronting Japan. First, China's strong and continued resistance has thrown the whole Japanese program out of gear. Second, economic sanctions, enforced under the leadership of the United States, which set a general example by freezing Japan's assets and embargoing the shipment of war materials to that country, have proved to the Japanese people the weakness of their whole economic position.
> It is evident that a prime object of Japan's present diplomatic moves is to bring about a cessation of the war with China, so that the so-called "Chinese incident" can be liquidated. This must be done because of American economic pressure upon Japan and Tokyo's need to restore trade relations with the domestic powers.[18]

A few days later columnist Ernest K. Lindley reminded his readers: "Japan is not yet bereft of bargaining power. She has a good navy, a fair army, and a third-rate air force.... But Japan's bargaining position is steadily weakening under economic pressure."[19]

On September 16, a correspondent reported from Tokyo on Japan's effort to increase trade with both China and Manchukuo to at least partially replace trade with other countries. The reporter began his article with the observation that "Japan's foreign trade with the outside world is virtually at a standstill."[20]

An unidentified author in Bangkok, Thailand, wrote of the repercussions of the trade freeze on southeast Asia. One indirect result was the inability of Japan to pay for any continuing purchases in an internationally recognized currency. So hard pressed were the Japanese to continue vital scrap, mineral, and rubber imports that they were reported to be sending gold to Thailand in order to purchase such supplies. Furthermore, available sources had dramatically jumped in price from their prefreeze levels, with increases ranging from 30 to 100 percent.[21]

The third week of the month, *Contemporary China*, a bimonthly reference published in New York City, predicted that the longest Japan could continue to hold out against the freeze would be six months. Thereafter, it asserted, Japan would have "to plea for an economic truce with America and Britain and sue for a military armistice with China." Its analysis indicated that scrap reserves would disappear by the end of the current year. The reserves of petroleum would evaporate by the end of March 1942. By the spring of that year, the silk industry would be two-thirds destroyed and the cotton industry would be 75 percent eliminated.[22]

A correspondent filing from Batavia in the Netherlands East Indies near the end of the month stressed the growing willingness of nations in that area to fight the Japanese if peace negotiations failed, which seemed likely. Buried in the report was a brief analysis of the Japanese economic situation, which might be boiled down to five words, hurting but not yet devastating:

> The semi-blockade of Japan that has been attained by the United States, the Netherlands East Indies, and the British freezing of credits and the cessation of trade, has not yet seriously affected Japan's supplies of oil and gasoline which, with economies, are probably sufficient for 18 months.
> But that her iron and steel shortages are already acute is evidenced by the recent decree of the ministry of commerce and industry forbidding the manufacture of upward to 150 articles, ranging from razors, bicycles, pans, baskets, chains, ballbearings, and safety razors to movie cameras and even cuff buttons.[23]

Writing in the October issue of *Contemporary Japan*, Masatoshi Matsushita (a Japanese-born scholar teaching in the United States) reminded his readers that "Japan is a trading country, and since 70 percent of its trade is with Anglo-American countries, economic pressure by these countries no doubt has a great effect on the economic structure of the country."[24]

In early October, retired Rear Admiral Yates Stirling, Jr., perceptively drew attention to the fact that the very success of the American embargo was posing the danger of shifting Japanese naval support toward a war with the Western powers:

> President Roosevelt's anti–Japanese oil embargo—which he himself admitted might lead to war with Nippon—now appears to be 100 percent effective. Britain and the Netherlands Indies also have stopped all oil supplies to Nippon, and Japanese-American conversations looking to a general understanding with regard to the Far East appear to be in a stalemate. All signs point towards a crisis, possibly within the next few months, if Russia collapses in Europe. . . .
>
> One of the most significant developments is the changing attitude of Japanese naval leaders. Traditionally conservative, highly respectful of British and American naval strength, and more keenly aware of Nippon's economic vulnerability than leaders of the army, the imperial navy always has sought to avoid war with the English-speaking powers.
>
> The very fact that Nipponese naval leaders are so keenly aware of their country's economic weaknesses, however, now appears to be making them war-minded. The Japanese navy, like all others, must have oil to exist. Cut off from adequate oil supplies it must be ready to fight to restore its sources of supply. Equally the imperial navy is keenly interested in Nippon's formerly large overseas trade. It needs a big and active merchant marine to maintain its position. But that merchant marine now is endangered, not only by a lack of fuel oil, but also because of diminishing trade.
>
> Nippon's markets in British and American-controlled areas and in Latin America have practically disappeared, routes to Europe are closed by the British blockade, and foreign exchange which international shipping must have—is impossible to obtain because of British-American financial pressure. All this the Japanese navy well knows and its leaders are beginning to say so.
>
> And if the imperial navy decides to throw its support to the imperial army for war—war is very likely to come whether Britain and the United States want it or not.[25]

Later in October, Henry C. Wolfe summed up in a lengthy article his firsthand impressions of economically besieged Japan. Things had gone so far that "many of the taxis are run on charcoal gas" because of the petroleum shortage.[26] Furthermore, though the Japanese were likely, on a psychological level, to hold up well against outside pressure, "the economic situation in Japan is growing steadily worse, there is no early prospect of a turn for the better, and even a tough race like the Japanese may some time reach the limit of human [endurance]."[27]

In the middle of the month, the *Washington Post* editorially suggested that "the danger of economic strangulation" lay behind Japan's recent willingness to negotiate. The *Post* thought it likely that Japan would further postpone any major military move but realized the situation was hard to predict: "Yet the economic noose around Japan's neck is steadily growing tighter. And Japan cannot afford to wait too long."[28]

A few days later, Barnet Nover wrote in his syndicated column: "Japan is in a vise. She is being squeezed dry." Those Japanese factions pushing for war against Russia had increased their pressure "as the economic noose around Japan's neck tightened."[29]

Soon thereafter, the International News Service (INS) distributed an article based upon comments by the Commerce Department's resident specialists. The first sentence summed up Nippon's current dilemma: "Perched uneasily on dwindling stockpiles of materials vital for war, Japan faces a future wiped clean of all imports except rice and other grains, some small amount of low-grade pig iron and a trickle of fuel from colonies in China." Several war-essential items "vital to any shooting campaign, are dangerously low."[30]

The Foreign Policy Association splashed a dash of cold water upon economic collapse advocates in November, however. It issued a statement that Japan was still capable of launching a powerful, though short-term, major offensive: "Careful estimates indicate that, despite the existing trade embargoes, Japan possesses stocks of war materials adequate to maintain a southern blitzkrieg for as long as six months."[31] Apparently it did not occur to the authors of the statement that heavy usage would quickly reduce this reserve buffer and that if a diplomatic solution could not be found before the situation reached a critical point, Japan would feel compelled to act militarily. Most significantly, that point would be in the near future.

In a report on Ambassador Kurusu's arrival in Washington later in the month, the *Washington Post* noted on November 16, 1941, that there was "evidence that Japan is feeling acutely [the] economic measures taken by this country that have cut off large supplies of materials needed for the Japanese war machine." Nor was the damage only to Japan's war-making capacity. The *Post* pointed out that the embargo measures "are said to be having a profoundly serious effect on the Japanese economy" as a whole.[32]

The same day, Ernest Lindley's column concurred in this judgment: "The economic life of Japan is slowly draining away."[33] On November 19, a column by Barnet Nover reminded his readers that more than one factor had produced the current situation: "Japan is suffering from the effects of four years of indecisive war [in China] upon which there is now being superimposed the equally debilitating effects of economic sanctions."[34] About two weeks later Nover embraced the assertion he attributed to unidentified others that "the trade embargo is slowly but steadily strangling Japan."[35]

On November 30, Ernest Lindley wrote: "The Japanese are growing weaker daily. The longer they wait the more hopeless their position will become—unless, as their militarists hope, the Nazis break through to the Indian and Pacific Oceans, or knock out England." Perhaps not aware of the irony, he noted that the Japanese "had followed the British pattern in seeking an economic empire."[36] This was a pattern Lindley found unacceptable for the Japanese to follow, but this did not preclude him from urging a staunch pro–British policy.

Lloyd Lehrbas, an Associated Press correspondent, reported that the diplomatic negotiations in Washington on the twenty-second had concentrated on economic matters and the tremendous stress the embargo had placed on Japan: "The United States, Great Britain and the Netherlands have embargoed oil shipments to Japan, imposed export restrictions on shipments of other goods vitally needed in Japan's daily life, frozen Japanese assets, and taken other economic measures designed to block Japan's threatened expansion southward."[37]

Although we have examined a substantial number of clear references to the economic devastation caused by the embargo (and the number could be multiplied in a more comprehensive study of the national press of that day), it should be stressed that these references were commonly "inside page" material or passing remarks by syndicated columnists. In other words, they were the type of material easily overlooked by the casual reader.

Perhaps it is for that reason that even supporters of a militant boycott could be unaware of the effectiveness of the existing measures. Less than two weeks before Pearl Harbor, for example, Clinton M. Howard, the general superintendent of the International Reform Federation, stood before a Methodist audience and demanded that the United States put into effect the very kind of comprehensive trade embargo that, in effect, was already in existence:

> Let the United States and England say to Japan, "get out of China or we will declare an all-out financial and economic boycott against you, and bar your flag from every American and English port in the world." Let the United States say "get out of China or we will not sell you another bale of cotton, another ton of scrap iron, another barrel of oil, another pound of food. Get out of China or we will not purchase from you another dime's worth of silk to make stockings for our women or another toy for our children."[38]

If activists such as this did not always understand the full scope of the damage already being inflicted, how much less did the general public? On the other hand, the information *was* there for those alert and persistent enough to pry out the publicly available facts. In light of this fact and the general anti–Japanese sentiment, even greater press coverage would have been unlikely to alter American support for the trade action. If the coverage had continued to be extensive and if it had equaled the early reports in their emphasis on the war potential of the embargo, then and only then might there have been the chance of serious second thoughts taking root. By this point the public equation had become "successful negotiations of war" rather than "trade embargo or war," thereby deemphasizing the major allied contribution to Japanese belligerency.

In the few days left of peace, reports continued to surface of how badly Nippon was suffering. On December 1, the National Industrial Conference Board released "The Effects of Allied Economic Blockade on Japan." The board estimated that 75 percent of Japan's imports had been terminated by the embargo.[39] On the same day, *Contemporary China* contended that the combination of the war in China and the trade freeze had brought Japan to the edge of economic collapse.[40]

A writer in the *Wall Street Journal* stressed the impact upon two industries in particular, the silk and cotton trades. The writer noted that 25 percent of the Japanese population "normally derive all or part of their income from silk." A similar situation existed for cotton; between 20 and 25 percent "of all her factory workers are employed in plants associated with the industry." These were identified as two of the three biggest "peacetime industries," indeed "the very backbone of the economy."[41] One can understand the desire to curb the Japanese military even though that course carried with it enormous risk. But the cynic might well ask: does one serve the cause of peace by cutting off the resources necessary for such nonmilitary sectors to operate? Or does one simply radicalize those sectors of the population into bitter hatred of the foreigner who denies them the opportunity to earn a living?

Finally, on the day of the Pearl Harbor attack, the *New York Times* reported: "Less than four months of blockade are said to have forced a curtailment of perhaps 40 percent in Nippon's factory operation."[42] Would the United States have tolerated such a blow without resorting to force of arms? Why, then, should it have been expected the Japanese to do so? When one factors into the situation a far greater militarism than has ever been prevalent in American culture, a military response was even more likely.

Government Statistical Data

There are various ways to stress the importance of foreign trade to a given nation. One way is by noting how much of its national product is derived from that source. In an analysis released just after the war ended, Edward Anderberg, Jr., wrote:

> Foreign trade is more important to the economy of Japan than it is to the economies of many countries of the world. Before World War II exports constituted about 20 percent of the value of production of all industry of Japan including agriculture, forestry, and fishing as well as mining and manufacturing. Imports also were of great importance, as they too, constituted approximately 20 percent by value of total national production.[43]

Hence Japan was heavily dependent upon a steady flow of trade. Later Anderberg reemphasizes this extreme reliance on foreign commerce: "The economic situation of Japan is, in fact, similar to that of Great Britain in many ways, except that it is many times worse. For Japan proper has a much larger population and fewer domestic raw materials than has the United Kingdom."[44]

One historian goes so far as to say that "With no substantial imports

Table 7.2. Dependence of Japan Upon Foreign Trade: Combined Calendar Year Imports and Exports, 1937–1939, with Various Trading Partners (In Thousands of Yen)

	1937		1938		1939	
	Imports & Exports	Percentage	Imports & Exports	Percentage	Imports & Exports	Percentage
Japanese Controlled						
Manchuria	465,163	6.7	655,594	12.2	941,242	14.5
Kwantung Leased Territory	441,112	6.3	596,640	11.1	817,693	12.6
British Controlled or Heavily Influenced						
United Kingdom	274,069	3.9	198,155	3.7	156,511	2.4
India	748,853	10.8	360,271	6.7	393,258	6.1
Australia	237,332	3.4	152,263	2.8	143,127	2.2
United States Controlled or Heavily Influenced						
United States	1,908,970	27.4	1,340,423	25.0	1,643,893	25.3
Philippine Islands	105,542	1.5	68,229	1.3	73,861	1.1
Central America	73,650	1.1	36,729	.7	47,138	.7
South America	272,130	3.9	151,386	2.8	182,841	2.8
Other Countries & Continents						
China	322,887	4.6	477,512	8.9	671,141	10.3
France	75,093	1.1	50,320	.9	40,198	.6
Germany	219,624	3.2	204,185	3.8	165,994	2.6
Africa	449,041	6.5	197,957	3.7	245,697	3.8
Netherlands Indies	353,501	5.1	192,294	3.6	209,431	3.2
All other countries	1,011,626	14.5	671,169	12.5	762,011	11.7
Total	6,958,595		5,353,117		6,494,036	

Note: The average value in United States currency of the yen in 1937 was $0.2879; in 1938, $0.2845; and in 1939, $0.2596.
Source: Adapted from "Monthly Return of Foreign Trade, Department of Finance, Tokyo, December, 1939" as reprinted in U.S. Department of Commerce, *Economic Review of Foreign Countries, 1939 and Early 1940*, Economic Series No. 9 (Washington: U.S. Government Printing Office, 1941), 319. Percentages computed by current author.

Impact of the 1941 Embargo Measures

other than China, Japanese foreign trade came to a virtual standstill."[45] Although one might quibble with that assessment a little, most would concur.

Soon after the war began, *Current History* estimated that 75 percent of Japan's trade had been eliminated before the outbreak of hostilities,[46] an approximate figure concurred in by several other contemporary writers, as noted earlier in this chapter. The 75 percent figure has also been cited by various later students of the war years.[47]

In order to obtain a more precise indication of the degree of impact, the reader should consult Table 7.2 (which provides an overall picture by combining together imports and exports for the years 1937 to 1939). Tables 7.3 and 7.4 deal respectively with Japan's dependence upon imports and exports, providing figures for 1938 and 1939 and the averages (for comparison purposes) of 1928–1932 and 1933–1937. Tables 7.3 and 7.4 are not fully compatible with Table 7.2 since they were based upon separate government surveys. In one table the Japanese possessions of Korea and Formosa are both included while in the other Korea and Formosa are omitted. In spite of this caveat, these tables provide us a good picture of Japan's "normal" foreign trade before it was disrupted by the European war in the second half of 1939. This latter event cut off trade with most European sources and must have therefore increased Japan's reliance upon non–European suppliers.

Japan's empire provided it some degree of protection in case of a trade cutoff. From Manchuria, Kwantung Leased Territory, Korea, and Formosa (see Tables 7.3 and 7.4), Japan imported 40.2% of its yen-value trade in 1938, and Japan sent 53.2% of its exports to these areas in the same year. In 1939 these figures (excluding Formosa, for which separate figures were not available) had declined to 33.0% (imports) and 52.4% (exports). Hence as of 1939 some two-thirds of Japan's imports originated in potentially unfriendly countries and about half of its exports went to such destinations. In view of these figures, one is hard pressed to come up with the 75% trade loss so confidently cited. Even so, one would seemingly be safe in speaking in terms of at least a 50% loss, itself an immense disaster even if it is not as dramatic as the larger figure. Using Table 7.2 for 1939, one sees a combined import-export reliance upon non–Japanese empire sources of 74.9%, which would yield the commonly cited figure when rounded off; quite possibly this is the original source for it. It should be noted that neither Formosa nor Korea are provided separate listings, thereby reducing Japan's actual yen-bloc trade. If one factors in an estimate for this trade of only about fifteen percent of the total yen volume, one still reduces the reliance upon potentially unfriendly sources to about sixty percent. Again, though this falls substantially short of the commonly cited figure, it could be nothing short of devastating to the Japanese economy.

Table 7.3. Dependence of Japan upon Imports from Various Trading Partners: 1928–1939 (In Millions of Yen)

	1928–1932 Average Imports	Percent
Japanese Empire Area[a]		
Manchuria	50.2	2.3
Kwantung	121.0	5.4
Korea	283.1	12.7
Formosa	214.6	9.7
British Controlled or Heavily Influenced		
United Kingdom	110.5	5.0
India[c]	200.7	9.0
Australia	121.0	5.5
United States Controlled or Heavily Influenced		
United States	514.9	23.2
Philippine Islands[d]		
Mexico, Cent. & S. America	9.9	.4
Other Countries & Continents		
China	125.9	5.7
Germany	108.4	4.9
Netherland Indies	67.3	3.0
Africa	28.9	1.3
All other Asia	102.6	4.6
All other Oceania	5.2	.2
All other Europe	86.7	3.9
All other North America[e]	51.3	2.3
Bonded mfg. warehouse	20.5	.9
Totals	2,222.8	

a Imports from the Mandated Islands small in amount have not been included in this table.
b Statistics not available for 1939.
c Includes Ceylon prior to 1934 and Burma prior to 1938.
d Not included as separate category.
e Excludes Mexico.
f Not reported separately, included in detail.
g Does not include trade of Formosa.

NOTES

Initial Estimates

1. "Crippling of Japan in Six Months by British-U.S. Blockade Is Seen," *New York Times*, 26 July 1941, 1.
2. "Import or Die," *Time*, 4 August 1941, 61–62.
3. "Loaded Gun," *Time*, 61.
4. "Import or Die," 61.
5. Ibid., 62.

Table 7.3.
(continued)

1933–1937 Average		1938		1939	
Imports	Percent	Imports	Percent	Imports	Percent
191.6	5.6	339.3	9.0	405.6	11.1
30.4	.9	60.3	1.6	61.7	1.7
460.0	13.5	710.5	18.8	736.9	20.2
310.7	9.1	408.7	10.8	b	b
82.7	2.4	63.2	1.7	24.4	.7
324.3	9.5	172.2	4.6	182.3	5.0
196.9	5.8	82.9	2.2	71.0	1.9
863.4	25.3	915.3	24.2	1,002.4	27.4
80.9	2.4	98.5	2.6	119.2	3.3
133.0	3.9	164.6	4.3	215.7	5.9
123.6	3.6	171.2	4.5	141.0	3.9
92.9	2.7	88.2	2.3	71.6	1.9
102.3	3.0	60.6	1.6	92.8	2.5
167.0	4.9	198.8	5.3	244.2	6.7
24.5	.7	15.0	.4	15.3	.4
146.7	4.3	141.9	3.7	144.5	3.9
66.3	1.9	91.3	2.4	126.0	3.5
f	f	f	f	f	f
3,414.5		3,782.5		3,654.6^g	

Source: Chart adapted from yen and percentage data of Edward Anderberg, Jr., *The Overseas Trade of Japan Proper, Including a Summary of the Prewar Trade and a Discussion of Postwar Problems* (prepared for the Foreign Economic Administration of the United States Tariff Commission, October 1945), 24–25. Reprinted by University Microfilms, Ann Arbor, Michigan, 1980. Anderberg's source was official annual and monthly statistics of Japan, Korea, and Formosa.

6. "Squeeze on Nippon," *Newsweek*, 4 August 1941, 20.
7. Robert P. Post, "London Joins U.S. in Freezing Action," *New York Times*, 26 August 1941, 5.
8. Unidentified author, "Stopping Japan's Trade / Essential Imports Hit / Facts and Figures," *Times* (London), 28 July 1941, 4.
9. "A Total Weapon Against Japan," *Times* (London), 29 July 1941, 5.
10. Associated Press, "Throttling of Japan Forecast in a Year," *Washington Post*, 27 July 1941, A-2.
11. Associated Press, "Throttling of Japan Forecast," A-2. The same dispatch was printed under the title "New Economic Blows Against Japan Loom," *Los Angeles Times*, 27 July 1941, I-2.

Table 7.4. Dependence of Japan upon Exports to Various Trading Partners: 1928–1939 (In Millions of Yen)

	1928–1932 Average	
	Exports	Percent
Japanese Empire Area[a]		
Manchuria	41.5	2.0
Kwantung	101.5	5.0
Korea	273.2	13.5
Formosa	127.6	6.3
British Controlled or Heavily Influenced		
United Kingdom	59.5	3.0
India[c]	155.3	7.7
Australia	33.6	1.7
United States Controlled or Heavily Influenced		
United States	623.4	30.7
Philippine Islands[d]		
Mexico, Cent. & S. America	21.7	1.1
Other Countries & Continents		
China	219.3	10.8
Germany	11.0	.5
Netherlands Indies	78.1	3.8
Africa	61.2	3.0
All other Asia	131.6	6.5
All other Oceania	9.9	.4
All other Europe	62.8	3.1
All other North America[e]	19.0	.9
Totals	2030.3	

a Exports to the Mandated Islands small in amount have not been included in this table.
b Statistics not available for 1939.
c Includes Ceylon prior to 1934 and Burma prior to 1938.
d Not included as separate category.
e Excludes Mexico.
f Does not include trade of Formosa.

    12. Edward T. Folliard, "Japanese Occupation of Indo-China Brings Swift Economic Reprisals," 27 July 1941, B-3.
    13. "On Guard in the Pacific," *New York Times*, 24 July 1941, 16.
    14. "Political Estimate, August 20, 1941," State Department document 894.000/1132, 42.
    15. Ibid., 44.

Later Contemporary Estimates

    16. "Japan's Weakening Positions," *Washington Post*, 3 September 1941, 11.
    17. "Oil at Vladivostok," *Washington Post*, 5 September 1941, 10.
    18. United Press, "Gen. Chiang Hopes U.S. Won't Relax Pressure on Japan," 10 September 1941, 3.

Table 7.4.
(continued)

1933–1937 Average		1938		1939	
Exports	Percent	Exports	Percent	Exports	Percent
136.5	4.2	316.3	8.0	535.7	11.1
312.1	9.7	536.3	13.7	755.9	15.7
544.3	16.8	921.3	23.5	1,229.4	25.6
205.9	6.4	312.6	8.0	b	b
126.4	3.9	135.0	3.5	132.1	2.7
255.5	7.9	188.0	4.8	211.0	4.4
66.3	2.1	69.4	1.7	72.1	1.5
532.1	16.5	425.1	10.8	641.5	13.3
107.0	3.3	89.6	2.3	110.8	2.3
142.6	4.4	312.9	8.0	455.5	9.5
27.5	.9	33.0	.8	25.0	.5
157.7	4.9	104.0	2.6	137.8	2.9
188.7	5.8	137.3	3.5	152.9	3.2
279.9	8.7	207.1	5.3	224.4	4.7
22.7	.7	27.2	.7	23.3	.5
113.4	3.5	93.1	2.4	81.2	1.7
11.7	.3	15.3	.4	17.2	.4
3,230.3		3,923.6		4,805.8[f]	

Source: Chart adapted from yen and percentage data of Edward Anderberg, Jr., *The Overseas Trade of Japan Proper, Including a Summary of the Prewar Trade and a Discussion of Postwar Problems* (prepared for the Foreign Economic Administration of the United States Tariff Commission, October 1945), 24–25. Reprinted by University Microfilms, Ann Arbor, Michigan, 1980. Anderberg's source was official annual and monthly statistics of Japan, Korea, and Formosa.

19. Ernest K. Lindley, "Tension Temporarily Eased," *Washington Post*, 15 September 1941, 3.

20. Otto Tolischus, dispatch from the *New York Times* reprinted under the title "Japanese Act to Become Self-Sufficient," *Washington Post*, 17 September 1941, 29.

21. *New York Times* dispatch reprinted under the title "Japan Ships Gold to Cover Purchases from Thailand," *Washington Post*, 18 September 1941, 8.

22. "Japan's Position Held Precarious," *New York Times*, 22 September 1941, 4.

23. Hallett Abend, *New York Times* article reprinted under the title "Far East Is Ready to Fight Japanese," *Washington Post*, 29 September 1941, 26.

24. Reprinted under the title, "America Is Real Ringleader of ABCD Front Encircling Japan," *Japan Times and Advertiser*, 14 October 1941 (morning edition), 6.

25. Rear Admiral Yates Stirling, Jr., in an article he wrote for the United Press, *Washington Post*, 9 October 1941, 15.

26. Henry C. Wolfe, "Tokyo, Capital of Shadows," *New York Times Magazine*, 12 October 1941, 6.
27. Ibid., 28.
28. "Eyes on Japan," *Washington Post*, 14 October 1941, 10.
29. Barnet Nover, "The Konoye Cabinet Resigns," *Washington Post*, 15.
30. "Japan's Only Resources: Silk and Workers," *Washington Post*, 19 October 1941, 2.
31. Quoted by Associated Press, "Policy Group Sees Japanese Power Offset," *Washington Post*, 10 November 1941, 3.
32. "Kurusu, Arriving Here, Sees 'Fighting Chance' of Accord on Far East," *Washington Post*, 16 November 1941, I-1.
33. Ernest Lindley, "Tightened Line in the Far East," *Washington Post*, 16 November 1941, II-7.
34. Barnet Nover, "What Japan Wants: Plain Speaking from Tokyo," *Washington Post*, 19.
35. Barnet Nover, *Washington Post*, 15.
36. Ernest Lindley, "The Choice Put to Japan," *Washington Post*, 30 November 1941, II-7.
37. Lloyd Lehrbas, "Leaders Taciturn on Japanese Talks, Economic Aspects of Far East Crisis Indicated Discussed," *Washington Post*, 23 November 1941, I-8.
38. "Howard Urges Strong Stand Against Japan," *Washington Post*, 24 November 1941, 8.
39. "Japan's Imports Cut 75% by War," *New York Times*, 2 December 1941, 6.
40. Ibid.
41. John O'Riley, "Japan: Its Industries Live on Borrowed Time; War Means Collapse," *Wall Street Journal*, 2 December 1941, 3.
42. "Trade Winds," *New York Times*, 7 December 1941, IV-3.

Government Statistical Data

43. *The Overseas Trade of Japan Proper, Including a Summary of the Prewar Trade and a Discussion of Postwar Problems* (Washington: Foreign Economic Administration of the United States Tariff Commission, October, 1945; reprint, Ann Arbor, Michigan: University Microfilms, 1980), 7.
44. Ibid., 1.
45. William L. Neumann, *America Encounters Japan: From Perry to MacArthur* (Baltimore: Johns Hopkins Press, 1969), 26.
46. George H. E. Smith, "Why Japan Chose to Fight," *Current History* (February 1942): 505.
47. Basil Collier, *The War in the Far East, 1941–1945: A Military History* (New York: William Morrow, 1969), 75; John Keegan, *The Second World War* (New York: Viking, 1989; reprint, 1990), 248; John Robertson, *Australia at War* (Melbourne: William Heinemann, 1981), 63; and Louis L. Snyder, *The War: A Concise History, 1939–1945* (New York: Julian Messner, 1960), 198.

Chapter 8
THE PETROLEUM SUPPLY CRISIS OF 1941

The Crisis of Ongoing Supply

Official restraint in public statements notwithstanding, the Japanese knew full well that they were not obtaining any further Western petroleum, and the careful reader of the American press was also aware of the fact. Rear Admiral (Retired) Yates Stirling, Jr., described as a "United Press naval expert," wrote in mid–October of 1941: "President Roosevelt's anti–Japanese oil embargo—which he himself admitted might lead to war with Nippon—now appears to be 100 percent effective."[1] A week later the *Wall Street Journal* reported: "Washington sources say that since last July Japan has not received gasoline or scrap iron from any source."[2] Less than a week before Pearl Harbor, the same journal informed its readers: "Since June the petroleum flow from the U.S. and the Dutch Indies to Japan has been nonexistent."[3]

This termination of petroleum supply enters the picture in two different but overlapping ways. Because of Japanese inadequacies in both areas, the two factors combined to create an even greater incentive to resolve the problem by military means.

In this section we will discuss the first factor, the crisis of ongoing supply. Although the exact figures vary from one source to another, they all testify to Japan's perpetual reliance on foreign suppliers for its industrial and military survival.

In the immediate issue after the embargo was proclaimed, *Time* stressed its impact upon Japan's oil supply, "Japanese-held East Asia is virtually unblessed with petroleum. Almost every drum of gas and gallon of oil that Japan burns in her tanks, planes and other empire-building machinery must be imported."[4] Japan's output was not only grotesquely inadequate for domestic needs, it palled into humiliating inconsequence when compared with that of its key Western rival. Japan possessed about four thousand wells operating prior to the war, each producing only about one barrel per day; in contrast the United States had some 400,000 wells

Table 8.1. Japanese Dependence Upon Imported
Petroleum: I Artificially Minimizing the Dependence
(Japanese Fiscal Years, 1937–1941)*
(In Thousands of 42-Gallon Barrels)

	Crude Petroleum			Refined Petroleum Products†		
	All Sources	Imports	% Imports	All Sources	Imports	% Imports
1937	22,701	20,231	89.1	29,224	16,651	57.0
1938	20,869	18,404	88.2	27,186	14,044	51.7
1939	21,175	18,843	89.0	23,799	11,818	49.7
1940	24,113	22,050	91.4	25,916	15,110	58.3
1941	5,071	3,130	61.7	21,239	5,242	24.7

*The Japanese fiscal year ran from April through March. For example, fiscal year 1941 extended from April 1941 through March 1942. The American embargo was in effect for three-quarters of fiscal 1941.

†The "All sources" column in this section includes previously imported crude and therefore results in an understatement of reliance on imports.

Sources: Refined petroleum statistics come from the Japanese Army-Navy Oil Committee as reprinted in "Table 1. Production, Consumption and Imports of Liquid Fuels and Lubricating Oil—Inner Zone" in Oil and Chemical Division, U.S. Strategic Bombing Survey, Oil in Japan's War (Appendix) (1946), 12. Also reproduced under the title "Table 26. Imports, Production, Consumption, and Inventories of Liquid Fuels and Lubricating Oil—Inner Zone" in Oil in Japan's War (1946), 69. Both charts carry a note indicating that what is tabulated consists of "Aviation gasoline, motor gasoline, diesel fuel, fuel oil, and lubricating oil."

Crude petroleum figures: Import figures come from the following source (total crude comes from adding together the chart's two columns on "imports" and "indigenous products"): "Table 2. Crude Oil, Imports, Production, and Inventories—Inner Zone," Oil in Japan's War, 15.

in operation in 1941, with a per-well daily barrel production almost ten times as large.[5]

Another article, much later in the first postembargo issue of Time, noted: "Oil is Japan's most obvious lack. She produces only 10% of her peacetime needs."[6] Writing about the same time, Edwin L. James noted that even that modest figure is slightly misleading: "It has long been evident that her supply of oil is the weakest spot in Japan's armor. She produces only about 10 percent of her normal consumption and that includes what she gets from Northern Sakhalin, which belongs to Russia [and was used on a long-term lease]."[7] Or, as one scholar pointed out part way through the war, the figure of 10% of Japan's "normal consumption" was arrived at by "including the shale oil in Manchuria" and supplies brought in from Sakhlain as well.[8] Others stressed this variety in intraempire sources by pointing to different occupied territories. According to a Tariff Commission analysis at the end of the war, "Forty years of drilling and testing brought in a meager supply from wells on the islands of Honshu and

Table 8.2. Japan's Dependence Upon Imported
Petroleum: II Domestic Contribution Basis*
(Japanese Fiscal Years, 1937–1941)
(In Thousands of 42-Gallon Barrels)

	All New Japanese Production	Combined Imports: Crude and Refined Petroleum Products	Total of Both Categories	% of Japanese Reliance on Imports
1937	2,470	36,882	39,352	93.7
1938	2,465	32,448	34,913	92.9
1939	2,332	30,661	32,993	92.9
1940	2,063	37,160	39,223	94.7
1941	1,941	8,372	10,313	81.2

*Domestic refined petroleum is excluded because what was refined included previously imported stocks.
Source: See Table 8.1.

Hokkaido in the main Japanese Archipelago and on Formosa [Taiwan], which together furnished Japan with an average of about 2.5 million barrels a year, or about 10 percent of her prewar civilian needs."[9]

Another factor affecting the percentage of "domestic" (i.e., intraempire) production versus the total utilized is the specific year under discussion. An internal State Department study of May 1941 brings this out well. "The petroleum sources within the Japanese Empire are small and can be said to contribute not more than 10% of Japanese peacetime consumption and 3% of her estimated wartime production."[10] This must be considered an approximate multiyear average since the report indicates that reliance upon domestic sources had been increasing from 7.55% (1937) to 8.48% (1938) to 10.51% (1939) and 13.00% in 1940.[11]

The figures of 90% imported and 10% "domestic" production are the figures most commonly given. Usually the imported percentage is provided and the smaller one not mentioned, though, less often, the procedure is reversed. One or the other is found both in contemporary sources[12] and among later historians.[13]

Based on an on-the-scene examination of the documentation shortly after the war ended, Jerome B. Cohen suggested modestly different figures: "Japan's 1941 production from wells and synthetic plants was less than 12 percent of her peacetime requirements,"[14] which would suggest an import figure between 88% and 89%. The postwar Strategic Bombing Survey analysis came to the conclusion that Japan's own production could only meet "about 12 percent of the peace-time civilian demand,"[15] again suggesting a figure of 88 or 89%. The 88% figure is cited by some later

Table 8.3. United States Exports of Petroleum and Related Products to Japan, 1936–1941 (In 42-Gallon Barrels)

Year	Crude Petroleum	Natural Gasoline	(Refined) Gasoline	Kerosene	Gas Oil & Fuel Oil	Lubricating Oil	Total§
1936	10,381,285	68,363	1,013,105	271	9,255,628	308,344	21,026,996
1937	15,994,669	309,277	1,093,029	181,557	10,353,193	444,405	28,376,130
1938	21,271,773	384,278	1,058,633	130	8,327,050	307,272	31,349,136
1939	16,086,176	181,210	1,197,722	104,501	9,908,936	513,545	27,992,090
1940	11,528,686	5,062	3,151,793	434,463	7,248,326	819,418	22,796,748
1941*	5,208,191	0	2,224,790	87,510	3,793,325	880,892	12,194,708
1941†	8,928,327	0	3,813,926	150,017	6,502,843	1,510,101	20,905,214

*Shipments for January through the first week in August (effectively, seven months).
†Hypothetical projection of the seven-month figure for the entire calendar year.
§Excludes small amounts of "Naphtha, solvents, and other finished light products."

Source: U.S. Department of Commerce, *Foreign Commerce and Navigation of the United States*. Each year's annual volume figures were cross-checked for accuracy by the author against the two-year comparative tables found in every other volume. The only discrepancy was for refined gasoline for 1936; the 913-barrel smaller figure in the body of tables is used in preference to that found in that volume's two-year summary.

Table 8.4. Approximate Japanese Reliance on U.S. Petroleum Total Import Basis (In Thousands of 42-Gallon Barrels)

	Total Petroleum Imported to Japan (Fiscal Year)	Total from United States (Calendar Year)
1937	36,882	28,376
1938	32,448	31,349
1939	30,661	27,992
1940	37,160	22,797
1941	8,372	12,195*
Total	145,523	122,709

Approximate Reliance on U.S.: 84.3%

*American exports effectively ended in late July; the Japanese fiscal year began only on April 1. Hence part of the United States exports were included in the preceding fiscal year of 1940.
Source: For Japanese total imports, Table 8.2; for United States exports to Japan, Table 8.3.

historians.[16] The 89% figure is given by at least three contemporary news reports.[17]

Even the individual sources are not always consistent within their own discussions. An internal State Department report of May 1941 gave the figure of "10% of Japanese peacetime consumption" but, on the same page, went on to add, "Of the oil Japan uses, 85% to 90% is imported."[18]

Table 8.1 indicates comparative Japanese reliance on foreign crude and foreign refined products. However, this statistical approach dramatically understates the total reliance since previously imported crude is, in effect, counted as part of the domestic supply when calculating the reliance on foreign refined petroleum. Even utilizing this artificially minimizing method, the figures still reflect a dangerously high reliance on suppliers who could only act with the tolerance of their own national governments. A fairer and more reasonable approach is found in Table 8.3, where all new Japanese production is contrasted with the total of crude and refined petroleum products being utilized. This produces a reliance on foreign suppliers exceeding 90% in all years except 1941, when the figure still exceeded 80% in spite of the American embargo imposed in midyear.

Although the imports from the Netherlands East Indies were not nearly as high as those of the United States, they amounted to at least as much as Japan's own domestic supply. Some set the figure at 10%.[19] An internal American government study in May 1941 lumped this Dutch possession in with other regional sources to come to the conclusion that "13% to 19% come from the Netherlands East Indies, British Borneo, and Malaya."[20] One prominent American liberal writer of the period wrote that "a

Table 8.5. Approximate Japanese Reliance
on U.S. Petroleum Total Supply Basis
(In Thousands of 42-Gallon Barrels)

	Total Petroleum Available to Japan: Imports and Domestic (Fiscal Year)	Total Petroleum Imported from United States (Calendar Year)
1937	39,352	28,376
1938	34,913	31,349
1939	32,993	27,992
1940	39,223	22,797
1941	10,313	12,195*
Total	156,794	122,709

Approximate Reliance upon U.S.: 78.3%

*Discrepancy caused by embargo beginning late July, while the 1941 fiscal year only began April 1, 1941. Hence much of this had been received in the previous fiscal year.

Source: For Japanese total supply, see Table 8.2; for United States exports to Japan, see Table 8.3.

fourth [of the oil] has come from the Indies,"[21] although it is possible that he uses the term in a geographic sense rather than just in regard to the Dutch colony.

As to the degree of reliance upon oil purchased from the United States, it was clearly substantial, though the proportion varies surprisingly when one compares the estimates of various writers. The most commonly cited figure is an 80% reliance on American oil.[22] A lesser number of contemporaries[23] and later writers[24] opt for a 60% dependency. Another popular cluster of numbers centers around the two-thirds figure. At least one contemporary arrived at a figure of 65%[25] and another at "about two-thirds,"[26] a proportion endorsed by a later close student of economic warfare.[27] According to Henry Morgenthau, in the late summer of 1940, top-level American oil men believed that the figure had been running higher: "Japan has been importing three-quarters of its oil supply from the United States."[28]

The huge volume the United States provided—regardless of what percentage one embraces—can be seen in Table 8.3. To calculate the degree of dependence upon American resources, one must compare these numbers with the total amount of imports found in Table 8.2. These two tables must be brought together with caution since the first is based upon Japanese fiscal years, while the latter is based on United States calendar years. This difficulty can, to a great extent, be remedied by resorting to a multiyear comparison, thereby minimizing the effect of the three-month difference between fiscal and calendar year numbers.

When one approaches the question on a multiyear basis from the standpoint of total importation (Table 8.4), we find that over 84% of all Japan's imported petroleum (including both crude and refined) came from the United States. This overstates the case, however, because it considers imports alone and does not take into consideration domestic production. When we shift to a total available basis (which adds in domestic crude to the import figures), the reliance on American purchases is reduced to a little in excess of 78% (Table 8.5). We take this as confirmation of the dominant assertion that Japan received about 80% of its oil from the United States.

For the purpose of our argument, an exact figure to the last decimal point is not required. No matter which of the estimates we have presented that an individual may prefer, they all indicate the precarious situation Japan found itself in because of the American-initiated embargo on petroleum. If the situation were permitted to continue, Japan would face nothing short of national economic collapse.

If the United States had been faced with a similar boycott which equally endangered its future, few Americans would have questioned the propriety of waging a major war to restore the prerequisites of American survival. (Indeed, one of the major rationalizations for the Persian Gulf War of 1991 was the possibility that a successful petroleum boycott might be launched at some indefinite future date.) The only reservations then (and now) would have surrounded the question of prudence—the "winability" of the war—not principle. A body blow of this caliber could have driven multitudes beyond even caring about "winability." National self-respect and even the quest for naked vengeance (always powerful emotions in a time of crisis) would have reinforced necessity and swept aside any objections. If the United States would have launched a preemptive war under such circumstances, why is it so surprising that the Japanese did so? With a militaristic tradition far more intense than that of America, it was even less likely that Japan would choose any other course.

The American side insisted that it would provide adequate oil if Japan reversed its policies. Unless the United States was willing to permit Japan to retain at least a "resonable" part of China and to agree to ironclad guarantees of how much petroleum was to be provided, Japan was faced with relying upon the naked goodwill of its (potential) occidental foe. Might not the Americans be acting restrained only as a ploy to force a further rollback of Japan's borders at a future date (when Japan would be even less able to resist the pressure)? Even assuming the best of goodwill at the present that was no guarantee of the policy of some future American administration. In the time frame within which Japan had to make its peace/war decision, the United States was unwilling to commit itself to concrete agreements which (from the Japanese standpoint at least) would resolve these questions. As the Japanese saw it, the alternatives were a kind of disgraceful surrender over the control of Japan's possessions and foreign policy (either immediate or postponed) or a dangerous war where victory was far from certain. Japan chose the latter when the petroleum supply left it no choice but to make a definitive decision.

The Crisis of a Shrinking Reserve

The lack of new imports of oil represented only half of Japan's problem; the other half was the swiftly diminishing petroleum reserve that kept the nation afloat while new supplies were nonexistent. When this reserve was drained dry, there would be no escaping total economic collapse and, with that collapse, the disintegration of Japan's society. Hence, regardless of the nature of the final choice, some kind of basic decision had to be made prior to the exhaustion of that strategic stockpile.

If Japan decided that war was inescapable, the conflict had to begin within a time frame permitting new petroleum-bearing territories to be conquered before the reserve was exhausted. Since major war-level military and naval action would consume the reserve even faster, that further reduced the interim during which a nonviolent solution could be sought. That date by which military action had to be initiated—if it were to be initiated at all—also formed the terminal date for negotiations. Otherwise a de facto rejection of the military option would have occurred and, no longer possessing even a remote possibility of a victory in war, Japan would have had to accept whatever terms were offered. Since this was the one option that was utterly unacceptable to all factions, the deadline for beginning war automatically became the maximum deadline for diplomatic action.

The most authoritative information about the size of the stockpile is summarized in Table 8.6. Using fiscal 1939 as the base year, this table charts the growth and decline in new petroleum stocks, consumption, and total inventories. The reserve reached its maximum in 1939 and continued downward from that point onward. The petroleum resources added to Japan's stockpile had (in the period covered by our chart) been at their highest in fiscal 1937, declining in 1938 and 1939 and reaching fifty million barrels once again in 1940. This dramatic increase in fiscal 1940 was more than balanced out by an increase in consumption, causing a net reduction in the level of the reserve in that year.

On-the-site information pieced together immediately after the Pacific war ended, indicated that when the conflict began, Japan had an oil storage capacity of some 60 million barrels, but these sites "were far from overflowing. In fact, Japan went to war with its oil storage tanks three-quarters filled," the most authoritative study tells us.[29] This translates into a reserve as of December 1941 of about 43 million barrels.[30]

Table 8.6. The Japanese Petroleum Reserve
(Japanese Fiscal Years 1937–1945)
(In Thousands of 42-Gallon Barrels)

	Added to Stock of Petroleum Resources (Crude & Refined)		Consumption		Total Inventories as of April 1	
1937	51.925	115.5%*	29,927	118.5%*	43,062	83.8%*
1938	48,055	106.9	27,951	110.6	44,356	86.3
1939	44,974	100.0	25,261	100.0	51,398	100.0
1940	50,029	111.2	28,558	113.1	49,581	96.7
1941	26,310	58.5	22,648	89.7	48,893	95.1
1942	28,888	64.2	25,794	102.1	38,229	74.4
1943	32,481	72.2	27,780	110.0	25,327	49.3
1944	16,175	36.0	19,401	76.8	13,816	26.9
1945†	2,742	6.1	4,582	18.1	4,946	9.6

*Columns reflecting percentages use 1939, the year with the largest inventory of reserves in the surveyed period, as the base year. For example, the 1937 consumption of 29,927,000 barrels is 118.5% of the 1939 consumption.
%April through September.
Source: The sources of Table 8.1 are drawn on and combined to obtain the above figures; the percentages are calculated by the author.

The exact size of the reserve was, for obvious security reasons, hidden from those outside the higher levels of the Japanese government. Indeed, even the Japanese army and navy were wary of sharing with each other the size of their respective petroleum stockpiles.

Japanese specialists of the time provided differing calculations of how long their supplies would last (see the chapter on imperial and liaison conferences for certain additional estimates beyond those we cover in this section). Western scholars who later surveyed these and other Japanese records commonly write that, as of the summer and fall of 1941, the Japanese believed that their reserves allowed survival for about two years maximum.[31] This assumed that the war in China did not escalate and that no other major conflict contributed to the depletion of their stockpile.

Some later writers have estimated that assuming the avoidance of war with the West, Japan could have even stumbled on for three years after the embargo went into effect.[32] A contemporary business correspondent with the *New York Times* estimated a two-and-a-half-year supply, which would permit the conflict with China to be continued at its existing level.[33] The more common estimate, in retrospect at least, has been a two-year period, either expressed directly or by implication via providing the size of the available Japanese oil pool and the amount of yearly consumption.[34]

In a midwar article, H. Foster Bain asserted that Japan's "oil in storage" at the war's beginning "is believed to have been the equivalent of about 18 months normal consumption. Though additional amounts may have been accumulated in secret underground storage places, this estimate is at least approximately correct."[35]

Others threw out a broad scatter-gun estimate that provided numbers that yielded little enlightenment because of their broadness. Upon the announcement of the trade freeze, the *Wall Street Journal* noted that a quick economic collapse was unlikely. "Japan is believed to have supplies of oil and steel to last one or two years—depending on demands."[36] The same publication alluded in October to unidentified Washington sources who provided an estimate in a slightly narrower range of "stores for from twelve to eighteen months."[37]

Given an all-out war, the available reserve would be eaten up far more rapidly, though Japanese officials hoped to be able to start quickly shipping crude from the conquered Dutch East Indies. This source, plus increased synthetic production, was relied upon to provide the necessary ongoing supply to permit Japan to continue any conflict.

An "estimate of Japanese national strength" prepared in early December for the Japanese government indicated that as of October 1, 1941, there were 9,050,000 kiloliters of oil in storage. Estimated wartime consumption would be 5,500,000 kiloliters a year, which would translate into 458,333 kiloliters a month for a little less than twenty months. Of this amount, it was estimated that the navy would consume about 2,500,000 kiloliters annually (45.5%), the civilian economy, 2,400,000 (43.6%), and the army the remaining 600,000 (10.9%).[38]

Although foreign sources at the time had only educated guesses to go on both in regard to the amount of fuel in storage and the probable consumption rate in case of conflict with the Western powers, estimates still had to be made both to meet civilian curiosity and as part of Western contingency planning. The upper limit for how long the supplies would last was two years. A May 1941 State Department study came to the conclusion that at that time Japan possessed sufficient "crude oil or fuel oil" in storage to last "for two years of war."[39] A one to two year full-scale war-making reserve was the contemporary estimate of one correspondent for the *New York Times*.[40] On August 2, Frank Knox, the secretary of war, publicly noted that the "general impression" in Washington was that Japan possessed an adequate petroleum reserve to wage war for a period falling within that range.[41]

The Office of Naval Intelligence estimated in March 1941 that the Japanese possessed a stockpile permitting a year-and-a-half of vigorous warfare.[42] Knox's personal view in August was that Nippon's reserves would support a fourteen- to sixteen-month war.[43] In March the British had provided a dramatically smaller estimate that suggested that Japan only had the reserves for about nine months of combat.[44]

Later students of the subject have perhaps tended to speak more in terms of supplies for an eighteen-month war. Ronald Lewin cites this figure of eighteen months in discussing what Japan could do under "war conditions."[45] Others embrace lower figures. Hanson Baldwin, a long-term military correspondent for the *New York Times*, wrote many years later that as of mid–October, "Japan's petroleum reserves [were] enough for about a year of war."[46] Since the embargo had been in effect for about three months as of that date, this would have meant a fourteen or fifteen month war-making capacity as of late July (which fits in well with Secretary Knox's contemporary estimate). Pacific fleet chief intelligence officer Edwin Layton later wrote statements that implied he had been convinced at the time that heavy naval usage had so dramatically reduced the stocks that as of the summer of 1941 Japan had the ability to sustain only a year's vigorous combat.[47]

It should have stood to reason that the lower the estimate of Japan's war-fighting oil reserve, the greater the danger of war in the short term if Japan chose to wage war at all. If there had been adequate reserves to be used on a reduced-supply basis, Nippon would have had the breathing room to allow negotiations to continue considerably longer. But because of the tight reserve, Japan simply did not have the luxury of indefinitely postponing action.

Hence the American decision to cut off all petroleum—no matter how emotionally satisfying it was—left a powerful foe with an extremely short time within which to either negotiate an agreement or strike out in bloody revenge. Japan did not voluntarily adopt these time limits; they were effectively forced upon it by the American decision to impose a comprehensive boycott of all commodities, especially of oil.

NOTES

The Crisis of Ongoing Supply

1. "2 Ocean War Threat Seen," *Washington Post*, 9 October 1941, 15.
2. "Fall of Konoyke Cabinet Upsets Talks on Far East Between U.S. and Japan," *Wall Street Journal*, 17 October 1941, 11.
3. John O'Riley, "Japan: Its Industries Live on Borrowed Time; War Means Collapse," *Wall Street Journal*, 2 December 1941, 3.
4. "Empire Game," *Time*, 4 August 1941, 21.
5. Oil and Chemical Division, United States Strategic Bombing Survey, *Oil in Japan's War (appendix)* (Washington, D.C.: U.S. Government Printing Office, 1946), 41.
6. "Import or Die," *Time*, 4 August 1941, 61.
7. Edwin L. James, "Once Again We Tease Japan on Oil Supply," *New York Times*, 3 August 1941, E-3.

8. H. Foster Bain, "Japan's Power of Resistance," *Foreign Affairs* 22 (April 1944): 426.
9. Tariff Commission, *Petroleum*, War Changes in Industry Series, Report No. 17 (Washington, D.C.: U.S. Government Printing Office, 1946), 148.
10. "Japan: Economic Estimate, May 27, 1941," State Department document 894.50/154, page 21.
11. Ibid., 22.
12. Edwin L. James, "Once Again We Tease Japan on Oil Supply," E-3; Edwin L. James, "Japan Marking Time as Moscow Holds Out," *New York Times*, 2 November 1941, E-3.
13. Basil Collier, *The War in the Far East, 1941–1945: A Military History* (New York: William Morrow, 1969), 75; John Keegan, *The Second World War* (New York: Viking, 1989; reprint 1990), 248; John Robertson, *Australia at War, 1939–1945* (Melbourne: William Heinemann, 1981), 62–63; Richard Collier, *The Road to Pearl Harbor, 1941* (New York: Bonanza Books, 1981; reprint, 1984), 156.
14. Jerome B. Cohen, *Japan's Economy in War and Reconstruction* (Minneapolis: University of Minnesota Press, 1949), 133.
15. *Oil in Japan's War (Appendix)*, Oil and Chemical Division Strategic Bombing Survey (Washington, D.C.: U.S. Government Printing Office, 1946), 3.
16. See the popular military historian, B. H. Liddell Hart, *History of the Second World War* (1970; reprint New York: Perigee Books, 1982), 206. Edwin T. Layton with Roger Pineau and John Costello, *"And I Was There": Pearl Harbor and Midway—Breaking the Secrets* (New York: William Morrow, 1985), 130, implies this figure because he refers to domestic production providing 12% of the needs. On the other hand, he mentions a 90% import rate, though he attributes it to American sources rather than all sources (84). This may be either a typographical error or else an accidental oversight, attributing to one nation what came from all foreign suppliers.
17. Associated Press article, "Dutch Indies to Curb All Trade with Japan; Tokio [sic] Hints Reprisals," *Richmond Times Dispatch*, 29 July 1941, 1; International News Service, "...Dutch Cancel Tokyo Oil Rights, Netherlands Indies Scraps Treaty, Puts All Nipponese Trade on a License Basis," *Washington Post*, 29 July 1941, 1; addendum to an Associated Press dispatch from Batavia, Dutch East Indies, "Indies Halt Japan's Trade," *Wall Street Journal*, 29 July 1941, 2.
18. "Japan: Economic Estimate," State Department, May 27, 1941, 22.
19. Robertson, *Australia at War*, 62.
20. "Japan: Economic Estimate," State Department, May 27, 1941, 22.
21. I. F. Stone, "Oil on the Pacific," *Nation*, 9 August 1941, 109.
22. Cohen, *Japan's Economy*, 134; Collier, *Pearl Harbor*, 156; Donald F. Drummond, *The Passing of American Neutrality, 1937–1941* (New York: Greenwood, 1955), 273; James H. Herzog, "Influence of the United States Navy in the Embargo of Oil to Japan, 1940–1941," *Pacific Historical Review* 35 (August 1966): 317; Robertson, *Australia at War*, 62; Irvine H. Anderson, Jr., "The 1941 De Facto Embargo on Oil to Japan: A Bureaucratic Reflex," *Pacific Historical Review* 44 (May 1975): 201.
23. "Showdown in Pacific Hastened by Firm Stand of Democracies," *Newsweek*, 4 August 1941, 12; Edward T. Folliard, "Japanese Occupation of Indo-China Brings Swift Reprisals," *Washington Post*, 27 July 1941, B-3.
24. Nobutake, Ike, trans. and ed., *Japan's Decision for War: Records of the 1941 Policy Conferences* (Stanford, Calif.: Stanford University Press, 1967), 187; R. H. P. Mason and J. G. Caiger, *A History of Japan* (New York: Free Press, 1972), 294.
25. Bertram D. Hulen, "Washington Gets Tokyo Complaint," *New York Times*, 4 August 1941, 1.

26. Stone, "Oil," 109.
27. W. N. Medlicott, *The Economic Blockade*, 2 vols., vols. 7 and 8 of *History of the Second World War*, United Kingdom Civil Series, ed. W. Keith Hancock (London: H.M.S.O., 1952), 1:480.
28. Morgenthau Diaries 294:120–32 as reprinted in *Morgenthau Diary (China)*, Internal Security Subcommittee of the Committee on the Judiciary, United States Senate (Washington, D.C.: U.S. Government Printing Office, 1965), 194.

The Crisis of a Shrinking Reserve

29. *Oil in Japan's War (Appendix)*, 11. It should be stressed that this was the capacity rather than the actual amount accumulated at any give point.
30. Survey, *Oil in Japan's War*, 1, 11.
31. Staff of *Asahi Shimbun*, *The Pacific Rivals: A Japanese View of Japanese-American Relations* (New York: Weatherhill/Asahi, 1972), 89; Herbert Feis, *The Road to Pearl Harbor: The Coming of the War Between the United States and Japan* (1950; reprint, Princeton: Princeton Paperback Edition, 1972), 252; Gordon W. Prange, in collaboration with Donald M. Goldstein and Katherine V. Dillon, *Pearl Harbor: The Verdict of History* (New York: McGraw Hill, 1986), 149.
32. Collier, *Pearl Harbor*, 156; B. H. Liddell Hart, *History of the Second World War* (1970; reprint, New York: Perigree Books, 1982), 206.
33. J. H. Carmical, "Japanese Oil Seen as Key to Policy," *New York Times*, 4 August 1941, III-1.
34. Mason and Caiger, *History of Japan*, 294; Akira Iriye, *Power and Culture: The Japanese-American War, 1941–1945* (Cambridge: Harvard University Press, 1981), 28; Robert Goraski and Russell W. Freeburg, *Oil & War: How the Deadly Struggle for Fuel in WWII Meant Victory or Defeat* (New York: William Morrow, 1987), 102.
35. "Japan's Power of Resistance," *Foreign Affairs* 22 (April 1944), 426.
36. "Japan's Trade," *Wall Street Journal*, 26 July 1941, 2.
37. "Fall of Konoye Cabinet Upsets Talks on Far East," *Wall Street Journal*, 17 October 1941, 11.
38. "Estimate of Japanese National Strength at the Outbreak of the Greater East Asia War as of December, 1941," Appendix A in the "Japanese Documents" section of United States Strategic Bombing Survey, *Japan's Struggle to End the War* (Washington: U.S. Government Printing Office, 1946), 14.
39. "Japan: Economic Estimate," State Department, May 27, 1941, 22.
40. James, "Once Again We Tease Japan," E-3.
41. Associated Press, "Knox Says Japan Has Oil for 16 Months of War," *New York Times*, 3 August 1941, I-22; "Tightening of Economic Noose Puts Next Move Up to Japan," *Newsweek*, 11 August 1941, 16.
42. Irvin H. Anderson, Jr., *The Standard-Vacuum Oil Company and United States East Asian Policy, 1933–1941* (Princeton: Princeton University Press, 1975), 163.
43. Associated Press, "Knox Says Japan Has Oil for 16 Months of War," *New York Times*, 3 August 1941, I-22.
44. Anderson, *Standard-Vacuum*, 163.
45. Ronald Lewin, *Churchill as Warlord* (London: B. T. Batsford, 1973), 122.
46. Hanson Baldwin, *The Crucial Years: 1939–1941* (New York: Harper & Row, 1976), 356.
47. Layton, *"And I Was There,"* 130.

Chapter 9

THE PUBLIC STANCE OF THE JAPANESE GOVERNMENT

We shall use the term *public* to refer to remarks made directly or indirectly to foreigners by civilian and military officials of the Nipponese government. In many cases, these were made literally to the public in speeches, public addresses, or statements to the press. These remarks were given domestic circulation in the government-controlled press, and they were also circulated abroad. In other cases, the objections and denunciations were initially behind the scenes but delivered (commonly by diplomatic personnel) in either writing or verbal discourse with American officials. The degree to which these various discussions enjoyed the prestige of being official communications varied, of course. What they all had in common was recognition of the harm being inflicted upon the Japanese economy and indignation that a long-term friend such as the United States would act in such a way. American objections to Japanese foreign policy (especially in China) were regarded as misconstructions of Japanese intent or essentially wrong-headed and unrealistic opinions, certainly beyond any legitimate concern of a major power half the world away. The sufferings inflicted upon Japan were maximized and the sufferings inflicted by Japan minimized.

Reactions to the 1940 Embargo Measures

The limited embargo measures of 1940, already examined in detail, were the result of both frustration with Japan's militaristic foreign policy and the inability to convince Japan to alter it substantially. By itself Japanese policy would have been unlikely to have convinced the United States to risk the antagonism that economic restrictions inevitably created. What made the difference was the ongoing public pressure to undertake an approach that would inflict some type of tangible damage upon the invaders of China. The Japanese government was well aware that many Americans were pressing for a bolder policy than that embraced by the existing "moral embargo." Hence on March 23, 1940, the Japanese prime minister implicitly warned of the danger of military conflict if the United States adopted strict trade limitations: "The question of a general embargo is a serious one both for the country imposing the embargo and the country upon which it is imposed. If one false step is taken, danger lies ahead for both countries."[1]

In November 1940, Admiral Kichisaburo Nomura was appointed the new ambassador to Washington. Talking with an American correspondent, he urged restraint against the temptation to adopt a wide embargo because, putting it discreetly, "cutting such a large trade channel might result in abnormal actions here." Furthermore, Nomura expressed both a fact and an implicit threat: "If the United States refuses to sell us oil and other supplies, we must get them elsewhere."[2]

Although Japanese publications were not permitted to publish actual figures documenting the degree of trade decline, economic writers in that country were indirectly conceding a substantial impact by their late 1940 stress on measures adopted to counter it. Regional commerce, trade with the Soviet Union, and greater imports from Germany were viewed as effective means to deal with the trade crunch. An unidentified American reporter surveying the available literature concluded that "the steel industry" had been "seriously handicapped by the embargo on scrap steel exports" and that, overall, "Japanese production has been slowed up considerably."[3]

On April 11, 1941, Vice Foreign Minister Chuichi Ohashi addressed a meeting of prefectural governors. In light of his position and the tense international situation, it is not surprising that the main focus of the speech was upon Japan's relations with the United States. He emphasized that the American government was heavily pushing assistance to the British and then added: "Both Britain and the United States are increasing their economic pressures on Japan. In these circumstances the future is unpredictable."[4]

In late May 1941, the Japan Foreign Ministry circulated in Tokyo reports that it had received concerning various resolutions and proposed laws that had been introduced by U.S. congressmen. These included such stern actions as a total petroleum ban. The official Japanese news agency Domei distributed the report with the comment "Although this message did not divulge details, in view of the prevailing international crisis, much significance is attached to the report as an indication of strong anti–Japanese sentiment among certain political leaders in that country."[5]

A few days later, the economic bureau chiefs of each of the prefectures were assembled to discuss the problems their country faced. The commerce and industry minister, Vice Admiral Teijior Toyoda, informed them: "In view of the difficulties in the importation of various important materials, which are increasing with the growing tension in the international situation—it is presumed that the supply of goods during the current fiscal year will be tightened more and more. The nation must be prepared for even greater control over demand and supply of goods."[6]

As to what Nippon was saying diplomatically, it would be useful to center upon one case study to illustrate its attitude: the late September 1940 expansion of export licensing requirements to iron and steel scrap. On October 7, the Japanese Embassy filed a protest note with the State Department which stressed that it found "it difficult to concede that this measure was motivated solely by the interest of national defense of the United States." If that were indeed the dominant motive, why was Britain excluded from the restrictions? Furthermore, the embassy pointed out that the measure would result in a clearly disproportionate impact upon only one country of all the trading partners of the United States: "In view of the fact that Japan has been for some years the principal buyer of American iron and steel scrap, the announcement of the administrative policy, as well as the regulations establishing [a] license system in iron and steel scrap cannot fail to be regarded as directed against Japan, and, as such, to be an unfriendly act."[7]

The case for a blatantly anti–Japanese bias was laid out even more clearly in a note filed with the State Department the following day:

> Since iron and steel scrap classified as No. 1 heavy melting scrap was placed under [the] export-licensing system on July 26, 1940, permission of the United States Government was obtained up to August 19 of the same year for 99 percent of applications for shipments to Japan.
>
> In the light of this fact, the sudden enlargement of the iron and steel scrap licensing system to include all grades of these materials is hardly explicable from the standpoint of national defense, on which the regulation of September 30, 1940, is purported to be based.
>
> The discriminatory feature of the announcement, that licenses will be issued to permit shipments to the countries of the Western Hemisphere and Great Britain only, has created a widespread impression in Japan that it was motivated by a desire to bring pressure upon her.
>
> The fact that the majority of essential articles and materials that Japan desires to import from America is placed under [the] licensing system is causing a feeling of tension among the people of Japan, who naturally presume that the system is intended to be a precursor of severance of economic relations between Japan and the United States.
>
> In view of the high feeling in Japan it is apprehended that, in the event of continuation by the United States Government of the present attitude toward Japan in matters of trade restriction, especially if it leads to the imposition of further measures of curtailment, future relations between Japan and the United States will be unpredictable.[8]

Although politely worded, the message is also clear: the growing willingness to restrict exports to Japan seemed destined to lead to a total severance of trade and the continuance of existing measures (much less their expansion) possessed an explosive potential.

Both of these statements were delivered by the Japanese ambassador in a meeting with Secretary Hull. After listening to a reading of the two notes, Hull responded that, by their very nature, national defense decisions must be made by the concerned nation and could not be subject to veto by other countries.[9] The restrictions were not arbitrarily adopted at the beginning of a prolonged military buildup but "only at the height of our national defense preparations." Nor should the significance of the measures be exaggerated since the United States was "imposing [only] a few embargoes on important commodities."[10]

Japan's sensitivity to any measures that impinged upon its own potential well-being but total lack of appreciation of other nations' concerns thoroughly annoyed Hull:

> I said it was really amazing for the Government of Japan, which has been violating in the most aggravating manner valuable American rights and interests throughout most of China, and is doing so in many instances every day, to question the fullest privilege of this Government from every standpoint to impose the proposed iron and steel embargo, and that to go still further and call it an unfriendly act was still more amazing in the light of the conduct of the Japanese Government in disregarding all law, treaty obligations and other rights and privileges and the safety of Americans while it proceeded at the same time to seize territory by force to an ever-increasing extent.
>
> I stated that of all the countries with which I have had to deal during the past eight years, the Government of Japan has the least occasion or excuse to accuse this Government of an unfriendly act. I concluded with the statement that apparently the theory of the Japanese Government is for all other nations to acquiesce cheerfully in all injuries inflicted upon their citizens by the Japanese policy of force and conquest, accompanied by every sort of violence, unless they are to run the risk of being guilty of an unfriendly act.[11]

The Japanese ambassador responded with the hope, to use Hull's summary, "that trouble may yet be avoided" and stressed "that strife between the two countries would be extremely tragic for both alike."[12] Hull responded that Japanese expansion in an area as vast as it had occupied could only destroy a positive relationship with other powers:

> The Ambassador undertook to repeat the old line of talk about how fair Japan proposed to be with respect to all rights and privileges of foreign nations within its conquered territory. He agreed that no purpose would be served now to go over the many conversations we have had with respect to these matters. I held up the succession of injuries to American rights and interests in China whenever he referred to the scrap iron embargo.[13]

If the Japanese government were this intensely upset with the prohibition of scrap exports, one could only expect an even more intense reaction if the dagger were struck at Japan's heart through a total embargo on petroleum exports.

Reports of Japanese Reactions to the 1941 Embargo Measures Appearing in Western Publications

The bedrock on which the Japanese reaction was built was a disavowal that foreign pressure could compel a change in the basics of Japan's foreign relations. Japan's finance minister asserted soon after the imposition of the trade ban: "Japan cannot retreat even one step from her fundamental policy of constructing a Great East Asia Co-Prosperity Sphere."[14]

In the first few days after the announcement of the new restrictions, the Japanese took pains to dispel the image of pending catastrophe while conceding the grave element of danger. In a July 27, 1941, statement to the Japanese press, the recently installed finance minister, Matasune Ogura, stated that since the freezing action "had been surmised beforehand" the government had already prepared "countermeasures" to deal with it.[15] Inter-Asian trade was so large that it could compensate for the American loss, he suggested.[16] He stressed that the trade between the two nations had already dramatically declined and that the Americans had not really frozen that large an amount.[17] In fact, the Japanese retaliatory freezing would actually tie up substantially more currency.[18]

Ogura emphasized that the current crisis must not be permitted to alter national policy. "The primary thing for Japan to do is to forge ahead toward fulfillment of the colossal task of establishing the East Asia Co-Prosperity Sphere."[19] In the short term, he stated, "I consider it imperative and necessary to perfect the wartime system" of economic management by the government.[20] Ogura was inconsistent in how he pictured the seriousness of the problem. On the one hand, he insisted that the impact would only be "comparatively slight,"[21] but he also conceded that the Western action had created a "super emergency."[22]

Japanese officials pressed on reporters that minimization scenario.[23] The news agency Domei—accepted as an "authoritative" spokesagency for official Japanese government viewpoints—stressed that the claim of the embargo to be impartial was very misleading. "The American embargo on motor fuels and aviation oils does not mention Japan, but it is competently pointed out that it is directed against Japan." Domei went on to provide a dose of consolation to its readers by stating that "Vegetable oils now have successfully been processed as aviation oils and 90 percent of used oils are being reclaimed."[24] The English-language *Japan Times and Advertiser* played up the negative impact of the embargo on American business due to the suspension of silk imports, "Thousands are likely to be thrown out of employment . . . an icy boomerang has returned to the hand of Uncle Sam."[25]

The Japanese stressed that they were going to try to fulfill their international commitments regardless of what the United States did. On the

28th, their financial commissioner in the United States announced that his government intended to attempt to continue its almost unique record of never having defaulted on payments due on foreign private and public debt: "If it [the United States] handles the matter so as to cut off all trade, payments will become increasingly difficult, but in any event we shall continue to meet them."[26]

Government actions belied official optimism. Immediately after the embargo was announced, "food regulations were tightened, the milk ration halved, and more restrictions placed on shipping."[27]

Some Japanese industrialists were privately cautious, stressing that it could only be known how serious the damage would be when it became clear how strictly the new policy would be followed.[28] Such thoughts did nothing to assure investors. The United Press reported that "near panic spread among traders on the Tokyo Stock Exchange" after the trade freeze was announced.[29] The Japanese stock plummeted to its lowest point in a decade.[30] This immediate sense of pessimism was widespread. The Tokyo correspondent of the *New York Times* reported that "as regards the American and British freezing order, it is generally admitted here that it is bound to have a crippling effect on Japanese trade, not only with the United States and the British Empire but also with South America."[31]

As in any de facto dictatorship, the government was able to use the press to express candidly the rage that diplomatic niceties made it impossible to state officially. Of course, since Japan's reliance upon foreign suppliers was far from a secret, it probably required little encouragement for nationalists to give vent to aggravation they were already feeling. The first *Newsweek* after the trade cutoff was embraced informed its readers that "The controlled Japanese press launched its most violent attack in history on the United States and warned flatly of possible war. In reply, the United States tightened the economic noose around the Nipponese neck."[32] An earlier July 30 dispatch filed by United Press in Tokyo used almost the same exact words ("the most violent attack in history") in describing the press reaction. It also stressed the emphasis in the local press on the danger of war.[33]

In late July 1941, one paper described Washington's recent policy innovations as "ten times as bad" as the policies of Russia prior to the turn-of-the-century Russo-Japanese War.[34] *Chugai* suggested that the impact "may be tremendous, since it affects Japanese trade in the United States, Central and South America, Britain and their spheres of influence. Japan must prepare to meet the United States move by establishing self-sufficiency in East Asia."[35] The response of the *Japan Times and Advertiser* was more restrained than many, although its allusion to the war danger was inescapable:

Although Japan has been seeking every possible chance to carry out her southward policy by peaceful economic means, should America, Britain and the Netherlands attempt to intensify their pressure this country would be compelled to take the most appropriate and most effective steps to cope with the situation. Needless to say, the responsibility for resultant developments must be borne by these countries.[36]

In the early days of August, Vice Admiral Seizo Sakonji warned that the embargo had gravely escalated the risk of war: "The current international situation is so tense that a single spark would be sufficient to cause an explosion."[37] The *Japan Times and Advertiser* chimed in, "This artificial exclusion of Japan from supplies merely hastens the course of self-sufficiency in the Western Pacific."[38]

On August 11, the Japanese government announced strong new moves to coordinate business and to deal with the difficulties imposed by the Anglo-American trade restrictions.[39] On the same day, Captain Hideo Hiraide, an official spokesman for the Japanese navy, charged that an economic war was already being waged against his nation and that Japan was effectively encircled by American and British military installations. "One step farther and Japan will be driven to make a decision involving life or death. No nation with any legitimate claim to life can be expected to accept its doom without question or struggle."[40]

The night of September 1, 1941 (Tokyo time; August 31 in the United States), the Japanese military headquarters in Tokyo had the chief of its army press section, Colonel Hayato Mabuchi, address the public on the general theme of protection against air raids. He took the opportunity to go far beyond this subject and lob a few verbal blasts at the United States and Great Britain.

Mabuchi labeled the embargo "a crime against humanity" and criticized the two nations for their "unpardonable crimes." If the embargo continued too long, he argued, the result would be disastrous: "If sources of materials in foreign countries are closed to us the day will come when we will be at the end of our domestic resources. . . . If Japan cannot reach a peaceful settlement through diplomatic negotiations, Japan must break through the encirclement fronts by force. This means engaging the countries included in the encirclement movement, notably America and Britain, in a long-drawn-out armed conflict. . . . The situation will compel us to stake all to save ourselves as a nation."[41]

On October 8, the Japanese commerce minister, Vice Admiral Masazo Sakonji, emphasized to the public that because of the trade ban, a war in effect already existed: "The expectation is that the economic situation in Japan will become further strained and the people will have to be prepared for a lower standard of living. In time of war, a new mode of living, suitable to the war situation should prevail."[42]

The following day Domei downplayed the significance of reports that a complete embargo had been agreed to by the Western powers:

> The effect of these hostile measures on Japan is small because she set up a wartime economic structure in anticipation of such actions before the freezing orders went into effect. Japan feels little pain from such an embargo, but will renew her firm determination to cope with various difficulties and hardships at home and abroad by establishing the projected Greater East Asia Co-prosperity Sphere.[43]

The American correspondent who reported this reminded his readers of its "remarkable contrast to previous declarations, such as that an oil embargo meant war."[44]

However much Japan might at this particular moment choose to downplay the danger of war growing out of the embargo, the very same day brought a belligerent statement from a spokesman for the Japanese cabinet. He pointed out that "because of developments in the past few months war is likely to spread to other regions at any moment." The same day the newspaper *Hochi* leveled the charge that the real danger to peace in the Pacific was "nothing other than the willful, arrogant intentions and actions of the United States."[45]

Perhaps reacting to these contradictory currents, in a dispatch dated October 11, Otto D. Toliscus sent an analysis suggesting that "the Japanese people are beginning to suspect that the change in the international situation calls for caution." Even militants were conceding the drastic impact of the termination of commerce: "Military spokesmen like Mabuchi, and nationalist radicals like Nakano, have told the people that the economic blockade is strangling the nation, draining its lifeblood—oil. In other words, Japan, even without plunging into a new war is using up more materials than it can replace."[46]

On November 1 the important *Nichi Nichi* newspaper editorially rebuked President Roosevelt for his "procrastination" in resolving outstanding issues between the two nations. If Japan's need for an external oil supply were not quickly resolved, "Japan will have to obtain it by extraordinary means, even if it should prove dangerous, because a modern state like Japan cannot exist without oil. This would be legitimate exercise of the self-defense right."[47]

That same day Domei attributed to "well-informed" sources (an euphemism for government officials) equally strong views. The release asserted that the "imminent fall of Moscow" and the likelihood of war in the Atlantic undermined American efforts to avoid conflict in the Pacific. Indeed, according to the news agency, at this stage "the clash in the Pacific ... now seems inevitable."[48] Having stressed the likelihood of war, Domei's press release immediately rebuked the American effort to reverse Japanese policy through the embargo:

It must be pointed out, however, that the United States vaingloriously assumes that it can force Japan to abandon her national policy for the establishment of an east Asian coprosperity sphere by general, aggressive economic pressure without resorting to arms, such assumption being evidently based on an American underestimation of Japan's national strength. . . .

Moreover, should the United States continue to enforce an economic blockade against Japan, there will be no other way left for Japan than to seek supply sources of vital goods and materials, as a measure of self-defense and protection. Japan will have to dare to proceed with such a measure in face of a situation where she must break through the encirclement that has been formed by hostile nations.[49]

On November 17, 1941, Foreign Minister Shigenori Togo addressed the Diet and conceded that the recent expansion into southern Indochina had been interpreted by the British and the Americans "as a menace to their territories and [as a result they] froze Japan's assets in their countries which constitutes a measure tantamount to rupturing economic relations." Unless the present alienation from these nations could be overcome, the situation could "ultimately end in catastrophe. Should such an eventuality occur it would entail great suffering not only on countries in the Pacific Basin but on all of mankind as well."[50] Togo warned that "there is naturally a limit to our conciliatory attitude."[51]

The same day, and before the same audience, Prime Minister Hideki Tojo reminded his listeners that there was only a thin line between economic and military warfare: "It hardly requires an explanation that the economic blockage resorted to constitutes a measure little less hostile in character than armed warfare."[52]

Reaction in the Government-controlled Japanese Press: Fall, 1941

So far we have stressed what was reprinted or quoted in American periodicals. Naturally, most of what the Japanese officials and press had to say was not reproduced abroad. Even so, these statements and publications were available to the foreign embassies in Tokyo and hence their content was known to key diplomatic officials. The *Japan Times and Advertiser*, which was controlled by the foreign office, made the task even easier for the diplomats in its twice daily editions.[53] Due to its special status, it represented a pipeline into foreign-office thinking. In addition, the evening edition reprinted, in translation, a cross-section of that morning's editorials from other Japanese newspapers.

Hence by examining the treatment of the ongoing story by the *Times and Advertiser* and the publications it reprinted, we can gain a further insight into Japanese thinking about the embargo—thinking that was available to the American Embassy. We will begin in September 1941: any initial panic was now over and long and hard thinking had been given to what came next. *And the press repeatedly warned of the danger if the trade freeze was not rolled back.*

In the September issue of *Nippon Hyoron*, Professor Tadao Takemura of Kei University pictured the economic embargo as a method of waging war by nonmilitary means. He was convinced that overt American military action was being restrained only by three factors: (1) insufficient unity to undertake such a war, (2) a navy unprepared to wage a two-ocean war until at least 1946, and (3) a preference for letting others do the fighting so the United States could reap greater influence in the postwar world than the bruised winners. Takemura asserted: "But America can avoid a war of attrition only when its economic war is effectively waged. Should it become no longer possible to deal a fatal blow to Japan through the economic warfare, America will be forced to appeal to arms." Professor Takemura was convinced that Japan's expansion throughout French Indochina had made an American economic squeeze ultimately futile, making quite possible a direct American exertion of its military strength.[54]

On September 6, *Chugai Shogyo* editorialized that because of the new trade restrictions "the supply of various materials has become tight," and the paper noted that "The asset freezing by Great Britain, the United States and other dollar and pound bloc countries has practically suspended third nation trade," that is, transshipment in either direction that used the ports of a third party. The newspaper pointed to the alleged havoc the cutoff had inflicted upon certain of those backing the action, especially in the southern Pacific and India.[55]

The paraphrase of a September 4, 1941, report filed from New York City by a correspondent for *Nichi Nichi* confirmed that "Since President Roosevelt froze all Japanese assets in America on July 15 [sic], commerce between the two countries has come to a dead stop." Treasury Department officials were still present in the offices of all American branches of Japanese-owned banks and major businesses to assure that the asset freeze was faithfully observed.[56] The seriousness of the situation was stressed in an article in the *Japan Times and Advertiser*:

> From the political angle, the United States is expected to accelerate its aid–Britain and aid–Soviet activities and to strengthen its encirclement of Japan because all feeling of friendliness toward Japan seems to have disappeared since the conclusion of the tripartite alliance. The common idea of both the Government and people is that the position of the United States on the Pacific has been markedly consolidated since last year. Half of the Pacific fleet was transferred to the Atlantic since the summer but the lacuna has been filled with a powerful air force. The Alaskan military bases have been strengthened so as to increase the possibilities of using the Siberian bases of the Soviet Union. The view that armed force should be used against Japan if necessary is running high in influential quarters. The United States policy toward Japan last year contained an element of bluff but that is not necessarily so any longer

and the United States may be regarded as facing Japan in full awareness of the consequences.[57]

A front-page column in the *Japan Times and Advertiser* on September 13 tore into the Western boycott and emphasized the damage it had inflicted upon the Chinese port of Shanghai, allegedly hurting Japanese commerce as a means of indirectly damaging Japanese business interests. "Financial warfare of this kind, carried out by the ABCD Powers cannot be tolerated. If retaliatory measures are launched the responsibility will rest upon the aggressive Powers."[58]

There were, of course, public relations articles attempting to downplay the signficance of the end of trade, useful perhaps in encouraging the less informed but hardly likely to deceive the diplomatic or business communities. One such article originating in the *Japan Times and Advertiser* in mid-September concerned the cotton textile industry and was optimistically headlined, "Spinners Are Equal to ABCD Pressures." Buried in the article, however, was an estimate that cotton availability was down by a quarter, according to nongovernmental estimates (official figures were no longer being released). The situation was actually worse than the percentage indication, as the article stated: "Because cotton available in this part of the world is inferior in quality to that from other spheres, the shortage must be considered to be larger than the above mentioned 25 percent." If this were not bad enough, transportation difficulties meant that the growth of cotton did not necessarily translate into its delivery to the plants where it could be processed. Hence the newspaper concluded: "At any rate, the situation is worse than the above figures indicate."[59]

On the following day the same publication carried the headline "Silk Industry Hit Little by Freezing." The report summarized a recent article by a representative of the Agriculture and Forestry Ministry. It attempted an upbeat message by emphasizing that the silk industry itself was not affected. Of course, the problem was not the industry itself but the availability of markets for its production, but the article downplayed the problem, stating: "The eventual stoppage of overseas shipments is of course a blow to Japan's silk industry, but its effect will be far smaller than [it] would have been around 1930 because silk exports to the United States have been on the decrease as contrasted to the market increase in home consumption in recent years." Since cotton availability had been reduced, it was hoped that silk products could be a partial substitute.[60]

Mid-September brought with it the tenth anniversary of the Manchurian Incident. To commemorate it, Major Kametaro Tominaga of the War Ministry's Press Bureau delivered an important speech that carried an implicit threat of war if the Netherlands East Indies participated in the embargo. (Its significance can be seen in that the heavily government-influenced *Times and Advertiser* reprinted the entire speech on September 18, 1941.) Tominaga observed:

> The situation in the South has been tense, vibrating and electrical. The ABCD aggression line is steadily narrowing its pressure circle against Japan. England and its possessions, the United States and Dutch East Indies proclaimed the freezing of Japanese assets simultaneously with the landing of the Imperial troops in Southern French Indo-China, adding another ugly feature to their economic warfare against Japan.
>
> That Japan needs, in realizing the new order in East Asia, materials from [the] Dutch East Indies situated in Japan's vital economic circle, goes without saying. The Japanese Government has been declaring that it seeks to carry on trade for mutual benefit, a peaceful progress, one may say, to obtain the needed raw materials. Should any Power or Powers go to the extent of forcing the Dutch East Indies to refuse Japan's legitimate demand and stop sending materials that have a grave bearing on Japan's life and death question, that will be the time for us Japanese to show them the folly of their maneuvering.
>
> The glorious tradition and mission of the Yamato people do not permit their country to remain under this ... economic oppression. Especially so, when the situation threatens to force Japan to suffer from gradual economic strangulation. We say it with conviction that a resolute step forward is the only way left for us in order to safeguard our honored history.[61]

A few days later the publication *Miyako* spoke in the past tense of the difficulties imposed by the freezing action and asserted that the minimization of its ongoing effect had been "due to the indomitable spirit and traditional wisdom of the Yamato race." In fact, the economic weapon was self-destructive, and Singapore and Hong Kong were already bearing its ill effects, according to *Miyako*. The publication claimed that the freeze would have no more impact upon Japan than spitting at the sky.[62]

On September 25, *Nichi Nichi* correspondents elaborated upon the theme of foreign damage caused by the elimination of Nippon-Western trade. Using its correspondents throughout southeast Asia, negative consequences were noted in every country. Rather than hurting Japan, these collaborators in the embargo had actually hurt themselves, this publication asserted.[63]

Retired officials and military men have a liberty of speech sometimes denied them while in active government service, so they represented an obvious means whereby indignation could be expressed. The former vice chief of the Naval General Staff told *Hochi Shimbun*, "Japan's southward advance is absolute which has no alternative whatsoever. It may be carried out peacefully by economic means or otherwise as the situation depends, but, in any event, we are to only trust in the policy of the Government." Then later, in what may be either a direct quote or a paraphrase, the former admiral pointed to the importance of foreign resources: "The absoluteness of our southward advance becomes even stronger under the present situation when we are forced to replenish necessary materials for the national existence." A discreet way of saying that the embargo was indeed seriously depleting Japan's reserves.[64]

In an October 8 dispatch from New York, the Domei news agency cited an Associated Press report that the British, United States, and Netherlands East Indies had decided to halt permanently all petroleum shipments to Japan. A paragraph presumably added after the dispatch's arrival in Japan provided a domestic commentary: "It was indicated here that such an agreement among these three countries would not be an economic blow to Japan. As the Japanese emergency structure was formulated long before the imposition of the freezing decree, it was stated here that this joint action would not have any tangible effect."[65]

Political commentator Yoshitaro Shimizu, writing in *Hochi* on October 11, blamed the current world crisis on a conflict between the "have-countries" (the United States and the British Empire) and the "have-not countries" (Japan and Germany in particular). He viewed the Co-Prosperity Sphere as a means of regional economic assertion. Even so he candidly conceded the seriousness of the West's trade measures: "Struggles with Britain and the United States cause heavy blows on Japanese industrial circles, since more than 40 percent of Japanese trade has been carried out with the Anglo-American bloc."[66]

In a quotation/summary from Domei's mid–October review of Japan's diplomatic stance, the war option was implicitly left open: "It should be pointed out here that the Japanese people are not so simple-minded as to believe that all problems can be solved through diplomatic parleys." The summary was subheaded with the same idea: "People Not So Simple As to Suppose Diplomacy Can Solve Everything."[67]

In *Contemporary Japan* (October 1941), Masatoshi Matsushita, a Japanese-born scholar teaching in the United States, vigorously criticized what he labeled America's key role in creating the military encirclement of his homeland. The economic cutoff did not go unnoticed in his analysis: "[The] embargo of war supplies to Japan is perhaps the most effective means of bringing pressure to bear on it. Japan is not self-sufficient as to war materials, it must either import them or resort to force in order to obtain them if it becomes necessary." Earlier in his essay, Matsushita had included oil among the nation's "war materials." For an English-speaking audience, his argument would have been improved by stressing that oil was equally important for both the civilian economy and the military one and that the denial of oil was, effectively, an attempt to destroy both.[68]

In a speech that gained front-page attention on October 17, 1941, Major-General Kiyofuku Okamoto, a director of one of the divisions of the General Staff Office, addressed a meeting of ex-servicemen:

> Although the Sino-Japanese and Russo-Japanese wars were two of the gravest crises that had ever confronted the nation, they were menaces surrounding only

Chosen and Manchuria. Confronted with various grave economic questions, the nation is now at the cross-roads of life or death. ... For the fulfillment of the national policy, this country has sought to reach an agreement of views with the United States by diplomatic means. There is, however, the limit for concession by us and the negotiations may end in rupture with the possible worst situation following. The people, therefore, must be fully resolved to cope with such a situation.[69]

An editorial in the *Japan Times and Advertiser* of October 22 took the line that America's hostility had, unfortunately, been a long-standing one and that there was a point beyond which Japan could not go: "This country has consistently tried to be friends with the United States, only to be met with such as the Stimson Doctrine, the economic pressure, the freezing and the encirclement. After all is said and done, there is a limit that Japan is resolved to maintain at all hazards. All this country can do is to point to the alternatives."[70]

When the first of November rolled around, that same Tokyo publication gave front-page coverage to the statement of an unidentified Japanese diplomatic official in Washington:

> If the crisis between Japan and the United States is to be avoided, the two countries must at least take measures to stop the economic war between them. The leaders of the Japanese Government have declared that it is impossible to maintain the Japan-American relation in the present condition.
>
> If the Japan-American relation is left to take its own course, it must either improve or turn worse. As the United States is prohibiting exports to Japan, it is an actual fact that the Japanese Government would come to a situation where they have to take measures of self-existence and protection to obtain oil and other materials.[71]

The evening edition gave front-page attention to a *Nichi Nichi* article that apparently elaborated upon the above interview:

> The Japanese spokesman in Washington is reported to have warned the United States that if there should not be any development in the Japanese-American negotiations, it will lead to Japan's application of self-defense measures.
>
> If the United States really desires to avoid war in the Pacific and maintain its supply of rubber, tin and other strategic materials from Malaya and the Netherlands East Indies, on which American industry leans, now is the time for the United States seriously to consider Japan's resolution and self-defense aims.
>
> With the advent of a fateful phase for Japan, the Japanese Government has fully completed all preparations for any eventuality through the close cooperation of the Army and Navy, officials and the people.[72]

A second translated article from the same day's morning issue of *Nichi Nichi* was reprinted in full on the inside of the paper:

> The Japanese-American negotiations are, so to speak, a game being played on the top of a steep precipice. A single mis-step will precipitate both countries into the bottom of a ravine. ...
>
> The one which constitutes the core of economic problems between the two

nations is oil. Frankly speaking, Japan will be compelled to devise measures to obtain oil even in the face of danger, if it is refused by the United States and the Netherlands East Indies to obtain oil through trade. This is a necessary measure for self-protection for a modern country to exist.[73]

Nichi Nichi proceeded to call attention to Roosevelt's own earlier warnings of how a cutoff of oil could lead to war.[74]

The following day, front-page coverage was given in Tokyo to "well-informed observers" and their concern over the danger of war resulting from the West's economic policies:

> Should the United States continue to enforce the economic blockade of Japan, there will be no other way left for Japan than to seek the supply sources of vital goods and materials as the measure of self-defense and protection.
> Japan will have to dare to proceed with such a measure even in the face of the situation where she must break through the encirclement formed by inimical nations.[75]

On the same front page, a radiotelephone conversation between *Nichi Nichi*'s European-American editor and its New York correspondent is quoted at length. The *Japan Times and Advertiser* summed up the conversation in a few introductory paragraphs. What is of special relevance in this context is the remark "They had a lively debate on the question [of American attitudes toward Japan], and eventually reached agreement on the view that the United States is determined to drive Japan into a corner economically."[76]

The following day the Japanese press became even more vehement. "Sharp comments were made by all Tokyo newspapers Monday upon the American attitude vis-a-vis the Japanese-American negotiations."[77] *Nichi Nichi* alluded to the complete success of the various restrictions: "the United States stopped even a trickle of oil or a fragment of scrap from reaching Japan."[78] The front page of that morning's *Advertiser* vehemently portrayed Henry Morgenthau, Jr. (U.S. secretary of the Treasury) as the villain behind the economic sanctions. The embargo he sponsored was a form of "persecut[ing] the poor"; it represented "economic oppression" and posed the danger of war. Furthermore, it was inherently futile: "There was no country that has fallen because of economic measures."[79]

On November 13, *Chugai Shogyo* emphasized that Western military and economic policy indicated the intention "of strangling Japan to death." The paper asserted: "Despair is taboo in diplomacy. Yet there is a limit to moderate policy or patience."[80] The same day *Nichi Nichi* took aim at the inclination of certain Americans to look upon trade with Japan as some kind of special favor. It pointed to Secretary of the Navy Frank Knox as a specific example of this frame of mind:

> Further he says: America has been patiently supplying Japan with materials. Not so fast, Colonel Knox. We have never obtained a single piece of anything from

America without duly paying for it. It has been a legal and commercial transaction. America has been realizing its own profit in this transaction, and while it may have reason to be grateful, there is nothing on Japan's part, to consider as a favor from the other side of the Pacific.[81]

Confidence-building articles were not abandoned. Efforts continued to be made to put the most optimistic interpretation on a disintegrating situation, presumably as a means of enhancing domestic morale and discouraging any foreign perception that Japan's position was untenable if the United States prolonged the trade/petroleum squeeze. On November 18, Finance Minister Okinori Kaya proudly announced, to use one newspaper's summary, that "Japan's economic power has advanced beyond all dreams since the start of the China Affair."[82] Yet the same day that paper carried an editorial which referred to the danger of a Pacific war under the title "By No Means Impossible."[83]

That night Major Kametaro Tominaga delivered a radio address tearing into the Western military-economic "encirclement" of Japan. As the result of such measures, he asserted, "the calmness of the western Pacific has been disturbed by these nations. . . . Japan has been maintaining patience in spite of their challenging actions and economic pressure solely desiring for the peace of the Pacific. . . . We will be forced to make them know that there is a limit to our patience."[84]

On November 20, 1941, Finance Minister Okinori Kaya encouraged the public by announcing that when one included into one's calculations the foreign loads that Japan no longer had to pay, it was the net gainer in the asset freeze to the tune of about 900 million yen.[85] On November 21, the president of the Japan Chamber of Commerce and Industry brought a similarly upbeat message to a Tokyo dinner meeting of his organization: "Far from being weak, Japan's economic power is really very stable and has enormous elasticity, and in case of any emergency it is sufficiently strong to surmount any difficulty with the support of the burning patriotism of the entire people."[86]

Premier Tojo presented a far grimmer picture in an address of the 25th. "The current situation is grave, which is unexempled [sic] in the glorious history of 3,000 years of Japan." Another speaker at the same meeting, Lieutenant-General Suzuki, spoke of the need to "break through the economic blockade by the encircling front and transform Japan's economic setup. If we think of [the] shortage of products from which our ancestors suffered when they arrived on [the] Islands of Japan, we should bear the difficulties in obtaining ample supply of commodities and materials."[87]

In an editorial of November 29, *Nichi Nichi* pointed to America's denial of needed "defense materials" and support of the Chinese foe as crucial impediments to a cordial relationship between the two nations. If these policies were altered, "there is no reason why it should not be at peace. The United States has the key to the problem of maintaining the peace of the Pacific area."[88]

Asahi weighed in on Sunday, November 30, with further criticism of the embargo. "All the trouble in the Pacific area has its genesis in efforts by countries hostile toward this country to deny it the most natural right to have access to materials which are needed for its existence."[89]

On December 2, *Nichi Nichi* went even further and attributed Pacific problems not just to an anti-Japanese bias but to an overweening American greediness. "The cause of the elements that disturb the East Asiatic peace is the fact that the United States, dissatisfied with its abundant natural resources and large territory, is still anxious to place even East Asia under its control."[90] On the same day, *Mikayo* emphasized: "The Japanese asset freezing is an economic warfare, pure and simple. It is an offensive. Should soldiers be satisfied with a mere message?"[91]

On December 4, Finance Minister Okinori Kaya spoke in extremely confident terms that "the freezing order has not dealt any serious blow to the countries against which the move was directed." He stressed that "any further economic pressure from countries opposed to us will not prevent us from looking to the future with equanimity."[92]

While proclaiming an exaggerated degree of self-reliance, Japan had repeatedly raised the prospect of war. On December 7, 1941, the total boycott was still in effect and a desperate Japan struck out to break it and to assure itself an empire that could stand against any occidental foe.

NOTES

Reactions to the 1940 Embargo Measures

1. Roger Parkinson, *The Origins of World War Two* (New York: G. P. Putnam Sons, 1970), 115.
2. Associated Press, "Nomura Holds U.S., Japan Needs Peace," *New York Times*, 27 November 1940, 10.
3. "Industry in Japan Seen Slowed Down," *New York Times*, 26 January 1941, III-3.
4. Quoted by Otto D. Tolischus, "Japan Warns of Long Struggle," *New York Times*, 11 April 1941, 14.
5. Quoted in unidentified author's "wireless" message, *New York Times*, 25 May 1941, III-2.
6. "Japanese Pressing East Indies on Pact." *New York Times*, 30 May 1941, 4.
7. "The Japanese Embassy to the Department of State, October 7, 1940," Department of State, *Peace and War: United States Foreign Policy, 1931–1941* (Washington, D.C.: U.S. Government Printing Office, 1943), Annex 1 to Document 186, p. 579.
8. "The Japanese Embassy to the Department of State, October 8, 1940," Annex 2 to Document 186, pp. 579–80.

9. "186. Memorandum by the Secretary of State Regarding a Conversation with the Japanese Ambassador (Horinouchi), Washington, October 8, 1940," *Peace and War*, 576–78 provides the complete text of Hull's summary of the meeting.
10. Ibid., 576.
11. Ibid., 576–77.
12. Ibid., 577.
13. Ibid., 578.

Reports of Japanese Reactions to the 1941 Embargo Measures Appearing in Western Publications

14. "Tightening of Economic Noose Puts Next Move Up to Japan," *Newsweek*, 11 August 1941, 16.
15. Domei's English translation quoted by the Associated Press, "Japan's New Financial Chief Calls for Fight," *Los Angeles Times*, 28 July 1941, I-6.
16. Ibid.
17. "Tokyo Freezes Assets of U.S. As Stocks Dive," *Washington Post*, 27 July 1941, A-2.
18. Associated Press, "Tokyo Stocks Drop in Panic," *Los Angeles Times*, 27 July 1941, I-1.
19. Domei's English translation, Associated Press, "Japan's New Financial Chief Calls for Fight," I-6.
20. Ibid.
21. "Tokyo Is Shocked by Economic War," *New York Times*, 27 July 1941, I-12.
22. Associated Press, "Japan's New Financial Chief," I-16.
23. United Press, "Tokyo Discounts Effect of Action, but Press Bitterly Rails at America," *Washington Post*, 26 July 1941, 1.
24. Associated Press, "Tokio [sic] Regime Warns Nation International Explosion Near, Rants at Newest U.S. Action, *Richmond Times Dispatch*, 3 August 1941, I-5.
25. Ibid.
26. United Press, "Japan to Make Debt Payments," *Wall Street Journal*, 29 July 1941, 2.
27. United Press, "Tokyo Discounts Effect," 1.
28. "Tokyo Freezes Assets," *Washington Post*, A-2.
29. "Tokyo Stock Prices Break," *Wall Street Journal*, 2 July 1941, 2.
30. Associated Press, "Tokyo Stocks Drop in Panic," I-1.
31. "Tokyo Is Shocked by Economic War," *New York Times*, I-12.
32. "Tightening of Economic Noose," *Newsweek*, 16.
33. This brief press summary was inserted in brackets—presumably by the editor—into an Otto D. Tolischus dispatch, "Japan Smolders over Oil Threat," *New York Times*, 30 July 1941, 1.
34. United Press, "Tokyo Press Flays U.S. and Hurls War Warning," *Los Angeles Times*, 30 July 1941, I-1.
35. Associated Press, "Tokyo Stocks Drop in Panic," I-1; also quote in "Tokyo Freezes Assets, *Washington Post*, A-2.
36. "Japan Smolders Over Oil Threat," *New York Times*, 4.
37. "Tokio [sic] Regime Warns," *New York Times*, I-5.
38. Associated Press, "Japan Determined to Supply Self from Indies, Paper Says," *Washington Post*, 2 August 1941, 3.
39. Associated Press, "...Japan 'Mobilizes' All Business," *Washington Post*, 12 August 1941, 1.
40. Otto D. Tolischus, "Japan's Press Turns Eyes on Soviet Role in 3-Power Line-

up," copyrighted by *New York Times*, as printed in the *Washington Post*, 18 August 1941, 1, 4.

41. Otto D. Tolischus, "Japan May Have to use Force to Break Out of 'Encirclement,'" copyrighted by *New York Times*, as printed in the *Washington Post*, 2 September 1941, 1, 6. Part of Mabuchi's address is also quoted by Barnet Nover, "The Japanese Blow Hot and Cold," *Washington Post*, 3 September 1941, 11.

42. "Japanese Warn U.S.," *New York Times*, 8 October 1941, 6.

43. Otto D. Tolischus, "Japanese Profess Unconcern on Oil," *New York Times*, 10 October 1941, 8.

44. Ibid., 8.

45. Both quotes cited by United Press, "U.S. Called 'Arrogant,'" *New York Times*, 10 October 1941, 8. Somewhat ironically this dispatch was printed on the same page as the Tolischus report cited in the two preceding footnotes.

46. "Hard Facts Restrain the Japanese," *New York Times*, 12 October 1941, IV-5.

47. United Press, "U.S. Risking War, Tokyo Paper Warns," *Washington Post*, 1 November 1941, 4.

48. Otto D. Tolischus, "Japanese Say They're Ready for Showdown," copyrighted by *New York Times*, as printed in *Washington Post*, 2 November 1941, I-15.

49. Ibid.

50. Associated Press, "Text of Address by Minister Togo," *Washington Post*, 17 November 1941, 6.

51. "Blockade Is Assailed," *New York Times*, 17 November 1941, 6.

52. Ibid., 6.

Reaction in the Government-controlled Japanese Press: Fall, 1941

53. The semiofficial role of the *Japan Times and Advertiser* was a well-known and accepted fact. A United Press dispatch of the period pointed to the fact that the paper "usually reflects the views of the foreign office" ("U.S. Risking War, Tokyo Paper Warns," *Washington Post*, 1 November 1941, 4). Associated Press dispatches in August called it an "organ of the Foreign Office" ("Japan Hurls War Threats on Squeezes," *Los Angeles Times*, 13 August 1941, 1) and "foreign-office-controlled" ("Japan Lists Steps for U.S. to Ease Crisis," *Washington Post*, 5 November 1941, 5). In a postwar investigation, United States ambassaor Joseph C. Grew testified that the Japanese government "constantly" used the press to air its views (testimony of Joseph C. Grew, *PHA*, 79th Congress, 2:595). He did not object when the *Japan Times and Advertiser* was described as "reflect[ing] the attitude of the war department" in Japan (2:597–98). Perhaps the explanation for the control being attributed to the war department instead of the foreign office is that General Tojo had taken power in October 1941.

54. Translated by "Contemporary Opinions," the essay is reprinted in condensed form under the title "Japan-U.S. Relations Analyzed from New World Development," *Japan Times and Advertiser*, 4 September 1941 (morning edition), 6.

55. "Asset Freezing and Third Nation Markets" (English translation), *Japan Times and Advertiser*, 6 September 1941 (morning edition), 3.

56. The report was paraphrased under the heading "Japanese Business in U.S. Paralyzed," *Japan Times and Advertiser*, 7 September 1941 (morning edition), 5.

57. Ibid.

58. "Aggressive Finance: Blocking Shanghai's Trade," *Japan Times and Advertiser*, 13 September 1941 (evening edition), 1. This subhead appears under the generic, ongoing headline of "The Times Today," the author(s) of which are never identified. Since the column usually consisted of several short paragraphs or miniarticles, it was probably compiled from the contributions of several staff writers.

The Public Stance of the Japanese 155

59. *Japan Times and Advertiser*, 16 September 1941 (evening edition), 5.
60. *Japan Times and Advertiser*, 17 September 1941 (morning edition), 5.
61. Text of entire speech printed under the title "Warning Bell Peals in East," *Japan Times and Advertiser*, 18 September 1941 (morning edition), 6.
62. The article was summarized under the title "Yamato Spirit Pins Anglo-U.S. Freezing / Expected Dire Economic Results Do Not Materialize As Japanese Inured," *Japan Times and Advertiser*, 23 September 1941 (evening edition), 3.
63. Their findings are summarized in an article entitled "Anglo-U.S. Freezing of Japanese Assets, Profess Boomerang to America, Britain," *Japan Times and Advertiser*, 25 September 1941 (evening edition), 1.
64. "South Move Vital, Admiral Declares / Notes Navalist Sankichi Takahashi Asserts Japan Has No Alternative," *Japan Times and Advertiser*, 2 October 1941 (evening edition), 2. The first quote is presented as a direct quotation by the newspaper; the second one is presented as part of the "summary" of his remarks.
65. "All Oil Shipments Banned to Japan by Allied Powers," *Japan Times and Advertiser*, 10 October 1941 (morning edition), 1.
66. Shimizu's article is quoted at length under the heading "Anglo-U.S. Policy in Asia Deplored," *Japan Times and Advertiser*, 11 October 1941 (evening edition), 1, 6. The "have"/"have not" comparison comes from page 1; the quotation from the continuation of the article appears on page 6.
67. "Situation of Japan Reviewed by Domei," *Japan Times and Advertiser*, 13 October 1941 (morning edition), 1.
68. The article is reprinted under the title "America Is Real Ringleader of ABCD Front Encircling Japan," *Japan Times and Advertiser*, 14 October 1941 (morning edition), 6.
69. "Japan-American Negotiations May Rupture Despite Peaceful Efforts, General Warns," *Japan Times and Advertiser*, 17 October 1941 (morning edition), 1.
70. "It's Up to Them," *Japan Times and Advertiser*, 17 October 1941 (evening edition), 6.
71. Asahi Service, "America and Japan Can Prevent Fight on Trade War End / ... Ban on Exports Only Forces Tokyo to Look for Other Solutions," *Japan Times and Advertiser*, 1 November 1941 (morning edition), 1. Asahi attributes the text we cite to "a New York Times report."
72. "U.S. Exhorted to Restudy Japan's Role to Snuff Out Match Held over War Keg" (English translation), *Japan Times and Advertiser*, 1 November 1941 (evening edition), 1. The *Advertiser* uses the odd expression that *Nichi Nichi* had spoken "semi-editorially."
73. "Japan's Self-Protection" (English translation), *Japan Times and Advertiser*, 1 November 1941 (evening edition), 3. This was in the daily "Japanese Press Comments" section.
74. Ibid.
75. "Japan Establishes Her War Structure to Meet Any Crisis," *Japan Times and Advertiser*, 2 November 1941 (morning edition), 1. Presumably to distance the government from potential American protests, these governmental opinions are presented not as direct quotations but as a "sum[ming] up to the following effect."
76. "Nichi Nichi's New York Correspondent Radiophones on U.S. Attitude to Japan," *Japan Times and Advertiser*, 2 November 1941 (morning edition), 1.
77. "American Attitude on Talks Excoriated by Tokyo Press," *Japan Times and Advertiser*, 4 November 1941 (morning edition), 1.
78. Quoted in continuation of previous article, under the title "U.S. Attitude on Talks Hit by Tokyo Press," 3.

79. "Morgenthau Economic Pressure Policy on Japan Is Viewed Contradictory Move."
80. "Japan and Moderate Diplomacy" (English translation), *Japan Times and Advertiser*, 13 November 1941 (evening edition), 3.
81. "America Peddles War" (English translation), *Japan Times and Advertiser*, 13 November 1943 (evening edition), 3.
82. "Economy of Japan Gains in Strength Says Minister Kaya," *Japan Times and Advertiser*, 18 November 1941 (morning edition), 1.
83. Ibid., 6.
84. "South Encirclement Discussed by Major," *Japan Times and Advertiser*, 19 November 1941 (evening edition), 2. The translation was provided by the Domei news agency. How much of the article was actual translation and how much interpretative paraphrase was left uncertain; though the words are presented within quotation marks, they are prefaced by the remark that "his speech in substance as translated by Domei follows."
85. "Y900,000,000 Is Gained by Japan on Freezing by Britain, U.S., N.E.I.," *Japan Times and Advertiser*, 21 November 1941 (morning edition), 1.
86. "Fujiyama Declares National Policies Will Be Supported," *Japan Times and Advertiser*, 22 November 1941 (morning edition), 1.
87. The addresses of both speakers were reproduced under the headline "Premier Describes People of Japan As United Nation," *Japan Times and Advertiser*, 26 November 1941 (morning edition), 2.
88. "Japanese-American Talks" (English translation), *Japan Times and Advertiser*, 29 November 1941 (evening edition), 3.
89. "'Tension' in Southern Asia" (English translation), *Japan Times and Advertiser*, 1 December 1941 (evening edition), 3.
90. "American-Japan Policy" (English translation), *Japan Times and Advertiser*, 2 December 1941 (evening edition), 3.
91. "Empty Principles" (English translation), *Japan Times and Advertiser*, 2 December 1941 (evening edition), 3.
92. "Economic Measures Against Japan Fail, Finance Chief Says," *Japan Times and Advertiser*, 5 December 1941, 2.

Chapter 10
TOP ECHELON DIALOGUE: THE LIAISON AND IMPERIAL CONFERENCES OF THE JAPANESE GOVERNMENT

In theory the emperor ruled; in actual fact, he was titular head of a regime over which he possessed virtually no authority. In order to make such a system work, it was essential that the emperor be spared the need of making any serious policy choices. This, in turn, required that basic decisions be worked out beforehand between competing factions and that a united front be maintained in his presence as the proposals were submitted for formal acceptance. To thrash out potentially divisive issues between government members, liaison conferences were held prior to (and on a more frequent basis than) the imperial conferences. The occasional imperial conferences were then held in order to obtain the emperor's approval for the predetermined policies.

The personnel attending the liaison conferences included the top-echelon officials (the prime minister, foreign minister, and navy and war ministers) as well as key military men from a slightly lower echelon (such as the army and navy chiefs of staff). Other officials were called to attend upon an as-needed basis. The prestige of the military contingent supplemented their substantial numbers and provided them a decided edge in these civilian-military exchanges held to iron out future government policy. On the other hand, there were sometimes profound differences of sentiment and emphasis between the military leaders themselves that made it impossible to take any bulldozer approach over the desires of the theoretically superior civilian components of the meeting. Within the confines of a militarist orientation to the solution of Japan's economic problems, the navy inclined toward moderation and the army toward more overt imperialism, the lines between the moderates and the hawks ever shifting according to the specific issue under discussion.

The liaison conferences were essentially unstructured affairs in which the number of participants varied from one stage of each meeting to another. Great candor was permitted in the discussion of matters on the agenda. Once a consensus was reached, however, only the broadest hint of dissent was permitted to be aired in the presence of the emperor. Formal written presentations were prepared by all parties and these were read at the imperial conferences so that the token, yet compulsory, imperial approval could be obtained. After this endorsement, a policy became official and extremely difficult to alter.[1]

The economic consequences of the foreign embargo were a natural subject of discussion at these meetings because the government was compelled to decide what policies to follow in reaction to it. At the liaison conference of July 24, 1941 (shortly before the trade freeze), the foreign minister predicted American retaliation for "the occupation of Indochina." He anticipated that the United States would "adopt a policy of putting an embargo on vital materials [and] freezing Japanese funds,"[2] and he expressed his opinion that "Among the items included in the embargo on vital materials will be raw cotton, lumber, wheat and petroleum. As for cotton and lumber, we have already taken steps. Since [America] is sending wheat to China, we can somehow or other get around the embargo on wheat. Although petroleum causes us some anxiety, it is unlikely that the United States will impose a complete embargo on it."[3]

In short, the item on the problem embargo list that appeared most difficult to compensate for was petroleum. Indeed, it was the one item mentioned that produced outright "anxiety" and that discomfort was tempered only by the belief that the embargo on oil would not be total. How much deeper, then, would the anxiety have been if the foreign minister had realized that the trade termination would be all encompassing?

As the foreign minister went on to discuss the matter further, it was not the freezing of funds in the United States that concerned him so much as the fact that such an act "will create a shortage of funds for importing petroleum, and will cause a good deal of hardship."[4] Again, petroleum supply was central.

At the September 3 meeting, the navy chief of state warned: "In various respects the Empire is losing materials: that is, we are getting weaker. By contrast, the enemy is getting stronger. With the passage of time, we will get increasingly weaker, and we won't be able to survive."[5] Because of the diminishing reserve, he feared that Japan's current "chance to win a war" would disappear entirely. Admittedly, a war could turn out to be either a short or a prolonged one. Prudence required preparation for either eventuality. If Japan could not quickly bring the enemy to a decisive battle, then "we will be in difficulty, especially since our supply of resources will become depleted. If we cannot obtain these resources, it will not be possible to carry on a long war." Hence to avoid the danger of a long-term defeat, it was "important" to obtain both the "essential sources" and to make "the best of our strategy." He cautioned against undue optimism: "There is no set series of steps that will guarantee our checkmating the enemy."[6]

At the imperial conference of September 6, the navy chief of staff endorsed the policy of negotiations for peace but warned that if military action were to be decided upon, there was a limited time frame within which it had to be undertaken. "A number of vital military supplies, including oil, are dwindling day by day." Although he spoke in terms of the second half of 1942 as the point at which the United States would "be difficult to cope with," this was surely his most optimistic projection, for the entire thrust of his remarks was upon Japan's rapidly declining ability to wage a successful war against its occidental enemies. Indeed, he candidly confessed that even as of the then current date there was no way to act decisively enough to compel the United States to abandon as hopeless any effort to regain seized territories.[7]

To protect against the inherent dangers of an extended conflict, the navy chief of staff recommended the seizure of those areas that would provide the necessary resources and establish a militarily "impregnable position" in the southwest Pacific.[8] He stressed that the navy would prefer a peaceful solution, but he emphasized that if war were to come, it was far better to wage it soon than to delay it to a time when Japan's resources would be even more limited.

At the same conference, the army chief of staff paid token praise to negotiations but made plain his own more hawkish sentiments. The nation was in a position where its military resources were inevitably bound to decline in comparison with those of Great Britain and the United States. If this were permitted to continue indefinitely, Japan's ability to wage a successful war might be compromised. To maximize the opportunity of success, war must be begun by the end of October.[9]

Of special relevance to our inquiry are the views presented at that meeting by the director of the Planning Board: Due to the Western embargo the empire was dependent upon its current Asian possessions. Resources were not coming in from any other source and reserves were declining.

> Our liquid fuel stockpile, which is the most important, will reach bottom by June or July of next year, even if we impose strict war-time control on the civilian demand.[10]

Hence by peaceful means or not, it was "vitally important for the survival of our Empire that we make up our minds to establish and stabilize a firm economic base."[11] A war would reduce the nation's "productive capacity" by one-half in order to meet military requirements. However, if the necessary areas could be seized within a period of four months or less, their new resources could be fully incorporated into the Japanese economy in a period of "two years or so."[12] War might prolong this time schedule, but planners were working out "means to cope" with any "unexpected situations" that might develop.[13]

In preparation for the September 6 imperial conference, slightly lower-echelon officials prepared a document for all participants, summarizing the consensus that had been reached and suggesting possible answers for any questions posed to them by the president of the Privy Council. (It was his duty to make inquiries so that the emperor could—in theory at least—be fully informed of the course proposed for the government.) The memorandum suggested that war was inevitable. It suggested a partial reversal of government policy, one that would place less faith in negotiations. Any agreement reached "for the sake of a temporary peace" would only result in a strengthened America which "is sure to demand more and more concessions on our part; and ultimately our Empire will have to lie prostrate at the feet of the United States."[14]

This fear that a negotiated settlement could be the means of Japan cutting her own throat was in the back of other minds as well. Later, at the liaison conference of November 1, the army vice chief of staff (one of the more extreme war hawks) argued, "If we withdraw our troops from French Indochina, our supply routes for materials from the South would come completely under the control of the United States, and we would be subject to American obstruction at any time."[15] Were these fears unfounded? Even assuming the most positive motives on the American side (both current and future), the temptation to interfere with these routes would clearly have been present.

At the October 27 liaison conference, the director of the Planning Board projected that in the short term the nation could almost sustain its current level of consumption of raw products: "Our ability to supply the natural resources needed in 1942 will probably be 90 percent of our ability in 1941. In doing this, we will be using up all of our stockpiles. However, only in the case of raw cotton can we manage until 1943 by using what is left in our stockpiles and by buying some from China."[16]

At the same meeting, the chief of the Navy Bureau of Supplies and Equipment stressed that the most optimistic scenario provided for only enough oil to wage war for two and a half years.[17] This scenario was based not on Japan's existing reserves but upon an expanded supply of additional oil from the Dutch Indies. However one looked at existing reserves, with or without possible supplements via conquest, the diminishing supply meant that Japan's war-making capacity was steadily going down hill, while that of its adversaries was increasing, an implication made explicit in the following day's liaison conference by the army chief of staff.[18]

At the imperial conference of November 5, the director of the Planning Board discussed at length a joint army-navy analysis that concluded that petroleum from a conquered Netherlands East Indies would make feasible a three-year conflict.[19] This analysis carried with it the implication that for either defensive or offensive purposes, Japan would need to gain access to that additional supply if its ability to wage either type of major conflict was to be maintained. The Planning Board chief conceded that "Concerning aviation fuel: it is expected that, depending on consumption, we might reach a critical stage in the second or third year."[20]

At the same official gathering, the navy chief of staff reported that the navy would be ready for war by late that month and assumed that war would begin in early December.[21] The army chief of staff carried the burden (appropriately, in light of his service's greater aggressiveness) of showing why delaying the war until the following spring was impractical. He emphasized the shift in weather patterns and the greater cooperativeness among the Western powers, and he noted that if the war were delayed, "the ratio of armament between Japan and the United States will become more and more unfavorable."[22]

Foreign Minister Togo also spoke, reviewing possible diplomatic solutions, although he was far from optimistic about their success. Astutely, he grasped what most Americans were unaware of, that the lifting of the asset freeze would not automatically resolve Japan's petroleum supply crisis. Since there had been a de facto cutoff of oil "even before the freezing order," he was convinced that any satisfactory agreement had to include a provision that "Japan would be able to buy the amount she needs, and not be limited to the amount prior to the freezing order."[23]

Togo reported to the November 13 liaison conference concerning a meeting he had had with the American ambassador. He stressed to the Western official: "Since the United States is applying economic pressure on us, which is *even stronger than military pressure*, we may have to act in order to defend ourselves. For the United States to insist that Japan disregard the sacrifice she is making in China is tantamount to telling us to commit suicide" (emphasis added).[24]

At the November 27 liaison conference, the army chief of staff stressed that if somehow, unexpectedly, the American-Japanese negotiations produced a breakthrough, it was essential to nail down a definitive agreement which assured Japan of its needed oil. He expressed considerable concern that this aspect of the two nations' relationship might be postponed to later as the result of "an American trap." If that were to happen, he insisted, "we will miss our opportunity" to act militarily in a decisive way.[25]

From these discussions, it is clear that top Japanese military and civilian officials were well aware of the economic vise imposed upon their nation as a result of the United States–instigated embargo. Even aside from the militaristic orientation of much of the government, a steady flow of adequate petroleum was essential to national self-respect and economic sufficiency. Any government with the ability to take direct action to assure itself of such supplies would have been forced to give the highest consideration to a military expansion into the major oil-producing areas.

Since the United States would not take kindly to the undoing of its boycott by military expansion, prompt retaliation was at least a fifty-fifty proposition. (As shown earlier, Americans were far more vehement in their anti-Japanese sentiments than in their anti–German ones.) This likelihood, in turn, encouraged the seeking of some type of decisive knockout punch (or, at least, a delaying punch) aimed at the American ability to intervene effectively in the Far East. Hence the American embargo leads, once again, to Pearl Harbor.

NOTES

1. For a useful survey of the function and purpose of these conferences, see the Introduction to Nobutake Ike, trans. and ed., *Japan's Decision for War: Records of the 1941 Policy Conferences* (Standford, Calif.: Stanford University Press, 1967), xiii–xix.
2. Ibid., 108.
3. Ibid., 109.
4. Ibid.
5. Ibid., 130–31.
6. Ibid., 131.
7. Ibid., 139.
8. Ibid., 140.
9. Ibid., 141.
10. Ibid., 147–48.
11. Ibid., 148.
12. Ibid.
13. Ibid.
14. Ibid., 152.
15. Ibid., 205.
16. Ibid., 191.
17. Ibid., 192.
18. Ibid., 194.
19. Ibid., 218–19.
20. Ibid., 218.
21. Ibid., 224.
22. Ibid., 225–26.
23. Ibid., 231.
24. Ibid., 246.
25. Ibid., 256.

Chapter 11
INTERNAL DIPLOMATIC COMMUNICATIONS OF THE JAPANESE GOVERNMENT

In determining the convictions of a given government, what it asserts publicly through its leading officials and diplomats is of obvious importance. The true significance of their remarks may vary immensely, however, from nation to nation and issue to issue. Governments are well known to assert claims for the record or for domestic consumption that are far different from their real beliefs. Likewise, the intensity of the government's concern may be dramatically escalated in its rhetoric, the result being the diplomatic equivalent of rhetorical brass knuckle fighting. All the passionate words may be a mere smokescreen to gain concessions on some other question of greater importance. Then again the words may actually mean what they say in all their grim seriousness and vigor, reflecting the real agenda of the objecting government.

How does one tell what is real and what is illusion? The host diplomatic establishment has the difficult task of separating the wheat from the chaff, the assertions from the genuine convictions, and the verbal overkill from sincere commitments. To accomplish this task, the diplomatic community of the host government must have a good working knowledge of the history, basic attitudes, and political convictions of the complaining nation. If they are fortunate, the objecting diplomats will—unofficially, of course—provide vital clues by which to determine what is of bedrock importance and what is for public consumption.

In the case of Japanese complaints about the American trade and petroleum embargo, the United States enjoyed an invaluable additional resource, the decrypted intercepted messages exchanged between the Foreign Office in Tokyo and its embassy in Washington.[1] Since these were obviously never intended for American reading, they gave the U.S. State Department an unusually clear picture of how the Japanese genuinely evaluated the importance of their protests. This view was the same one the American officials were obtaining from other sources: the embargo was hurting the Japanese economy, seriously and without respite, and the Japanese were unwilling to go on indefinitely without a clear resolution of the issue.

In a message of July 23, 1941, an official from Tokyo stressed that though much of future policy was still undetermined, the Americans should be warned of the potentially dangerous environment that might be created by a cutoff of trade:

> You were correct in assuming that I have not as yet determined upon a definite policy because of the fact that I have not been in office very long.
>
> As was pointed out in my message #368, our occupation of French Indo-China was unavoidable. This step has been decided upon by the Cabinet even before I assumed office. It is to be carried out peacefully for the purpose of jointly defending French Indo-China. It is my intention to continue to make an effort to decrease the friction between Japan and Britain-U.S.
>
> Should the U.S., however, take steps at this time which would unduly excite Japan (such as closing of [garbled] for all practical purposes and the freezing of assets), an exceedingly critical situation may be created. Please advise the United States of this fact, and attempt to bring about an improvement in the situation.[2]

In a response of the same date, the embassy reported that the State Department had been candidly informed that an embargo "would lead to national suicide." The Americans responded with cynicism that they seriously doubted the French were acting freely in allowing Japanese expansion into their southeast Asian colony:

> Since Wakasugi had called on the Acting Secretary of State, as reported in my message #545, I called on Welles myself this afternoon. I explained to him that our southern occupaion was *absolutely essential from the standpoint of national security and economic safety*. I further pointed out the impossibility of Japan to pursue a "do nothing" policy in the face of the embargoes being clamped down against her by various countries, for *such a policy would lead to national suicide*.
>
> After carefully explaining the above situation, I said that according to press report[s] the French Indo-China affair was apparently being carried out peacefully with the full approval of the Vichy government. I added that in view of those circumstances, it was my hope that the government of the United States would restrain itself from jumping to hasty conclusions, and instead would watch the trend of further developments for a little while yet.
>
> I told him that I feared considerable repercussions among the general public, if measures such as an export embargo on oil is put into effect at a time such as this.
>
> The new Cabinet in Japan, I advise[d] the Undersecretary, is as anxious to bring the U.S.-Japanese "Understanding Pact" to a successful conclusion, as was the previous cabinet.
>
> To the above, the Undersecretary replied that he would not reiterate his statements to Wakasugi. He w[c?]ould not, he said, reconcile the Japanese policy with regard to French Indo-China with the basic principles of the plans being discussed by Secretary Hull and myself. Neither Great Britain nor the United States had any intention of attacking French Indo-China, he said. The concensus [sic] here is, he said, that Vichy's submission came as a result of pressure from Hitler and that Japan

intends to use French Indo-China as a base from which to make further southward moves.

The U.S. Government, he continued, has not for the past many years made any hasty conclusions. Her actions are governed by Japan's policies.

Although he did not mention what steps the United States is planning to take in the future, he did say, as I was about to depart, that Secretary Hull was expected back at his desk very shortly and that he would no doubt welcome an opportunity to discuss matters with me.

In reply to my inquiry, the Undersecretary said that traffic through the Canal has been indefinitely suspended while it is undergoing repairs. He asserted that no particular nation was suffering discriminatory action [emphasis added].[3]

Tokyo was hoping against hope that the Americans would avoid reacting with an embargo which carried such explosive potential. In a communication labeled "secret outside the Department," a Japanese official repeatedly alluded to the danger of war occurring as the result of a trade freeze:

> That the leaders of the United States Government will at this time display a high degree of statesmanship is what I am secretly hoping for the sake of maintaining peace in the Pacific. The Japanese Government would do likewise and would like to reciprocate. However, according to information received by us lately, especially according to newspaper reports, there is the possibility of the United States freezing Japanese funds or of instituting a general embargo on petroleum, thus strongly stimulating public opinion in Japan. Should this plan of freezing Japanese funds be put into effect, it would have an adverse effect on many aspects of our domestic life and might compel us to resort to diverse retaliatory measures. This would lead to a breakdown of Japanese-American economic relations and we cannot be certain that it would not in turn hasten the development of the worst situation. Will you please get in touch with Finance Official Nishiyama and, in accordance with the contents of the caption telegram, request the United States Government to favorably treat this question.[4]

Ambassador Nomura informed Tokyo on July 30, 1941, "Today I knew from the hard looks on their faces that they meant business and I could see that if we do not answer to suit them that they are going to take some drastic steps."[5] (This was during the period when the true degree of "totalness" of the embargo remained unclear, but it was deeply feared that American officials would make it just as comprehensive as the public assumed it was designed to be.)

Nomura proceeded to put himself on record that so far as he was concerned the timing of the Indochina expansion was disastrous, "I can see just how gravely they are regarding it. Think of it! Popular demand for the freezing of Japanese funds was subsiding and now this has to happen. I must tell you it certainly occurred at an inopportune moment." He regarded it as essential that some kind of action be taken to calm down the American government. "Things being as they are, need I point out to you gentlemen that in my opinion it is necessary to take without one moment's hesitation some appeasement measures."

On July 31, 1941, the foreign minister sent to his representatives in Washington and Berlin a summary of the government's foreign policy in light of Germany's invasion of Russia.[6] Since the military (the army in particular) and the civilian government did not always seem to be supporting the same policies, it is of significance that the "policy and views" laid out in this communication were the result of "a conference with the military." Hence the summary represented the consensus of both the civilian and the military elements in the regime.

As to Germany, the Foreign Ministry stressed the need for "a certain flexibility" in the implementation of the Tripartite Pact. "What I mean to say is that each should understand that real cooperation does not necessarily mean complete symmetry of action. In other words, we should trust each other and while striving toward one general objective, each use our own discretion within the bounds of good judgment."

The Germans were clearly unhappy with this refusal to intervene. Although the Tripartite Pact represented a convenient excuse for intervention (if such were desired), the actual text of the agreement required entering the conflict only when a signatory was the victim of an external assault. Since Germany had clearly initiated the war, legal obligations to assist her were completely absent.

The Nazi regime in Germany was also disquieted by the Japanese determination to continue negotiations with the United States. The Japanese foreign minister insisted that these efforts were being continued out of a twofold motive. On the one hand, he stated, "we wish to settle the Chinese incident" (the on-again, off-again war in China). On the other hand, he noted that the "determination" of Japan's diplomatic posture had been "indelibly impressed upon the United States." This determination and the act of continuing negotiations "restrained" the Americans "from plunging into the conflict against Germany." Presumably, the intended implication was that rather than criticizing Japan, the Germans should be appreciative of Japanese efforts to keep the United States out of the European war. (One suspects that the German government easily dismissed this self-serving reasoning.)

Of concern to us is the Japanese evaluation of the dire consequences of the Western embargo; the Foreign Ministry even found a way to stress this as a benefit to the German regime:

> Commercial and economic relations between Japan and third countries, led by England and the United States, are gradually becoming so horribly strained that *we cannot endure it much longer*. Consequently, our Empire, *to save its very life*, must take measures to secure the raw materials of the South Seas. Our Empire must immediately take steps to break asunder this ever-strengthening chain of encirclement which is being woven under the guidance and with the participation of England and the United States, acting like a cunning dragon seemingly asleep. That is why we

decided to obtain military bases in French Indo-China and to have our troops occupy that territory.

That step in itself, I dare say, gave England and the United States, not to mention Russia, quite a set-back in the Pacific that ought to help Germany, and now Japanese-American relations are more rapidly that ever treading the evil road. This shows what a blow it has been to the United States [emphasis added].[7]

In a communication dated August 5, Tokyo assured its Washington representatives that "The Imperial Government is trying to give its attention to the all important matter of Japanese-U.S. relations."[8] It conceded, however, that "This is not an easy task for there are numerous obstacles involving domestic politics." This surely alludes to the existence of chauvinistic elements (especially, though not exclusively, in the army) like those existing in all nations, elements which always assume the worst about other major powers.

Tokyo noted that "according to the various reports you have submitted on the subject," the Washington administration was far more restrained than "the trend of general public opinion" in America. Even so, the "economic pressure on Japan is being daily increased in intensity." In this message, Tokyo further emphasized:

> If it is believed by many that our people and our country can be threatened into submission by the so-called strengthened encirclement policy or by the application of economic pressure, it is a mistaken notion. As a matter of fact it is erroneous to the extreme as should be obvious to any who understands our national characteristics.
>
> If such a policy as the above is adopted, we cannot guarantee that the trend will not be in directly the opposite direction from our goal of an improved U.S.-Japanese relationship. One should be able to see this clearly from the example set forth above. . . .
>
> For the purpose of preventing the possibility of letting anyone, either within or out of the country, be under the impression that the negotiations were conducted under the threat of economic pressure, all measures which may be construed as being economic pressure should be abandoned at once. That we shall reciprocate in kind was made clear in the recent statement issued by the Minister of Finance.[9]

On August 7, Tokyo suggested a face-to-face meeting between Prime Minister Konoye and President Roosevelt because "Japanese-U.S. relations are, today, critically tense. We feel that a policy of laissez faire should no longer be pursued."[10]

On the same day, a message from the Washington embassy noted that the major barrier between the two nations lay in the fact that "the United States is under the impression that the ties between the Axis partners are closer than appear on paper. It is convinced that the East is working in close cooperation with the West, and vice versa." The embassy was convinced that in the past progress had been made on correcting this misapprehension.[11]

Those gains had been lost. The U.S. officials absolutely refused to accept the Japanese claim that "the occupation of French Indo-China" was merely "a peaceful occupation." The takeover had revived and strengthened the deep American suspicion that Japan and Germany were cooperating closely in aggression. Not only had the Americans enforced the freeze and embargo, "There is no doubt whatsoever that the United States is prepared to take drastic action depending on the way Japan moves, and thus closing the door to any possibility of settling the situation."

In a dispatch of August 16, Ambassador Nomura warned that Tokyo could not count on American foreign policy divisions to undo its assertive policies in the Far East: "As I have already informed you, the United States has not yet attained sufficient unity of mind with regard to participation in the European war, and the President himself is hesitant. However, the people are unanimous with regard to taking a strong hand in the Far East."[12]

Prudence restrained Roosevelt, in the ambassador's view. Expressing a sentiment that anti–Roosevelt revisionists later found appealing, Nomura was suspicious of British agitation: "I hardly think that the President will go to the extreme, inasmuch as he and the naval leaders realize what a tremendous undertaking a Pacific war would be. I understand that the British believe that if they could only have a Japanese-American war started at the back door, there would be a good prospect of getting the United States to participate in the European War."[13]

Some ten days later, the Foreign Ministry was boiling at the United States' determination not only to do economic injury to Japan but also to implement the policy in a way that was deemed highly insulting. The entire Foreign Ministry dispatch reads:

> Notwithstanding representations made by us on successive occasions the United States is treading a course which seems to be bent on exciting public opinion within our country. Beginning the first day of September they are exercising stringent limitations on gasoline shipments essential to our civilian population. At this time they are planning to pass through waters adjacent to our shores with cargoes of petroleum products which should be coming to us. The fact that they are transporting these petroleum products to Vladivostok has dealt a severe blow to the sensibilities of our government and people. At the same time that this brings about grave effects upon Japan and American relations, a terrific blow is being dealt by those in Washington to the whole country far more than you can realize.
> This being the case, we are forced to cry out our disapproval of the realization of such measures and the Ministry of Interior as well as the War Ministry are very apprehensive. Therefore, because such measures are not in keeping with the neutrality treaty between Japan and Soviet Russia nor in accord with the interpretation of international law, I would like to have you make representations again to the Secretary of State in order that he may reconsider an immediate cessation of these measures from the general view point of the current Japan-American diplomatic relations. Wire me back as soon as you have filed these representations.
> In the event the United States assumes the position that it is impossible to cut

off shipments of petroleum products to the Soviet, then as it seems advisable to your Excellency make suggestions that they change the transportation route. However, should they not comply with this request, either, I think it would be wise to try to persuade the American authorities that they revive shipments of petroleum products to Japan immediately.

Furthermore, additional representations have been filed with the Soviet too, as of the 26th.[14]

In its instructions to Washington of September 4, 1941, the Foreign Ministry urged the embassy to present various suggested reasons for removing the embargo but noted, "As to the withdrawal of the orders for freezing of assets by both countries, you should avoid giving the impression that this freezing measure taken by the United States had proven to be damaging to Japan."[15]

Ambassador Nomura noted in a dispatch of October 3, that America's economic pressure was so intense that she had every chance of producing the results of a successful war without ever firing an actual shot in anger:

> The United States has not decreased her economic pressure against Japan one iota. It should be carefully noted that the United States is proceeding along a policy of making this her threatening power. Should the United States continue along her present economic policy, without resorting to the force of arms, she shall gain her objectives of a war against Japan without once resorting to a battle. Moreover, I am of the opinion that unless there is a radical change in the world situation or unless Japan changes her foreign policy, the United States will not alter this policy of hers against Japan.[16]

Nomura reported on October 27: "On the 25th, I met and talked with Admiral Pratt. The Admiral is one who recognizes the fact that in the final analysis, the aims of economic warfare and actual armed conflict are one and the same."[17]

Two days later the ambassador reported that even traditional antiwar segments of opinion were unsympathetic to Japan:

> Admiral Standley, Retired, told Member of Parliament Kasai that the more influential Congressmen from the Middle West (where there are many Americans of German descent) state that the majority of Middle Westerners are opposed to a war against Germany, but that at the same time a great number of them favor a U.S.-Japanese war. . . . I have heard O'Laughlin, who is familiar with that area, express similar opinions.[18]

Tokyo informed its Washington representatives on November 10 that it had told the American ambassador, Joseph Grew, that though many Japanese believed "extreme steps" were called for, the government itself was still reluctant to implement such an approach. Grew was told:

> Though I have all along fully appreciated the efforts of Your Excellency, I do not feel that the Government of the United States has as yet fully appreciated the situation. The feeling in favor of stability and peace is, as a matter of course, the feeling

of the majority of the people. Then too, insofar as the question of resources is concerned, if we take the example of the recent situation wherein the supplying of raw materials to Japan was suspended as a result of America's actions in the freezing of assets, such strong-arm measures of economic pressure, in addition to being a threat indicate the probability of even more severe measures in the future. The people of Japan, though they may feel deeply within themselves that extreme steps for self-defense must be brought to bear, cannot bring themselves to the point of carrying this out.[19]

On November 10, Ambassador Nomura quoted a report of Frederick Moore (legal adviser to the Japanese Embassy in Washington) based upon his meetings with Secretary of State Hull and Senator Thomas of the Senate Foreign Relations Committee: "The United States is not bluffing. If Japan invades again, the United States will fight with Japan. Psychologically the American people are ready. The Navy is prepared and ready for action."[20] The ambassador relayed the anti–Japanese sentiment of most of the American press: "In the newspapers and magazines, with the exception of the Daily News and the Hearst Papers, it is reported that the Americans are much more eager for a war with Japan than they are for one with Germany." Hence public opinion would not restrict the president's alternatives nearly as much in the Pacific as in the Atlantic.

The ambassador at the same time reported a private conversation with a major government official. That cabinet member had stressed American suspicions of future Japanese expansion, and the ambassador had in response emphasized the growing aggravation felt by the Japanese over the freezing of assets (the flip side of the total embargo). As Nomura remembered the dialogue:

> Yesterday evening, Sunday, a certain Cabinet member, discarding all quibbling, began by saying to me:
> "You are indeed a dear friend of mine and I tell this to you alone." Then he continued: "The American Government is receiving a number of reliable reports that Japan will be on the move soon. The American Government does not believe that your visit on Monday to the President or the coming of Mr. Kurusu will have any effect on the general situation."
> I took pains to explain in detail how impatient the Japanese have grown since the freezing; how they are eager for a quick understanding; how both the Government and the people do not desire a Japanese-American war; and how we will hope for peace until the end.
> He replied, however: "Well, our boss, the President, believes these reports and so does the Secretary of State."[21]

Nomura was candid in a November 10 discussion with President Roosevelt concerning the serious impact of the embargo upon the welfare of the Japanese state:

> My interview with the President, referred to in my #1069, was held in a private room in the White House in order to avoid publicity. It was as follows:

Prefacing my remarks with the fact that I was speaking on instructions, I said: "I have had no talks with the Secretary of State for about three weeks: ever since the resignation of the Konoye cabinet; and since the present situation between Japan and the United States is such that it could not be left as it is, I am very pleased to have this opportunity of speaking with you. The conversations on this question have lasted for more than six months. From their inception, Japan has been wishing to arrive at a quick settlement. The people of Japan also looked forward to these conversations with much hope; however, the conversations have dragged on and in the meantime the relation between the two countries has grown worse. It has become increasingly difficult for the people of my country to be patient.

"Now, the Government of Japan has in the meantime made many concessions, but the Government of the United States has held to its arguments and has shown no willingness to respond to our compromises. As a result, some people in Japan have begun to doubt if the United States is really sincere in this matter. *The Japanese people regard the freezing of funds as a kind of economic blockade, and there seem to be some who say that modern warfare is not limited to shooting alone. No country can exist without the supply of materials indispensable to its industry.* From what reports I have received from Japan, the situation seems to be *serious and threatening* and, therefore, the only way to keep peace is for Japan and the United States to come, without further delay, to some kind of a friendly and satisfactory agreement. It is for no other purpose than that of keeping peace in the Pacific that the Japanese Government is endeavoring so hard to arrive at a satisfactory agreement by continuing our conversations" [emphasis added].[22]

Within the limitations of polite diplomatese, one could not have made it clearer that the choice was between war or a compromise acceptable to both sides.

In a pessimistic message of November 14, Nomura noted that the Americans were using economic weapons (as well as a military build up) in order to exlude any further expansion of the Japanese Empire: "As I have told you in a number of messages, the policy of the American Government in the Pacific is to stop any further moves on our part toward southward or northward. With every economic weapon at their command, they have attempted to achieve this objective, and now they are contriving by every possible means to prepare for actual warfare."[23]

By November 17, Tokyo was worried that the wording of a proposed agreement might be of such a nature that Japan might sign it and still find itself faced with restrictions on receiving the amount of petroleum it regarded as essential:

The contents of 3 of paragraph 2 pertaining to Japanese-U.S. relations, seems to be about the same as the terms contained in the supplementary provision of the United States' 21 June proposal. In view of the fact that "materials necessary for one's own country's safety and for self-defense" shall be an exception, there is a danger that even after the agreement is entered into, they will put some restrictions on the exporting of petroleum. We cannot accept that phraseology, therefore, unless they agree not to restrict exports on articles needed by us which will be clearly listed.[24]

The next day, Ambassador Nomura wrote that Secretary of State Hull had proposed that Japan withdraw from the Tripartite Pact:

> Then I and Kurusu explained that it was an impossibility to settle such a basic point in any specified time limit. However, to ease the exceedingly critical situation, the first step would be to mutually return to the situation which existed prior to the date on which the freezing of assets order was put into effect, (in other words, Japan would withdraw from South French Indo-China and the United States would rescind her order to freeze the assets). Talks should then be continued in a more congenial atmosphere, we suggested.
>
> He did not seem particularly receptive to this suggestion. He said that if the government of Japan could make it clear that it wants to pursue a course of peace, then the United States would confer with the British on the subject of returning to the conditions which existed prior to the time that the freezing order went into effect. It is essential, however, that under those conditions, Japan continue to pursue a peaceful policy with ever increasing vigor.
>
> There were indications that Hull, because of his usual cautious nature, was somewhat influenced by the exaggerated reports carried in the press regarding the Premier's speech in the Diet in which he expressed the three basic principles of international relations and intention of increasing the troops in French Indo-China.[25]

On the 22, Ambassadors Nomura and Kurusu again met with the secretary of state. On the 23, Nomura quoted Hull's summary of the views of the ambassadors from Britian, Australia, and the Netherlands, with whom he had met for over two hours earlier the same day:

> The diplomats who called on me also pointed out that just prior to the application of the freezing order, Japanese imports of petroleum took a very sudden upward swing, disproving any contention that it was to be used solely for peaceful undertakings, but that it was being stored away by the navy.
>
> They further expressed the opinion that the embargo should be lifted only in slow degrees.[26]

Such extended gradualism could, of course, only be viewed as utterly humiliating by the Japanese. It would have created the worst-case scenario of Japanese nightmares: potentially forfeiting freedom in foreign policy for the needed petroleum. The very idea of "slow degrees" implied a prolonged period during which Japan would face the potential of overwhelming economic coercion being used to force it to adopt whatever policies were demanded by the Western powers, whenever and wherever they insisted upon changes. The reasonableness of such a dangerous course would have rested totally upon Western restraint and goodwill, a potentially fragile foundation.

On November 26, Tokyo officials once again indicated their suspicion that even after the signing of a treaty, they might be denied what they considered were essential supplies. To avoid this danger in regard to their most vital import (petroleum), it was especially necessary that specific figures be included in any agreement:

When you reach a settlement in accordance with our new proposal, it is essential that you secure guarantees for the acquisition of goods in connection with clauses 2 and 3 of that proposal. Of these goods, the acquisition of petroleum is one of the most pressing and urgent requirements of the Empire. Therefore, in accordance with the course of negotiations, prior to the signing of an understanding, and at as early a date as possible, I would like to have you make our wishes known insofar as petroleum imports are concerned along the following lines:

4,000,000 tons per year from the United States. (This figure is the average amount of imports during the years 1938, '39, and '40 from the United States. The breakdown according to type, aviation gasoline included, corresponds to the actual figures covering imports before the freezing legislation went into effect.) That is to say roughly 333,000 tons per month.

In addition, on the basis of past negotiations and roughly in the agreed amounts, we hope to import from the Netherlands East Indies 1,000,000 tons per year.

After the establishment of a verbal agreement, I would like to have a definite promise of the above incorporated into an exchange of documents between Your Excellency and the Secretary of State.

Furthermore, these figures are to be taken as the basis for negotiation (however, they can not be called our absolute minimum figures). On the other hand, as far as we are concerned, along with a restoration of trade in the future, we hope for an increase of these figures over the past. Therefore, after you have read all this, please negotiate along these lines to the best of your abilities.[27]

It is important to remember that these messages were never intended for American readers or for public consumption. They represent the private view of the embargo as seen by the Japanese in speaking with each other. And their judgment is quite clear: the embargo was extremely hurtful to their nation and required that *something* be done to remedy the situation. Short of a reversal of the American or Japanese policy, the only other realistic option was open war to gain control over the natural resources denied by the Western embargo.

Top American officials were kept aware of the seriousness of the Japanese economic crisis because the American "Magic" decryption system gave them access to such messages. Supplementing their own evaluations, it left them with no reason to doubt the disintegrating economic situation within the Japanese nation. The American policymakers did not continue the trade/asset freeze with all its dangerous war-making potential because they were unaware of the havoc it was producing; they had a competent awareness of its dire results. The ensuing war was not the solution these policymakers sought, but it was the result of a policy they consciously persevered in while knowing the catastrophe it was inflicting upon a proud and militarily strong Japan.

NOTES

1. Joint Committee on the Investigation of the Pearl Harbor Attack, *Pearl Harbor Attack: Hearings Before the Joint Committee on the Investigation of the Pearl Harbor Attack*

(Washington, D.C.: U.S. Government Printing Office, 1946). These messages are printed in volume twelve of *PHA*. For clarity, the volume number is given, followed by a slash [/] and then the page(s). Relevant message and translation identification numbers are provided, as available, to accompany each entry.

2. *PHA* 12/4–5; #397, JD-1:3986. The word "garbled" represents a series of hyphens included by the decryption team, presumably because a few words were missing or uncertain.

3. *PHA* 12/5–6; #555. Several typographical errors appear to have been made in the translation, and for clarity the missing letter(s) have been inserted in the text within brackets. None are of any importance in themselves and possibly represent errors due to pressure to complete the translation work as quickly as possible.

4. *PHA* 12/6; #406, Army 20034.
5. *PHA* 12/8; #609, Army 20423.
6. *PHA* 12/8–10. The message from Tokyo was #433; the identical message from Tokyo to Berlin was #708. Sent in four parts, Army intercepts 20461, 20462, 20463, 20464.
7. Ibid.
8. *PHA* 12/10–11; #447.
9. Ibid.
10. *PHA* 12/12; #452.
11. *PHA* 12/13–14, #663.
12. *PHA* 12/17; #703, part 1, Army 21150; part 2, Army 21151.
13. Ibid.
14. *PHA* 12/21; #505, Army 21482.
15. *PHA* 12/26; #528, part 2 of 2, Army 21791.
16. *PHA* 12/51–53; #894.
17. *PHA* 12/85; #1004, JD-1:6175.
18. *PHA* 12/88; #1010.
19. *PHA* 12/110–11; #757, part 3 of 3, Army 24585.
20. *PHA* 12/111–12; #1066, part 1, Army 24655; part 2 of 2, Army 24656.
21. *PHA* 12/111.
22. *PHA* 12/113; #1070, part 1 of 4, Army 24714.
23. *PHA* 12/127–28; #1090.
24. *PHA* 12/145; #785, JD-1:6589.
25. *PHA* 12/146; #1127, JD-1:6722.
26. *PHA* 12/167–69; #1159, JD-1:6839.
27. *PHA* 12/177; #833, Army 25346.

Chapter 12
CONFIDENTIAL AMERICAN EVALUATIONS OF THE EMBARGO'S IMPACT

No government, however repressive, can keep secret all it wishes, no matter how intense and energetic are its efforts. Even so, Japan must be counted as among the more successful suppressors of such information. It enjoyed special success in hiding domestic military and naval movements from the United States. It also effectively prevented the establishment of any domestic spy apparatus aimed at providing such data. Strenuous efforts were made to eliminate even that normal leakage that occurs in all countries. Ambassador Joseph C. Grew testified before Congress of how "their secret police were constantly watching all foreigners and all Japanese who were regarded as possibly pro–American or in any way pro-foreign, watching them continually, and if they felt there was any chance of them having imparted information they would generally arrest them immediately."[1]

During this period, only the spy network of German newspaperman Sorge was able to obtain detailed military intelligence, and Sorge was operating on behalf of the Soviet Union rather than the British or the Americans. In spite of the attempted information blackout, Grew conceded that "things dripped through from various channels from time to time."[2] Just as the Japanese hid military-related matters, they also attempted to obscure the details of their economic situation, though the broad outlines (and sometimes even the particulars) seeped through.

Reports from the Ambassador and the Tokyo Diplomatic Staff

Ambassador Grew informed his superiors in one dispatch that much economic harm had been done but dissented from the common prediction that the pressure would quickly compel a change in official policy.

> The theory put forward by many of our leading economists that depletion and eventual exhaustion of economic and financial resources would in a short time bring about the collapse of Japan as a militaristic power has never seemed convincing to us for the reason that forecasts of this character were unconsciously based on the assumption that retention by Japan of the capitalistic system would be a dominant consideration.
>
> Despite a *loss of the greater part of her commerce, drastic curtailment of industrial production and depletion of her national resources* the predicted outcome has not transpired. On the contrary the process of integrating the national economy, without which the predicted collapse might well have occurred, is being dramatically prosecuted. The view therefore that war in the Far East can best be averted by continuation of trade embargoes and, as proposed by some, the imposition of a blockade is not supported by what has thus far occurred [emphasis added].³

The ambassador warned that the failure to come to mutually agreeable terms would have disastrous results:

> The pendulum in Japan will in all probability swing back once more to its former position, or still farther back, leading to what I have called "an all out, do or die" attempt to render Japan impervious to foreign economic embargoes, even risking national hara kiri rather than cede to foreign pressure. Those of us who feel the national psychology and temper from day to day realize beyond her adventure that such a congency is not only possible but probable.⁴

Grew noted that more than one approach could be adopted in the ongoing negotiations. He contended that these specific options were actually of secondary importance. The fundamental decision that the United States had to reach was, "whether our national needs, policies and objectives justify war with Japan in the event that diplomacy, our first line of national defense should fail."⁵

The long-serving United States ambassador had originally opposed the use of an embargo as saber rattling because of the inherent risk it carried for war. He testified before the army investigation of Pearl Harbor:

> During the period up to, I think it was, the autumn of 1940, I took the position that economic embargoes against Japan—and embargoes are in the nature of sanctions and therefore are *always interpreted as international insults*—I took the position that we should not put embargoes on Japan, until we were prepared to go all the way through with whatever might result from those embargoes.
>
> I pointed out that when we put embargoes against Japan into effect, our relationship with that country were bound to go steadily downhill and it *might, and probably would, end in war,* and that until we were prepared to go to war with Japan, I felt it would be very shortsighted to go into a situation where we might be obliged at a later date to withdraw those embargoes. There is nothing so conducive to a lowering of national prestige, reputation and authority as to make threats and then have to recall those threats or modify those threats [emphasis added].⁶

During the second half of 1940, Grew reversed himself and decided that Nippon's foreign policy had become so obnoxious that there was no real alternative to risking war. Before the Army Pearl Harbor Board, he indicated that the decisive turning point in the relationship between the two major powers was the trade restrictions—first the limited embargo in 1940 and then the total cessation of trade in the summer of 1941. Grew testified:

> In the autumn of 1940, I telegraphed the Secretary of State that I felt that time had come, since Japan was threatening not only our national interests, but, I would say, our vital national interests; I felt that the time had come to consider, not whether we must call a halt to Japan's expansion, but when. It seemed to me at that time, whether we were fully prepared for war or not, that we must in our own interests put those embargoes into effect; and shortly thereafter, those embargoes were put into effect.
> Our relations then started directly on a downhill course, and they ended in war but at least we were more prepared for war at that time than we had been three years earlier.
> It was in the fall of 1940 that we cast the die and adopted economic sanctions.[7]

The comprehensive freeze occurred so late in July 1941 that there was little time for much more than the initial shock to register before the month was over. Even so, Ambassador Grew's monthly report for July emphasized its ominous implications:

> The full significance of the freezing of Japanese assets in the United States, Great Britain and the Netherlands East Indies was not brought out by the end of July but there was no reason to doubt that it came as a very heavy blow to Japanese industry and presented Japanese business interests with the most discouraging outlook they had ever faced.
> Unless the restrictions on Japanese foreign trade to the countries mentioned are lifted, Japan's industrial, economic and financial structure will be very substantially weakened through the inability to maintain those foreign commercial relations upon which her prosperity depends. Besides the disruption of the trade with the United States, Great Britain and the Netherlands East Indies the action of the United States and the withdrawal of most of the Japanese ships from trade routes to South America brought Japanese trade with Latin America practically to a standstill. These four areas had account[ed] for *almost all* of Japanese foreign trade outside of the Yen Bloc as because of the European hostilities trade with that continent had almost entirely ceased. What compensation Japan could obtain in developing her trade with China, French Indochina and Thailand could only in small measure make up for her trade losses with the other regions [emphasis added].[8]

The ambassador's August report on conditions in Japan emphasized that the embargo had already had a prompt and clear effect on the local economy:

> General business operations were severely hampered during August by the Japanese and foreign freezing orders, stricter control measures and the widespread concern over the strained international situation. . . . Plans were being rapidly formulated and put into effect to conserve more efficiently stocks of materials and supplies formerly obtained from the United States and the British Empire. In the meantime domestic prices rose further and there was an intensification of the scarcity of foodstuffs as a result of new control measures and extensive flood damages throughout the country to crop and transportation facilities.

All foreign trade business outside of the yen bloc remained at a complete standstill with the exception of a few negligible transactions with South America. Evidencing the effect of the curtailment of foreign trade was an announcement of the Federation of Cotton Spinning Companies that it had been decided to restrict the spinning mills in operation to fifty percent of the total in existence.[9]

Moving forward in time about a month, we find Commercial Attaché Frank S. Williams filing his second "Strictly Confidential Fortnightly Background Report" to cover September 12–27, 1941. He pictured the embargo as dramatically worsening an already serious situation:

> The complete cessation of trade with the United States and the major portion of the British Empire as a result of the freezing orders has notably intensified the already serious financial situation which had gradually but steadily been developing during the past four years. Today Japan is practically isolated from the money and commodity markets of all nations. Her ocean going steamers are either tied up in harbors or being utilized by the military authorities as transports. Her export warehouses are filled with stocks of merchandise which cannot be moved and on which interest and storage charges are eating away profits. Corporate business excepting munitions is being severely restricted by control measures and shortage of supplies—and profits are dwindling.[10]

Williams refers to "the prevailing shortage of practically every vital material"[11] And Japan's "increasing financial burdens and decreasing resources."[12] He cited as a particularly vivid example the state of the silk industry:

> The loss of a cash business running into the neighborhood of Yen 450 million annually with no prospective substitute market would be a serious blow to any industry in any country. To Japan the impact is particularly staggering because of her inability to consume the surplus silk, the disorganization it has caused in agriculture and the total loss of income in foreign currencies sorely needed for the purchase of vital materials and equipment if and when the freezing orders are terminated.[13]

Oddly enough, the attaché's third report (they are numbered consecutively on the title page) skipped the next month and covered the period of October 27–November 8.[14] He laid out so starkly and bluntly Japan's desperate situation and alternatives that the document deserves to be quoted in full:

> *Japan's economic structure cannot withstand the present strain very much longer.* For three months no supplies of oil, copper, iron, steel, aluminum and other essential products have been received from abroad. No exact data is available on present stocks of these commodities but from unofficial reports and personal studies of Japan's economy over a period of several years it is firmly believed that on the average the volume of these stocks, with the exception of fuel oil for the Navy, is relatively small—probably adequate to maintain the already unbalanced level of production and consumption for from ten to twelve months. The Navy's supply of fuel oil is generally estimated at sufficient for two years' wartime consumption.
>
> To assure any substantial degree of success in the execution of declared wartime policies Japan's vast economic structure must be continuously nurtured. Her

industries must be supplied with innumerable kinds of materials, her people must be fed, her national defenses must be substantially extended and strengthened, her transportation facilities must be improved and maintained, domestic business must be carried on and public utilities must be operated at full capacity. All of these activities demand materials and supplies, and more materials and supplies, and these in an uninterrupted flow. *Japan has never even moderately been self-sufficient in these essential materials and supplies but has always leaned heavily upon contributions from the United States and the British Empire.* Today these supports have been completely removed and this nation left entirely on its own. Extensive geographical areas have been added to Japan's sphere of influence during the past ten years but these have proven very small donors of vital resources and have permitted only a slight reduction in the nation's dependency upon the United States and Great Britain.

That strenuous efforts have been and are being made to remedy this dangerous situation is all too obvious. It is equally apparent that little real progress has crowned these efforts. Given a period of another ten years some measure of success might be achieved but unfortunately for Japan her problems must be solved immediately.

No nation can erect a wall around its national defense structure. Every phase of national economy must contribute heavily to its development and maintenance. Japan in her present economic position cannot long continue without replenishment the consumption of such large quantities of essential materials in efforts to create a defense force sufficient to withstand the self-inflicted encircling pressures from the United States and Great Britain. *The bottom of the barrel is plainly in sight.* She must have access to foreign supplies of oil and other vital products in order to keep her industrial wheels turning. If she cannot obtain these supplies she must accept the inevitable or fight, and the writer firmly believes that the military leaders of Japan decided months ago that it would be far better for the Japanese Army to go down fighting a major power than to withdraw from China for any other reason.

Stripped of all pretense the glaring fact is that Japan has steered her course to the point where she now must choose one of three routes. She must either, (1) Curtail production of all types of goods, conserve her supplies of materials and drift with the current of international developments, or (2) Make an all-out effort to establish her Greater East Asia Co-Prosperity Sphere and finish the China Affair, or (3) Reach some definite understanding with the United States.

The first route would mean that in another twelve months Japan's economy would be so weakened she would be unable to forcefully resist any demands imposed by the United States. The second road leads to war and national suicide. The third to the preservation of her Empire, the security of her people and the continuation of her existence as a major world power—but the probable loss of a certain amount of "face."

It appears, therefore, that Japan's present position briefly is this: On the one hand she can exist for say another twelve months on material now in stock and new supplies available within the Empire and her "sphere of influence." At the end of this period, however, the nation will be a weakling from both a military and economic standpoint. On the other hand by pooling her entire resources and taking a desperate gamble on victory in a short "blitzkrieg" she could, from an economic standpoint, wage what might be termed a fairly efficient war for a few months, at the end of which time she would be economically bankrupt. The remaining alternative is to forago [sic] her aggressive action in the Far East, and "make the best out of a bad bargain."

There are definite signs that most Japanese leaders and very large segments of the people have conclusively abandoned the first alternative. This leaves only two moves, i.e., war or an agreement with the United States. A decision must be made in the very near future. On this decision rests the nation's destiny.[15]

Ambassador Grew endorsed this evaluation in a covering letter accompanying the report: "I entirely concur in Mr. Williams' appraisal of the situation in Japan."[16]

Military Intelligence Analyses

In accordance with its official duties, Army G-2 (Military Intelligence) prepared periodic reports concerning foreign affairs, with a predominant stress upon potential foes (Germany and Japan) and beleaguered unofficial allies (Britain and China). Several of these reports during the second half of 1941 mention Japan's imperiled economic situation.

Just before the late July asset freeze and trade abolition were announced, G-2 called attention to economic mobilization measures taken by the Japanese government. (The less restrictive embargo of 1940 had already increased Japan's difficulties.) "The new policy is obviously a belated attempt to improve the deplorable economic conditions in Japan."[17]

On August 28, Major General Saburo Isoda, the Japanese military attaché in Washington, had an off-the-record session with Colonel R. S. Bratton, chief of the Far Eastern Section of Army Military Intelligence. As the result of a long acquaintanceship spanning eighteen years, the discussion was candid and to the point. Bratton summarized Isoda's remarks: "Due to restrictions imposed by our export control, the Japanese have begun to use a portion of their war reserve of petroleum. . . . Japan has her back to the wall. She can be pushed just so far, then will have to fight us to save her national honor and integrity, though war with the United States is the last thing desired by Japan."[18]

In an evaluation of probable events during the three following months (early September to early December), Brigadier General Sherman Miles reported that the Japanese economic squeeze was already serious:

> Because of the ever-increasing stringency of the embargo placed on Japan by the United States, Great Britain and the Netherlands East Indies, the economic situation in Japan is slowly but surely becoming worse. The Japanese have always lacked war materials, adequate foreign exchange and sufficient foreign trade; the embargo has served to increase the deficiencies in these categories. These deficiencies are serious but are not likely to become dangerous before December 1, 1941 [The Pearl Harbor attack was less than a week later]. The fact that Japan is also encumbered with financial problems connected with the "incident" in China prevents any curative steps being taken. . . .
>
> The action of the Netherlands East Indies in joining with the United States and Great Britain in embargoing goods to Japan was undoubtedly a severe blow, both economically and in prestige. . . .

> The fact remains that Japan lacks essential raw materials to support either her manufacturing industries or a major war effort. To procure them she must have foreign exchange; in order to obtain foreign exchange, she must have foreign trade, which, at present, is seriously curtailed. The stoppage of trade is reducing Japan's raw materials *drastically*—raw materials which are *vital* to the organic well-being of Japan and to her ability to wage war successfully. No other country even approaches the United States in importance to Japan's economic welfare, both as a source of raw materials and as a market for the exports of Japan. Thus through the advantage the United States has gained through the embargo, Japan finds herself in a very poor bargaining position [emphasis added].[19]

The memorandum predicted that the Japanese would use a combination of "threats and promises to soften the impact" of the embargo.[20]

In an early October memorandum, Army Military Intelligence advised against any international conference between the United States and its Oriental foe "unless a definite commitment to withdraw from the Axis were obtained from Japan prior to the conference." Unless such political concessions were first obtained, "economic concessions" would not be appropriate, either. Also needed was "a guarantee, backed by substantial evidence of sincerity, not to attack Russia in Siberia."[21] The memorandum went on to argue that the growing economic strangulation was the best course to preserve peace in the Pacific:

> Since it is highly improbable that this condition can be met by the Japanese Government at the present time our course lies straight before us. This Division still believes that forceful diplomacy vis-a-vis Japan, including the application of *ever increasing military and economic pressure on our part*, offers the best possibility of preventing the spread of hostilities in the Pacific area, and the best hope of the eventual disruption of the Tripartite Pact. The exercise of increasingly strong "power diplomacy" by the United States is still clearly indicated [emphasis added].[22]

In the middle of October, G-2 discussed the fall of the current Japanese government and the reasons behind it. "This resignation was the logical result of Foreign Minister Toyoda's failure to secure a relaxation of the economic pressure on Japan by the U.S. Government."[23] As a result, the even more militaristic government of Lieutenant General Hideki Tojo came to power.

In an analysis in early November of the Far East situation, General Miles reported that "After four years of war in China, Japan is militarily over-extended on the mainland of Asia, economically weak, and psychologically aware of the fact that her *economic structure is crumbling*" (emphasis added). His second point was that "For obvious reasons both Germany and China would like to embroil the United States in a large scale war with Japan. While Japan is reluctant to go to war with us, her political and economic situations demand action." The general surveyed several possible courses of action available to the Japanese and ended with a kind of cop-out conclusion: "Japan's most probable line of action, therefore, will be to continue her efforts to secure a relaxation of American economic pressure while completing her plans and arranging her forces for an advance in the direction which will be most fruitful of quick results."[24]

In an early December "Brief Periodic Estimate of the Situation December 1, 1941–March 13, 1942," Army G-2 drew attention to the growing success of the embargo:

> Because of the ever increasing stringency of the embargo placed on Japan by the United States, Great Britain, and the Netherlands East Indies, the economic situation in Japan is slowly but surely becoming worse. The Japanese have always lacked war materials, adequate foreign exchange, and sufficient foreign trade; the embargo has served to *increase sharply* the deficiencies in these categories. . . .
> Japan lacks essential war materials to support either her manufacturing industries or a major war effort, even continued effort against China. The stoppage of trade and freezing of credits has *drastically reduced* Japan's supply of raw materials, and has caused her to begin using her reserves. *Many* of her industries are suffering from shortages, rationing has been extended and intensified; in short, *economically Japan is in perilous plight* [emphasis added].[25]

Army G-2 was convinced that there was no available strategy whereby Japan could quickly secure the military upper hand. Hence, it was confident that the cessation of trade had produced a Japanese policy stalemate: "The situation calls for strenuous measures; yet, if she goes to war, she may use up her reserves, especially of oil and steel, before she can force a decision favorable to herself. Thus her economic situation contributes largely to the indecision of her leaders. This is a problem which she must solve *within the next few months*" (emphasis added).[26]

In other words, war would not be the likely result. "Our influence in the Far Eastern theater lies in the threat of our Naval power and the effort of our economic blockade. Both are primary deterrents against Japanese all-out entry in the war as an Axis partner."[27]

The embargo had encouraged even smaller nations (Thailand was cited in particular) to stand up to Japanese pressure. Deciding how to deal with the continuing crisis would be central in the minds of Japanese planners. That nation is pictured as being in a classical no-win situation, "If she goes to war to achieve her economic objectives, Japan faces ruin; but at the same time she feels that achievement of these objectives are vital to her existence."[28] Consideration was not given to the matter of national psychology—that such a coercive situation (both in the short term and in terms of long-range policy reversals) meant that national "face" and "honor" might well require hostilities, regardless of whether a permanent military victory could be obtained. For comparison, it is worth noting that the United States was dominated throughout the cold war by various forms of a "better dead than Red" mind cast. Although a nuclear war could never produce a meaningful victory for either side, it was deemed essential to be willing to inflict such retaliation to maintain national honor and to deny the foe the sought-for triumph. If the collective American psyche required such a policy of defiance at any and all costs, so to an even greater degree did the collective psyche of the Japanese, who had far more overt and acknowledged stress on the absolute necessity of maintaining "face" and "honor."

The American navy also recognized Japan's dire economic straits as well. In an internal "Memorandum for the Chief of Naval Operations" dated October 21, 1941, it was noted that the economy of the Nipponese opponent remained in steady decline and that its reserves of most essential materials would not last more than six additional months:

> The basic weakness in Japan's economic situation is her lack of raw materials to feed her war industries. She depends on overseas imports for 65% to 100% of her supplies of nickel, cotton, rubber, molybdenum, aluminum, lead, mercury, oil, tin, mica, iron; this dependence is partly offset by stockpiles, particularly oil, molybdenum and aluminum, but existing stocks are not sufficient to meet current requirements for more than six months. ...
> The living standards of Japan's industrial and agricultural workers reflect the condition of Japan's foreign trade, particularly the export of silk and the import of industrial raw materials. The steady decline of foreign trade has caused the living standards of the entire nation to deteriorate.[29]

In the summary of the memorandum (which serves as the document's front page), it was noted:

> Economically food is not a problem for Japan but in order to supply her war industries which are essential for her present war effort Japan must have access to over-seas markets or must open up an over-land supply route to Europe through Russia. Failing in either of these two alternatives, she must face a situation in which she will see her total war effort gradually decline which must eventually result in her eviction from the Asiatic continent and her *decline as a world power* [emphasis added].[30]

Was it realistic to expect any proud and militarily strong nation to accept peacefully eviction from its world power status? That there was a definite possibility of a military response is alluded to in vague terms: "The report that General Tojo is filling the Home Ministry and War Portfolios in addition to the Premiership indicate clearly however that the Army intends to take the reins of the Government, and such being the case, the intimation is clear that positive action detrimental to United States' interests may be expected."[31]

Other Analyses

Although the State Department and the military had special, vested concerns in the Japanese situation, that did not mean that other departments were totally lacking in either interest or awareness of what was occurring. At the Treasury Department, Secretary Morgenthau had been playing a vigorous role in encouraging the imposition and enforcement of vigorous anti–Japanese restrictions. When the September issue of *China Today* circulated an optimistic picture of Japan's rapid decline and collapse, Morgenthau was more than modestly interested in how accurate the publication's estimates were. The Treasury Department's own specialists concurred that the situation was disintegrating but not as rapidly as the publication had claimed. On October 1, H. D. White responded in writing and began with a "Summary of Appended Memorandum"

> 1. "Contemporary China" states that at the current rate of consumption, Japan will have exhausted her reserves of oil and gasoline by the end of March, 1942.
> This underestimates Japan's petroleum reserves. Our earlier studies indicated that they are probably sufficient for about a year, rather than for the six months suggested by the press.
> 2. "Contemporary China" concludes that Japan will have used up her stocks of imported iron and scrap before the end of the current year.
> Japan may exhaust her stocks of imported iron and steel before the end of this year. However, since Japan is reducing the amount of scrap used in the mixture with pig iron, her total stock of scrap, i.e., domestic as well as imported, may possibly be sufficient for a year. Of more importance is her shortage of iron ore, pig iron, manganese ore, and coal.
> 3. "Contemporary China" claims that the silk industry will be at least two-thirds ruined next spring.
> This conclusion seems to be based on the pre–1939 importance of foreign markets to Japan's silk industry. During this year considerably more than half of Japan's production of silk is for domestic consumption.
> 4. "Contemporary China" states that the cotton industry will be operating at 25 percent of normal capacity next spring.
> This estimate is probably too low. Our figures seem to indicate that if Japan is cut off from all non-yen supplies of raw cotton, her cotton industry will probably be operating at about 35 percent of normal output in the near future. If, however, Japan is able to continue obtaining supplies from Latin America, her cotton textile industry will have sufficient raw cotton to maintain production at more than 50 percent of normal output.[32]

Even these "mark-ups" of Japan's supplies provide evidence of the degree of harm inflicted upon the civilian economy. Whether Japan's cotton industry worked at 25% or 50% of capacity, it would be a disaster. Whether Japan's silk industry was two-thirds destroyed or only about 50% devastated, it would be a body blow to an industry which in no shape or form would seem to have any connection to the military excesses of the system. In peacetime, does one wreck havoc throughout an entire economy when measures can be aimed specifically at the military aspects of the system? And if one chooses to do so, does not one fan the bitter flames of hatred and rage that encourage rather than discourage war? In short, if one in supposed peacetime destroys an entire people's well-being, is not one waging war against a *people* when the proper target is the regime that is abhorred? This is an ethical question well worth meditating upon because the imposition of economic embargoes represents a nonmilitary war-making tool that seems to tempt every generation.

NOTES

1. Joint Committee on the Investigation of the Pearl Harbor Attack. *Pearl Harbor Attack: Hearings Before the Joint Committee on the Investigation of the Pearl Harbor Attack* (Washington, D.C.: U.S. Government Printing Office, 1946), 2/578.
2. Ibid.

Reports from the Ambassador and the Tokyo Diplomatic Staff

3. Photographic reproduction of telegram, *PHA* 14/1049–51.
4. *PHA* 14/1052. The word "adventure" is presumably an error in decryption at the State Department. The following page of the photographed telegram is unreadable.
5. *PHA* 14/1054.
6. *PHA* 29/2144.
7. *PHA* 29/2144. Grew himself quoted this before the Joint Congressional Investigation, 2/584–85.
8. "Report of Conditions in Japan During the Month of July, 1941," State Department document 894.00PR/163 (pages 25–26 of report).
9. "Report of Conditions in Japan During the Month of August, 1941," State Department document 894.00PR/164 (pages 28–29 of report).
10. *PHA* 20/4042 (page 2 of report); the entire document is photographically reproduced, 4041–49.
11. *PHA* 20/4047 (page 7 of report).
12. *PHA* 20/4048 (page 8 of report).
13. *PHA* 20/4047–48 (pages 7–8 of report).
14. *PHA* photographically reproduced, 20/4053–57.
15. This report is complete except for the title page and a few final lines pertaining to State Department identification number and distribution.
16. *PHA* 20/4051–52.

Military Intelligence Analyses

17. "Memorandum for the Chief of Staff" by Brigadier General Sherman Miles, dated 25 July 1941, *PHA* 14/1344.
18. "Memorandum for the Chief of Staff" by Brigadier General Sherman Miles, dated 2 September 1941, quoting Colonel Bratton's summary, *PHA* 14/1348.
19. "Memorandum for the Chief of Staff" by Brigadier General Sherman Miles, dated 5 September 1941, *PHA* 14/1353.
20. *PHA* 14/1353.
21. "Memorandum for the Chief of Staff" by Colonel Hayes A. Kroner, dated 2 October 1941, *PHA* 14/1359.
22. *PHA* 14/1358–59.
23. "Memorandum for the Chief of Staff" by Brigadier General Sherman Miles, dated 16 October 1941, *PHA* 14/1359.
24. "Memorandum for the Assistant Chief of Staff, W.P.D. [War Plans Division]" by Brigadier General Sherman Miles, 2 November 1941, *PHA* 14/1363.

25. By Brigadier General Sherman Miles, dated 5 December 1941, *PHA* 14/1382.
26. *PHA* 14/1382.
27. *PHA* 14/1378.
28. *PHA* 14/1382.
29. *PHA* 15/1845.
30. Ibid.
31. Ibid.

Other Analyses

32. Morgenthau Diaries 447:48–49, as reprinted in *Morgenthau Diary (China)*, vol. 1, Internal Security Subcommittee of the Committee on the Judiciary, United States Senate (Washington, D.C.: U.S. Government Printing Office, 1965), 472.

Chapter 13

THE AMERICAN RECOGNITION OF THE WAR-MAKING POTENTIAL OF AN EMBARGO

Retrospective Recognition of the Linkage Between the Embargo and the Outbreak of War by Commentators

Although most writers appear to pay little attention to the relationship between the embargo and the Pacific war or to recognize the potential significance of this relationship, from the time of the war onwards a more perceptive minority have recognized that the two events are definitely linked together. Some have been fervently pro–FDR and others his bitter opponents, while yet others have steered clear of those bitter controversies. Hence the linkage arises not out of some ideological hostility to the president but out of the search for a fairly based understanding of the events that led up to the eruption of hostilities.

During the war itself, W. F. Kernan, a lieutenant colonel in the U.S. Army artillery, wrote a popular volume entitled *Defense Will Not Win the War* (six hardback printings in two months). In his book he contended that a combination of American economic pressure and long-standing Japanese internal policy failures made the Pearl Harbor attack an act of desperation:

> In this order of ideas, the Japanese attack on Pearl Harbor from the standpoint of the Axis was a forlorn hope. This attack must therefore be regarded, not as an insolent gesture of an enemy who believed victory to be within his grasp, but as the last throw of the dice of a gambler who has staked his shirt. For Japan, gutted by a decade of war, *suffering from economic strangulation*, wholly possessed by the eviscerating demon of militarism, had no other chance for survival except in sharing the spoils won by a victorious Germany [emphasis added].[1]

Immediately after the war, one study of the Pearl Harbor attack conceded of the sanctions: "We know that it risked precipitating them into war. But nothing less would now serve."[2] Later pro–Roosevelt writers agreed that the policy carried the risk of producing a Pacific conflict. Leonard Baker, for example, spoke with approval of the sanctions[3] while quoting

Roosevelt's warning that a petroleum cutoff would result in war.[4] The veneration with which he viewed FDR can be seen in the jacket subtitle (missing from the title page), "A Great President in Time of Crisis."

Revisionists have likewise been alert to the connection between the embargo and the eruption of hostilities. Charles A. Beard called attention to President Hoover's refusal to adopt an embargo because of the war danger inherent in such an act.[5] In a footnote, this vehement critic of Roosevelt discussed the fact that Admiral Stark had prepared a lengthy memorandum for the president in regard to the proposed embargo. After quoting brief extracts, Beard concluded: "In short, when President Roosevelt began his program of economic sanctions in the midsummer of 1941, he had been advised by his naval experts that such actions should be postponed and that, if taken, they would almost certainly inflame the war party in Japan and probably result in a fairly early attack by Japan in the Pacific."[6]

Over fifty pages later, Beard inserts into the main text a reference to "economic sanctions likely to lead to war" and provides a long footnote summarizing the gradual implementation of sanctions on Japan.[7] If one were to set the entirety of Beard's various references to the matter in text-size type, one would perhaps have not much over five pages—out of a complete work running almost six hundred. For an economics-centered historian such as Beard this represents an astounding lapse.

A year before Beard's better-known work appeared, George Morgenstern turned his attention to a Beardian-style conspiratorial interpretation of the war's beginning: "For years before Pearl Harbor Mr. Roosevelt had talked of peace. For months he had schemed for war. His deeds belied his words."[8] Publicly, the administration raged about the treachery of Japan attacking the United States on December 7: "The administration conveniently forgot to remind the American people of the part played in bringing about the result of December 7 by its campaign of economic warfare, its secret diplomacy, its covert military alliances, the submission of demands which Japan found 'humiliating,' and its own complete abandonment of neutrality in favor of nondeclared war."[9]

Although he did not devote much more space to the significance of the embargo than did Beard, Morgenstern at least placed his discussion of the issue exclusively in the main text, thereby increasing its visibility. He also repeatedly stated the economic accusation in such explicitly clear language that even the most casual reader could not escape the point, while that is quite possible to do when reading Beard.

Since these books appeared in the late forties, the drama and tragedy of Pearl Harbor has commonly distracted attention from the underlying events that turned the possibility of war into a grim reality. The fact that the Japanese fired the first shot has blotted out the question of whether

American foreign policy needlessly and excessively encouraged our Oriental foe to take that step.

Yet the correlation between embargo and war has not been totally lost. Among historians who are in neither the "hate Roosevelt" nor the "worship Roosevelt" camps, attention has been drawn to the problem. Michael A. Barnhart has argued that due to the asset freeze, "the doors to any peaceful settlement of Pacific differences would be all but shut tight."[10] Jonathan G. Utley contends that without the embargo, war "might have been avoided indefinitely" because of the dramatic growth in visible American military might.[11]

William L. Langer and S. Everett Gleason, in their analysis of American conduct during the two years preceding formal entry into World War II, point to the trade embargo as the critical step:

> When, in July, 1941, the Japanese marched into Indo-China, Washington had taken the bit in its teeth. The freezing order was probably the crucial step in the entire course of Japanese-American relations before Pearl Harbor. It was not initially intended to end all American trade with Japan, but rather to serve as a means of exerting pressure as the circumstances warranted. But in practice no exports of any consequence reached Japan after August, nor was Japanese silk or any other commodity imported into the United States. Thanks to the cooperation of the nations of the British Commonwealth and of the Netherlands Indies, the ensuing economic blockade of Japan was all but complete. If one thing was more certain than another, it was that Japan could not continue under such pressure for more than a few months.[12]

Many years after his service with the "Magic" decryption effort at Pearl Harbor, W. J. Holmes wrote a lengthy and authoritative account of its workings. Writing in the late seventies, he still viewed Japan as having had only two basic options:

> The Anglo-Dutch-American oil embargo had impaled Japan on the horns of a cruel dilemma. If she remained on the defensive, the depletion of her oil reserves would cripple her military operations in China and shortly render her completely impotent. This energy crisis forced her either to knuckle under to Allied demands or to move against the Netherlands East Indies and to seize the essential supply of oil.[13]

An early 1980s historian of the Australian role in the Second World War pointed to the importance of the embargo when he wrote, "For Japan, 1941 was a crucial year as her shortage of some important raw materials forced her leaders to choose between war or a humiliating abdication of great power status."[14] On the following page, he returned at greater length to the repercussion of the trade decision:

> As British and American policy-makers, including Eden, recognized, this forced her to choose between a reversal of her pro–Axis policy, or war to obtain control of raw materials. Eden thought she might opt for the former, the United States

Navy for the latter. In fact, by this stage, if not earlier, war had emerged as a very likely eventuality, as it could be avoided only by one side or the other making a humiliating backdown. But it was not until the last week of November that the tortuous American-Japanese negotiations reached the stage where Japan made the irrevocable decision for war, ratified at an Imperial Conference on 1 December.[15]

Far Eastern diplomacy specialist George Alexander Larsen speaks of the pivotal role the embargo played in causing Japan to reject a possible anti–Soviet campaign and to launch one against the Americans instead:

> Japan had decided to strike the United States rather than the Soviet Union, because she was in urgent need of the raw materials in the South Pacific and the United States blocked—or at least seemed to block—her expansion in that direction. (The American attempt to bring the Japanese war machine to a halt by withholding the fuel on which it ran had had the opposite effect; unable to buy what she needed, Japan, in desperation, had determined to seize it.) Furthermore, at the same time, the United States with her soft life and lack of discipline had seemed less formidable an opponent than the U.S.S.R., particularly since the might of the Japanese navy could be brought to bear on the former more readily than on the latter.[16]

Jeffrey G. Barlow makes brief reference to the economic impetus to war in an essay on naval strategy in the Pacific: "Japan's decision to go to war with the United States had been dictated in large part by strategic circumstances. Because of the U.S.-led embargo on the sale of oil and other materials to Japan, the Japanese government looked to the oil-producing and mineral laden territories in Southeast Asia to make up its losses."[17]

James J. Martin, in his massive survey of liberal and left-wing periodicals between the two world wars, is clearly disturbed by the contemporary unwillingness of those publications to recognize the war-making potential of their demands for an uncompromising policy, including massive trade limitations. He notes that "an economic squeeze of formidable proportions had been in progress since mid–October, 1940, with the British, French and Dutch collaborating with the United States."[18] By October 1941, "the embargo and the absence of a trade treaty were creating a frightful economic crisis."[19] Martin rebukes "the liberal editorial staffs" for ignoring available evidence that such policies could easily provoke Japanese expansion into Southeast Asia. They "chose to ignore the subject, as it was in complete conflict with their cheerful line that economic pressure on Japan would not make the Japanese the least bit active but would result in their meek collapse in a short while."[20] To Martin, the first post–Pearl Harbor issue of the *New Republic* revealed "the course of American liberalism over the previous decade" in its insistence upon an ever-stronger anti–Japanese foreign policy. On the page where its main editorial was printed, the *New Republic* had pulled the usual masthead and had printed in equally large letters "*Our War*" (emphasis added).[21]

Recognition of the Danger by the Contemporary Press

As soon as the asset freeze/trade stoppage was announced, the military affairs analyst for the *New York Times* provided a detailed appraisal of whether the Japanese would strike south (against the British and, perhaps, the Americans) or would turn north (against the Soviet Union while it was tied down in a bloody war with Germany). His judgment was that they would do neither in the short term:

> Because of the strength of these southern positions [Hong Kong and the Philippines in particular] and because of the likelihood of American intervention should Japan attack the Netherlands Indies or Singapore, there is little possibility that these southern sectors will be attacked *unless* (1) *Anglo-American economic reprisals should threaten to strangle Japan*, (2) Britain should be threatened with defeat in Europe and the Anglo-Dutch-American defense in the Far East should be weakened [emphasis added].[22]

Writing in the first days of August, Edwin L. James was concerned that the United States might allow (as it had in the past) large loopholes to exist which would undermine what appeared to be substantial restrictions upon Nippon-American commerce. "In other days it was the feeling in Washington, and in London as well, that a real curb on oil imports by Japan would *force her* to try to seize the Netherlands East Indies" (emphasis added). James thought that if such a "feeling remains," the United States was likely to only "tighten the reins slightly on Japan" and to save the draconian measures for such contingencies as a Japanese attack on British Singapore.[23]

Newsweek, in its issue immediately after the freeze/embargo announcement, described the action as "striking the Nipponese in their economic solar plexus." Yet, somehow, simultaneously (and in the same sentence), they were able to call it an effort "to stir the less aggressive element in Japan, composed of the big business trusts, the intellectuals, and the Navy moderates, into action to stymie the Army and other jingoes."[24] It noted that the war potential had been immediately recognized on both sides of the Pacific. "Economic warfare, the newspaper *Nichi Nichi* in Tokyo was frank to admit, is 'one step from armed warfare,' and accordingly the United States girded itself for the next step, if it should come."[25] The American publication conceded: "If a strict blockade is instituted Japan's *only alternative* might be to cut the noose by armed force, perhaps by attacking the oil fields of the Netherlands Indies. But the democracies by their stern action showed they are ready for such a showdown" (emphasis added).[26]

In the same issue, Retired Admiral William V. Pratt provided an article in which he saw only two alternatives for Japan, retreat or war: "There is no mistaking the warning that we have given, nor any doubt but that Japan must heed it, or take the plunge into a new war which is certain to be her economic ruin and leave her with no friend anywhere in the world and nothing to depend on beyond the dangerous promises of Hitler."[27]

In its first postembargo issue, *Time* combined together the asset freeze and the calling into federal service of the Philippine militia as proof of how far the American government was now ready to go. "The two acts were more than a warning to the Japanese of war to come—they amounted to a declaration of economic war with military war to follow soon unless the Japanese decided to reverse their course." And the next paragraph began: "That fact could not be mistaken."[28]

The following week, *Newsweek* once again returned to the fact that "the declaration of economic war in the form of freezing $131,000,000 in Japanese assets in the United States"[29] could lead to a shooting war as well:

> Japan was learning that American economic biceps were capable of strangling it, even though the United States hoped to avoid the war with Japan which Germany would like to see. The question of war was up to Japan, if it should fail to respond to the economic pressure and recklessly race ahead with its expansionist policy. And if Japan should force the issue, it would have no right to complain that the United States had failed to make its policy clear.[30]

In the following months (as documented elsewhere in this volume), American press reports repeatedly indicated that the American boycott was producing the very kind of crippling success that maximized the prospect of the war option being chosen. In an irony of timing, the *New York Times* reported on the day Pearl Harbor was attacked that a continuation of the embargo would compel the Japanese government to feel that war was essential:

> Less than four months of blockade are said to have forced a curtailment of perhaps 40 percent in Nippon's factory operation. ... One of the main goals of the Japanese in the Washington talks was relaxation of the blockade. What Tokyo might give in return for such a concession remained obscure. From her Premier down, it was emphasized that the nation would not retract her aggressive steps. If the blockade were not lifted, the implication seemed clear, Japan would be compelled to seek new sources of materials by arms. That the blow might come in the south seemed apparent from a sudden acceleration in the flow of Japanese troops— their number was put at 100,000 or more—toward Indo-China.[31]

American Military Awareness of the Explosive Potential of the Embargo

Because each officer brought his own unique background to his interpretation of the severity of the war danger, it is not surprising that the relative seriousness given to the threat varied from individual to individual. As one travels through the testimony given before the various Pearl Harbor investigations, however, it is clear that even those who in retrospect sought to minimize that danger were quite alert to what could happen.

General Walter C. Short, army commander in chief at Pearl Harbor, caught much flak for his alleged inadequate preparations for a Japanese onslaught. Samuel H. Kaufman, an associate general counsel for the joint congressional investigation, apparently thought that the embargo should have greatly heightened the general's consciousness of the danger:

> Mr. Kaufman. Now coming down to 1941, you read in the paper, of course, about the deterioration of relations as between the Japanese and the United States?
> General Short. Yes, sir.
> Mr. Kaufman. And you knew of the freezing of Japanese funds in the United States?
> General Short. Yes, sir.
> Mr. Kaufman. And you knew of the oil embargo against Japan?
> General Short. Yes, sir.[32]

And then came the logical inquiry, "Did that create in you a consciousness that trouble might come with Japan?" "Yes, sir," was the response. But the general promptly pointed out why his alarm had been restrained: "but I was also told by the War Department that they did not expect a reaction causing the use of military forces on these acts. In their message of July 25, they stated definitely that they did not expect a military reaction."[33] Yet he was sufficiently concerned to order a reevaluation of the air defenses of the Hawaiian Islands,[34] an action which would suggest that the general desired to protect against excessive optimism on the part of his superiors.

In his congressional testimony, Admiral H. E. Kimmel, the commander in chief of the Pacific fleet, looked upon the embargo as but another step in the process that led to the war. He indicated that he was not quite as pessimistic in his evaluation as some of his superiors:

> Senator Ferguson. Well, were you aware from your own judgment, like Admiral Stark and Admiral Turner have stated here, that Anglo-Dutch-American embargoes on Japan oil supplies, regardless of their justification for such embargoes, constituted an actual and a logical cause of war with Japan?
> Admiral Kimmel. Well I thought that the embargoes would irritate Japan considerably and I knew about the embargoes.
> Senator Ferguson. Well, did you think it would irritate them enough, as has been stated by Admiral Stark, that we should have anticipated war over that?
> Admiral Kimmel. Not necessarily; no.
> Senator Ferguson. You did not go that far?
> Admiral Kimmel. No.
> Mr. Murphy. Will the Senator yield?
> Senator Ferguson. Yes.
> Mr. Murphy. In the previous hearing the witness said that he thought it was another step on the road to war.
> Senator Ferguson. Is that the way you want to put it, just another step?

Admiral Kimmel. Well, I think there is very little difference betwist that and what I have just said.

Senator Ferguson. Of course, another step would not be definite unless we knew how many steps we were away from war.

Admiral Kimmel. Yes, sir.

Senator Ferguson. Well, at that time about how many steps were we away from war, if we can clear that up?

Admiral Kimmel. That depended upon the attitude of our Government and the attitude of the Japanese Government and had I known what was known in Washington I could have estimated much more accurately how many steps we were away from war.[35]

At the very minimum, Admiral Kimmel clearly conceptualized the freeze/trade cutoff as an action that brought the war nearer, though he could not be fully certain how much nearer.

Captain Edwin T. Layton, chief intelligence officer for the Pacific fleet under Admiral Kimmel, was uncertain in the fall of 1941 whether the Japanese would undertake military action. He was convinced, however, that they would have to, by some means, obtain the petroleum supplies that they were being denied. As he told the Hart inquiry: "The freezing of credits wherein their supplies from America were cut off, crystalized my belief in the "expansion to the South" being for the means of obtaining, by military means, if necessary, the petroleum products for which they had fruitlessly negotiated with the NEI [Netherlands East Indies] through Yoshizawa earlier in the year."[36]

Admiral Raymond K. Turner was chief of the War Plans Division of the navy. On July 19, 1941, the division issued a study of the likely results of a complete petroleum and trade embargo. Turner predicted war in the near future as one quite possible result:

> It is generally believed that shutting off the American supply of petroleum will lead promptly to an invasion of the Netherlands East Indies. While probable, this is not necessarily a sure immediate result. ... Japan has oil stocks for about eighteen months war operations. Export restrictions of oil by the United States should be accompanied by similar restrictions by the British and Dutch. ... An embargo on exports will have an immediate severe psychological reaction in Japan against the United States. It is almost certain to intensify the determination of those now in power to continue their present course. Furthermore, it seems certain that, if Japan should then take military measures against the British and Dutch, she would also include military action against the Philippines, which would immediately involve us in a Pacific war. ... An embargo would probably result in a fairly early attack by Japan on Malaya and the Netherlands East Indies, and possibly would involve the United States in early war in the Pacific. ... Recommendation: That trade with Japan not be embargoed at this time.[37]

One copy of this analysis was forwarded to the president with an accompanying note from Admiral Stark: "I concur in general. Is this the kind of picture you wanted?"[38]

In his capacity as the War Plans Division chief, Admiral Turner sent to the American fleets in the Pacific a warning on October 16, 1941, about the dangerous situation in that region. The memorandum asserted, among other things, "There is a *strong possibility* of hostilities since the United States and Britain are held responsible for her present desperate situation" (emphasis added). Senator Owen Brewster of Maine inquired concerning this dispatch: "To what did you refer in the words 'desperate situation.' Were you referring to her economic condition?"[39] The admiral replied:

> Very largely to her economic condition, and to the fact that through our action, her trade had been cut off not only with the United States, but with the British possessions and the Dutch had reduced their commitment to furnish oil, a certain amount of oil annually, to something like one-third or two-fifths of that. That meant that since the United States and the Dutch possessions were the sources of nearly all of the petroleum products that Japan was using, in a comparatively short time her own large stocks maintained in the Empire would be exhausted. She could not get cotton from India, upon which she depended for a large part of her cotton industry, and she also got rice from the Dutch and India.
> It meant, of course, that her trade with the world was practically stopped and that was a very serious matter for an industrial nation.
> In addition to that, of course, was her very large extension in China, and the help that the United States and the British were giving to the nationalist government in China.[40]

Turner was convinced that, given the respective positions of Japan and the United States, war was inevitable and the embargo accelerated the deteriorating relationship between the two countries. "I did not say that I opposed putting on the economic sanctions. I merely said—which I believed and which is borne out to be correct—that putting the economic sanctions on would hasten war, and I think it had a very decided influence in hastening the war."[41]

Although Turner did not oppose the idea of sanctions, he quickly admitted that a reasonable case could be made for maintaining the shipment of exports. "The only object that I could see in putting off the war with Japan was so we could get our war potential higher. We were improving at a rate considerably greater than the Japanese were during the fall of 1941."[42]

Admiral Harold R. Stark, chief of naval operations, recalled before the Navy Court of Inquiry that the navy had operated on the periphery of the decision to declare a total trade halt. The decision "was more economic than otherwise," and the navy "had no organization to study" such aspects of the proposal.[43] Furthermore, he testified:

> The outstanding thing in my memory as regards my stand so far as the Navy Department is concerned, with reference to pressure on Japan, was in reference to oil. *I made it known to the State Department in no uncertain terms that in my opinion if Japan's oil were shut off, she would go to war.* I do not necessarily mean with us, but I mean if her economic life had been choked and throttled by inability to

get to oil, she would go somewhere and take it, and I stated if I were a Jap, I would.

I did state in that connection that unless we were prepared for war—I do not mean prepared in the sense of complete readiness for war, but unless we were ready to accept a war risk, we should not take measures which would cut oil down to the Japanese below that needed for what might be called their normal peace time needs for their industry and their ships. I never waivered [sic] one inch on that stand [emphasis added].[44]

When Stark later appeared before the congressional investigative committee, Congressman Bertrand W. Gearhart of California demanded to know whether certain acts either contemplated or considered by the United States had been "overt act[s]" (of war). One would think that once one conceded that the embargo virtually guaranteed a war that the trade freeze could hardly be classified as anything else. In spite of this, the admiral justified a negative answer to the question by stressing that "there were certain stipulations there whereby it was made possible for the unfreezing of assets as necessary to carry on certain trade, if we desired to do so. It was not a loophole, but it was left open for certain essentials, that it could be done."[45] In other words, since it was theoretically possible to grant exceptions, the import/export prohibition was not quite the act of war his earlier testimony seemed to imply. When one considers the intensity of Stark's earlier remarks before the Navy Court of Inquiry, one would seem compelled to conclude that he was using this theoretical loophole as the means to escape the legitimate conclusions required by his own assertions.

At the time of the Pearl Harbor assault, Captain Charles Wellborn, Jr., was administrative aide to the chief of naval operations, Admiral Stark. Wellborn conceded to the Hart Inquiry that the officers he worked with most closely were "not entirely in agreement" in their individual evaluations of the degree of war danger posed by the total cessation of trade. Nor could he "recall the particular shading of views held by the individual officers" because several years had passed.[46] He noted that "I can't recall opinions of individuals, but I do recall that it was *generally* felt that the stoppage of crude oil would probably result in a warlike step on the part of Japan. The *consensus of opinion*, as I recall, was that the stoppage of shipments of aviation gasoline, the freezing of credits, and shutting off of steel scrap were probably moves which would *not* provoke war" (emphasis added).[47]

It is difficult to reconcile how the embargo would simultaneously "result in a warlike step on the part of Japan" while it "would not provoke [a] war." Perhaps Wellborn's idea was that although the embargo could initiate a war, the Japanese were more likely to limit themselves to saber rattling and other steps just short of open conflict. Even under such a generous interpretation, however, Wellborn's testimony still makes plain that others were far from certain of such a peaceful outcome.

American Recognition of the War Potential

Army chief of staff General George C. Marshall recalled before the Navy Court of Inquiry that Admiral Stark had repeatedly warned of the danger of any complete termination of trade:

> I was certain that they were going ahead in the Far East but whether they would do it overtly or whether they would do it over some severance of diplomatic relations or moves of that kind, I wasn't clear in my mind, I might say that we had a *number of discussions*, particularly Admiral Stark with members of the State Department and with the President at which I was present, with relation to the imposing of economic sanctions against the Japanese, particular in regard to fuel oil and gasoline, and *it was the opinion that if you moved so far you provoked them to the point where something overt would happen right away*. I mustn't speak for him but this was discussed by him *very often* as to what would happen if you caught them on the fuel oil business cold; whether or not they would be provoked into action, all of which meant, in my mind, whether they moved directly—as they did—or whether they moved more circuitously under the cover of various diplomatic ruptures and things of that sort [emphasis added].[48]

Note that Marshall refers to "*the* opinion" that war would happen rather than just "*his* (Stark's) opinion," which seems to indicate that it represented a considerably wider sentiment. Be that as it may, it is immediately obvious that the general himself drew a direct line between the embargo and the outbreak of war. The only real question was how the Japanese would proceed from one to the other, whether "directly" or "under the cover of various diplomatic ruptures and things of that sort."

The President's Admission of the Danger

Roosevelt repeatedly referred to the danger of war as grounds for holding off on implementing any stringent embargo. In a cabinet meeting during December 1939, there was a discussion of efforts to prevent important and scarce metals finding their way to Germany. Ickes called attention to the fact that "in California particularly" there was "growing opposition" to continuing the existing "vast shipments of oil and gasoline from this country to Japan." Ickes was convinced that "our own moral situation" required a prohibition of such exports. The president took a utilitarian approach, suggesting that "perhaps it was just as well for us to ship these supplies to Japan because otherwise Japan might raid the Dutch East Indies."[49] In February 1940 even Ickes himself was conceding to his diary "a possibility" of such intervention.[50]

In his diary entry of October 10, 1940, Assistant Secretary of State Breckinridge Long discussed a meeting the president held with Sumner Welles, Secretary of State Hull, and him:

> There came up several other questions, among them that of partial embargoes against Japan. The President's position was that we were not to shut off oil from

Japan or machine tools from Japan and *thereby force her into a military expedition against the Dutch East Indies* but that we were to withhold from Japan only such things as we vitally needed ourselves, such as high test gas and certain machine tools and certain machinery which we absolutely now needed ourselves; that there was to be prodding of Japan and that we were not going to get into any war by forcing Japan into a position where she was going to fight for some reason or other [emphasis added].[51]

In November of the same year, Eleanor Roosevelt gave her husband a note with the challenge, "Now we've stopped scrap iron, what about oil?" His reply was that not only could Japan increase its purchases from Mexico but also that it "may be *driven by actual necessity* to a descent on the Dutch East Indies. At this writing, we all regard such action on our part as an encouragement to the spread of war in the Far East" (emphasis added).[52] The author who quotes these words immediately adds the commentary that Roosevelt was quite right in his prediction, "but the ban on oil would come eight months later, and the Japanese attack on American forces at Pearl Harbor came less than five months after that."[53]

The later revisionist scenario of a Pacific war as the back door into the European conflict sought by the administration was not unknown among at least some policymakers. Secretary Ickes wrote the president on June 23 seemingly suggesting such a European intervention might be a desirable side-effect to the cutoff of all fuel to Japan, "There might develop from the embargoing of oil to Japan such a situation as would make it not only possible but easy to get into this war in an effective way."[54] The president's response to the suggestion was standoffish, and he, in effect, argued: would you really continue to endorse a petroleum ban if you knew the result would be a Japanese attack on Russia or the Dutch East Indies?[55]

On July 26, Roosevelt ordered the freezing of all Japanese assets. Yet only two days earlier he had spoken to a civilian defense committee explaining that he had not previously cut off oil because such an action would have resulted in war:

> Here on the East Coast you have been reading that the Secretary of the Interior, as Oil Administrator, is faced with the problem of not enough gasoline to go around the East Coast and how he is asking everybody to curtail their consumption of gasoline. All right.
> Now, I am—I might be called an American citizen, living in Hyde Park, N.Y. And I say, "That's a funny thing; why am I asked to curtail my consumption of gasoline when I read in the papers that thousands of tons of gasoline are going out from Los Angeles—West Coast—to Japan; and we are helping Japan in what looks like an act of aggression?"
> All right. Now the answer is a very simple one. There is a world war going on and has been for some time—nearly two years. One of our efforts, from the very beginning, was to prevent the spread of that world war in certain areas where it hadn't started.
> One of those areas is a place called the Pacific Ocean—one of the largest areas

of the earth. There happened to be a place in the South Pacific where we had to get a lot of things—rubber, tin, and so forth and so on, down in the Dutch Indies, the Strait Settlements and Indo-China. And we had to help get the Australian surplus of meat and wheat, and corn, for England.

It was very essential from our own selfish point of view of defense to prevent a war from starting in the South Pacific. So our foreign policy was—trying to stop a war from breaking out down there.

At the same time, from the point of view of even France at that time—of course, France still had her head above water—we wanted to keep that line of supplies from Australia and New Zealand going to the Near East—all their troops, all their supplies that they have maintained in Syria, North Africa, and Palestine. So it was essential for Great Britain that we try to keep the peace down there in the South Pacific.

All right, and now here is a nation called Japan. Whether they had at that time aggressive policies to enlarge their empire southward, they didn't have any oil of their own up in the north. Now, *if we cut the oil off, they probably would have gone down to the Dutch East Indies a year ago, and you would have had war.*

Therefore, there was—you might say—a method in letting this oil go to Japan, with the hope—and it had worked for two years—of keeping war out of the South Pacific for our own good, for the good of the defense of Great Britain and the freedom of the seas [emphasis added].[56]

Two days later, the United States apparently decided it was essential to order a total trade prohibition with Japan. Was it at all likely that the perceived probable results of such an action had in any way been altered? If on July 24, the president felt that an embargo carried an extremely grave risk of war, how could he avoid having the same conviction only two days later when he signed the necessary paperwork to invoke the policy change?

It is interesting that the evening of the same day that the president addressed the civilian defense committee, he met with the Japanese ambassador and mentioned once again the war danger as an explanation for why he had held off on terminating petroleum exports. Preparing the way for a possible reversal of policy, he cited public pressure against continuing such supplies. He then made explicit reference to Japan's option of seizing the Netherlands East Indies and implied the virtual inevitability of American intervention. Because of the importance of recognizing the fact that the president was fully aware of the war danger from his new policy that was about to be announced, it is worth quoting at length a substantial extract from Welles' summary of the meeting:

> At the request of the Japanese Ambassador, the President received the Ambassador for an off-the-record conference in the Oval Room at the White House at five o'clock this afternoon. At the President's request, Admiral Stark and I were present.
>
> At the outset of the conference the President made approximately the following statement to the Ambassador. The President said, referring to a talk which he had made this morning to a home defense group under the leadership of Mayor LaGuardia [see above], that for more than two years the United States had been

permitting oil to be exported from the United States to Japan. He said that this had been done because of the realization on the part of the United States that if these oil supplies had been shut off or restricted the Japanese Government and people would have been furnished with an incentive or a pretext for moving down upon the Netherlands East Indies in order to assure themselves of a greater oil supply than that which, under present conditions, they were able to obtain. The United States had been pursuing this policy primarily for the purpose of doing its utmost to play its full part in making the effort to preserve peace in the Pacific region.

At the present time, the President said, the Ambassador undoubtedly knew that there was a very considerable shortage in the oil supply in the eastern part of the United States and the average American man and woman were unable to understand why, at a time when they themselves were asked to curtail their use of gasoline oil, the United States Government should be permitting oil supplies to continue to be exported to Japan when Japan during these past two years had given every indication of pursuing a policy of force and conquest in conjunction with the policy of world conquest and domination which Hitler was carrying on. The average American citizen could not understand why his Government was permitting Japan to be furnished with oil in order that such oil might be utilized by Japan in carrying on her purposes of aggression.

The President said that if Japan attempted to seize oil supplies by force in the Netherlands East Indies, the Dutch would, without the shadow of a doubt, resist, the British would immediately come to their assistance, war would then result between Japan, the British and the Dutch, and, in view of our own policy of assisting Great Britain, an exceedingly serious situation would immediately result. It was with all of these facts in mind, the President said, that notwithstanding the bitter criticism that had been leveled against the Administration and against the Department of State, the President up to now had permitted oil to be shipped by Japan from the United States.[57]

NOTES

Retrospective Recognition of the Linkage Between the Embargo and the Outbreak of War by Commentators

1. V. F. Kernan, *Defense Will Not Win the War* (New York: Pocket Books, 1942), 73.
2. Walter Millis, *This Is Pearl! The United States and Japan—1941* (New York: William Morrow, 1947), 116.
3. *Roosevelt and Pearl Harbor* (New York: Macmillan, 1970), 173.
4. Ibid., 176.
5. Charles A. Beard, *President Roosevelt and the Coming of the War, 1941: A Study in Appearance and Realities* (New Haven: Yale University Press, 1948), 178.
6. Ibid., 179.
7. Ibid., 235.
8. George Morgenstern, *Pearl Harbor: The Story of the Secret War* (New York: Devin-Adair, 1947), 85.
9. Ibid., 310.
10. Michael A. Barnhart, *Japan Prepares for Total War: The Search for Economic Security, 1919–1941* (Ithaca, N.Y.: Cornell University Press, 1987), 214.

11. Jonathan G. Utley, *Going to War with Japan, 1937–1941* (Knoxville: University of Tennessee Press, 1985), 180.
12. William L. Langer and S. Everett Gleason, *The Undeclared War: 1940–1941* (New York: Harper & Bros., for the Council on Foreign Relations, 1953), 708.
13. W. J. Holmes, *Double-Edged Secrets: U.S. Naval Intelligence in the Pacific During World War II* (Annapolis, Md.: Naval Institute Press, 1979), 27.
14. John Robertson, *Australia at War, 1939–1945* (Melbourne: William Heinemann, 1981), 62.
15. Ibid., 63.
16. George Alexander Larsen, *The Strange Neutrality: Soviet Japanese Relations During the Second World War, 1941–1945* (Tallahassee, Fla.: Diplomatic Press, 1972), 37–38.
17. Jeffrey G. Barlow, "World War II: U.S. and Japanese Naval Strategies," in Colin S. Gray and Robert W. Barnett, *Seapower and Strategy* (Annapolis, Md.: Naval Institute Press, 1989), 251.
18. James J. Martin, *American Liberalism and World Politics, 1931–1941: Liberalism's Press and Spokesmen on the Road Back to War Between Mukden and Pearl Harbor* (New York: Devin-Adair, 1964), 2:1302. See 2:1302–12 for a detailed discussion of the liberal treatment of Japan during the prewar decade.
19. Ibid., 2:1310.
20. Ibid., 2:1305.
21. Ibid., 2:1312.

Recognition of the Danger by the Contemporary Press

22. Hanson W. Baldwin, "Japan Gets in Position," 26 July 1941, 4.
23. "Once Again We Tease Japan on Oil Supply," *New York Times*, 3 August 1941, E3.
24. "Showdown in Pacific Hastened by Firm Stand of Democracies," 4 August 1941, 13. The title of the article itself bears testimony to the editors' interpretation of the danger posed by the termination of trade.
25. Ibid., 12.
26. Ibid., 13.
27. "Japan's Move South: A Quest for Naval Empire," *Newsweek*, 4 August 1941, 19.
28. "The Last Step Taken," *Time*, 4 August 1941, 11. Again the title of the article reinforces the point we are making.
29. "Tightening of Economic Noose Puts Next Move Up to Japan," *Newsweek*, 11 August 1941, 15.
30. Ibid., 17.
31. "Trade Winds," *New York Times*, 7 December 1941, IV-3.

American Military Awareness of the Explosive Potential of the Embargo

32. Joint Committee on the Investigation of the Pearl Harbor Attack, *Pearl Harbor Attack: Hearings Before the Joint Committee on the Investigation of the Pearl Harbor Attack* (Washington, D.C.: U.S. Government Printing Office, 1946), 7/2975.
33. Ibid.
34. *PHA* 7/2975–76.
35. *PHA* 6/2868.
36. *PHA* 26/236.

37. James H. Herzog, "Influence of the United States Navy in the Embargo of Oil to Japan, 1940–1941," *Pacific Historical Review* 35 (August 1966): 317–28.
38. Ibid., 327.
39. *PHA* 4/1945.
40. Ibid.
41. *PHA* 4/2013.
42. Ibid.
43. *PHA* 32/43.
44. Ibid.
45. *PHA* 5/2299.
46. *PHA* 26/421.
47. Ibid.
48. *PHA* 33/831.

The President's Admission of the Danger

49. Harold L. Ickes, *The Secret Diary of Harold L. Ickes*, vol. 3, *The Lowering Clouds, 1939–1941* (New York: Simon and Schuster, 1954), 96.
50. ibid., 132.
51. Breckinridge Long, *The War Diary of Breckinridge Long: Selections from the Years 1939–1944*, ed. Fred L. Israel (Lincoln: University of Nebraska Press, 1966), 140.
52. Wayne S. Cole, *Roosevelt and the Isolationists, 1932–1945* (Lincoln: University of Nebraska Press, 1983), 355.
53. Ibid.
54. Ickes, *Secret Diary*, 557.
55. Ibid., 558.
56. The text of Roosevelt's off-the-cuff remarks can be found in a number of sources:

"221. Informal Remarks of President Roosevelt to the Volunteer Participation Committee, Washington, July 24, 1941" (extract), Department of State, *Peace and War: United States Foreign Policy, 1931–1941* (Washington, D.C.: U.S. Government Printing Office, 1943), 703–4.

"67. The President Explains Our Policy Concerning the Exportation of Oil to Japan. Informal, Extemporaneous Remaks to Volunteer Participation Committee of the Office of Civilian Defense. July 24, 1941." In Franklin D. Roosevelt, *The Public Papers and Addresses of Franklin D. Roosevelt*, ed. Samuel I. Rosenman; 1941 volume: *The Call to Battle Stations* (New York: Harper & Bros., 1950), 280.

"President on Defense and Far East," *New York Times*, 25 July 1941, 4.

57. "220. Memorandum by the Acting Secretary of State (Welles) [Washington], July 24, 1941," *Peace and War*, 699–700.

Chapter 14
DISAVOWING THE LINKAGE BETWEEN EMBARGO AND WAR

After World War I, peaceful and disillusioned men and women longed for some nonviolent means to curb military aggression. Hence economic boycotts were advocated as peaceful means of hindering and even reversing the successes brought about by the imperialistic invasion of other lands.

What such proposals overlooked was that if a nation were simultaneously a major military power and suffered extensively from boycotts/sanctions, it might find it far more profitable to launch an attack against the power(s) backing the trade cutoff than to repudiate its own past and successful expansionism. Indeed, as we have seen from the evidence presented in this volume, that scenario perfectly reflects the events that led up to the Pacific war of 1941-1945.

In regard to active involvement in the European war that began in 1939, President Roosevelt was clearly ahead of public opinion in his policy of promoting intervention. In regard to a more militant anti–Japanese policy, it has been suggested, with considerable justice, that the president was lagging behind the consensus: the public was prepared to take stern economic measures before he was.[1] A Gallup Poll in the summer of 1941 found that almost two-thirds of the American people (62 percent) wished the government to take action "to keep Japan from becoming more powerful, even if this means risking war." Even the isolationist Midwest mustered majority sentiment behind that proposal.[2]

Hence, FDR was not deceitfully imposing upon an unsuspecting populace a policy that went against its own inclinations. That in no way changed the fact that such a course would be, to use Gallup's expression, "risking war." From the American perspective, such measures were viewed (rightly, we might add) as retaliation for Japanese militarism.

No matter how emotionally satisfying or how well deserved a punitive policy may be, prudence requires the careful consideration of other considerations as well. *In self-interest it may be desirable to avoid implementing fully deserved retaliation.* (Whether Japanese actions "fully deserved" retaliation or simply "deserved" it is not a matter we need resolve. Aggressors nearly always deserve punishment, but whether this nation should be the one to inflict it is, of course, an entirely different question.)

For one thing, in evaluating the desirability of a proposed retaliation, one must intellectually step back from the fray and put oneself in the other people's shoes: How will they interpret the action? Will it actually cause them to back away or will it provoke their pride to stubborn resistance? Will they be able to understand the reasonableness of the basis on which we act or will it sound far too much like a gratuitous insult that we would never accept if it were applied to us?

Consistency in application plays an obvious key role in how other powers will evaluate one's sincerity. Here the United States had an automatic credibility dilemma. Britain had a well-established policy of colonialism and a major Commonwealth aligned with it. Although elements of the Commonwealth had already forged their independence from the mother country (Australia and Canada, for example), most were still colonies and there was every indication they would retain that status indefinitely. Although American imperialism was far more restrained and the Philippines had even been pledged it would gain independence in less than a decade, the American bases were likely to be retained. (And they represented potential military bases for assault upon Japan.)

From the Japanese standpoint, who were these foreign powers to lecture them on the evils of colonialism? The American government found itself in a philosophical dead end; on the one hand, it viewed British imperialism with great skepticism, while on the other hand, it dared not say anything that would even potentially undermine British Empire support for the European war. Yet without such a balanced policy of open opposition, it would be naturally tempting for the Nippon regime to view American protests as racist imperialism.

Furthermore, interests were at stake which were viewed as essential ones: the concept of national self-sufficiency was far from a radical one at that time. There was no way Japan seemed able to obtain such a position unless through an empire. (Neocolonialism—economic imperialism—would have been an alternative but at this stage the concept had not evolved nor had its potential for effective dominance while removing the public relations burden of overt control become apparent).

In light of such facts, to the degree the American economic boycott was successful, it tempted the Japanese to strike out at their oppressor who seemed so determined to deny them the international prestige and empire it seemed to concede so willingly to the British. Since the Japanese were of a different color and there had been decades of racialist anti–Japanese bias in the United States, a sense of racial injustice and oppression was stirred into the intellectual/ideological ferment of the time. Indeed, when perceived in terms of surrender or military counterattack, the American economic stranglehold seemed to require a military response. Had not the Americans prolonged the negotiations and refused to commit themselves to any diplomatic solution that was acceptable to Japanese interests?

To us today, a half-century later, all this may seem grotesque exaggeration if not paranoia, but it remains the kind of picture the Japanese had at the time and the frame of reference within which they worked. In light of this situation, strong military counteraction was a highly probable result.

And the American government was fully aware of it. That has been documented at length. The government's own analyses anticipated this outcome. Its own analyses (and those decrypted from Japanese sources) confirmed the devastation that was being wreaked upon the Japanese economy. If the United States had been on the receiving end, it would have been just as willing to stake everything on a risky military enterprise to reverse the balance of power. Hence, no matter from what perspective one views the situation, war was the ultimate stake and war was the certain result once a mutually acceptable diplomatic settlement became impossible.

Yet there have always been those who have sought to deny this close linkage between embargo and war that the psychology of the period, the close chronological linkage of the two events, and the success of the trade freeze argue so strenuously.

Perhaps least defensible is the insistence of Richard Overy and Andrew Wheatcroft that the asset freeze and trade termination "was not a stranglehold." They prefer to say, simply, that "the noose was tightening."[3] With a 60–75 percent cut in trade and a 90 percent reduction in petroleum, how long does it take for a "noose [that] was tightening" to become a "stranglehold"? Does it only become one at the final deathrattle? Japan had time left, it is true, but only a few months in which military action could credibly be launched. With its economy dying around Japan, what else could the Western action be called but a "stranglehold"?

Gordon W. Prange, perhaps the most well-versed researcher on Pearl Harbor, insists that "The final break in Japanese-American relations cannot be laid upon the sanctions of the summer of 1941." He contends that "In actual fact, the Japanese neither used the sanctions as an excuse to declare war nor did they sever diplomatic relations."[4] The Japanese did warn, however, officially and unofficially, of the dangerous situation produced by the embargo. Indeed, who can read some of their statements that have been presented throughout this book without concluding that the war option was a very viable one in their minds, however discreetly they might allude to it? The fact that so many Americans also recognized the war-making potential of the trade freeze (as previously documented) bears witness that there was considerable Western alertness to the danger of a Japanese response. Were they perceiving a fictitious, nonexistent danger?

Looking back from a perspective of several decades, Joseph Alsop, a respected journalist of that period, also contends that the economic factor was not decisive: "To begin with, it is obviously incorrect to suppose that either American diplomacy or American economic sanctions had very much to do with the Japanese decision to make war on the United States. ... What really mattered in this pre–Pearl Harbor period ... was not what the United States and Japan said or even did to one another. What really mattered, rather, was how each country saw its own situation and interpreted the purposes of the other."[5] Alsop argues that barring direct action against the territories of the United States, there was virtually nothing the president could do militarily in the Pacific. Hence the potentially powerful offensive bases in the Philippines and Hawaii were "politically neutralized by American domestic politics."[6] The Japanese only saw the potential of these bases and overlooked the presidential inability to use them. Due to this oversight, according to Alsop, the Japanese provided the president with the only viable excuse for American involvement in a Far Eastern war, explicit aggression against United States forces.

Although arguably valid as far as it goes (its validity is limited to FDR's ability to respond militarily to an assault on *British* Far Eastern possessions), this analysis overlooks the pivotal role of economic restrictions in compelling the Japanese to choose between a rollback of their colonialism and an attack upon American territories. The Japanese would not have made their misjudgment of the "need" to attack the Americans at Hawaii unless their economic situation had been so degraded that some kind of military solution seemed imperative.

Furthermore, there seems to be no question that Roosevelt was seeking a way around his "inability" to act decisively if the Japanese committed further aggression that did not involve American losses. British resources were already pushed to the breaking point. There was no way possible that Britain could have successfully coped with a Pacific conflict in addition to the immense war load it was already carrying in the Atlantic and Mediterranean.[7] If the Japanese had chosen a British-only strategy, what would have been the result if Roosevelt had still found a means to justify an intervention (such as inviting attack on some prearranged "losable" American war vessel)?[8] In such a case, would not later historians have critiqued the Japanese for not acting against the even greater potential danger from Hawaii and the Philippines?

Japan made a conscious decision to protect itself against both the immediate and the longer term threat posed by the two American territories. From the standpoint of the attacked, we Americans naturally deeply resented the Pearl Harbor attack (far more because it was successful than because it was attempted). From the Japanese standpoint, the attack seemed essential in order to neutralize American military power (at least

Disavowing the Linkage Between Embargo and War 207

in the short term) and American economic clout (in the long term). Both calculations proved ill-founded, but with a little more foresight and luck, the Japanese might just have been able to accomplish their goal.

In his study of Churchill's role as a military leader, Ronald Lewin at first leaves the impression that he is taking an antilinkage approach: "All the protestations and proposals, therefore, all the warnings and sanctions initiated by Washington in 1941—even the economic embargo imposed in July—lacked final authority (and in Tokyo were seen to lack it) because Roosevelt was unable to threaten or even to hint at the ultimate sanction of war."[9]

Unlike Alsop or Prange, Lewin quickly retreats from the ramifications of this attitude, backing off from delinking the embargo and the decision to go to war:

> [Churchill] failed to penetrate the mentality of his enemy and to realize that the Japanese were in a box from which they must inevitably strike out. The containment was psychological and economic. If the price of accommodation exacted by the United States was to be a surrender of the Japanese strangle-hold on China, it was inconceivable that the High Command in Tokyo would accept the consequent loss of face. *And unless the economic embargoes imposed in July by America, Britain and Holland were lifted, the Japanese must fight or wither* [emphasis added].[10]

When United States government officials touched on the matter at all, how did they handle it? What might be called the "official method" (due to its State Department source) was that of considering the embargo in isolation. Instead of considering the untenable economic and military situation it put the Japanese government in, this method puts the exclusive stress upon the embargo as a justifiable act of reaction to the Japanese takeover of Indochina:

> President Roosevelt discussed this question [of petroleum exports] in an informal talk at the While House on July 24. He explained the essential necessity, from the standpoint of our own defense and of that of Great Britain, of preventing war from breaking out in the South Pacific. He said that if oil supplies from the United States had been cut off, Japan probably would have attacked the Netherlands Indies to obtain oil and war would have resulted; that the policy of the United States in allowing oil to go to Japan had succeeded in keeping war out of the South Pacific, "for our own good, for the good of the defense of Great Britain, and the freedom of the seas."

>> Freezing of Japanese Assets in the United States

> The Japanese move into southern Indochina, in disregard of the entire spirit underlying the exploratory conversations, was unmistakably an overt and flagrant act of aggression. Japan's constant expansion of its military position in the southwest Pacific had already substantially imperiled the security of the United States along with that of other powers. By this further expansion of its field of aggression Japan virtually completed the encirclement of the Philippine Islands and placed its armed forces within striking distance of vital trade routes. This created a situation in which the risk of war became so great that the United States and other

countries concerned were confronted no longer with the question of avoiding such risk but from then on with the problem of preventing a complete undermining of their security. In these circumstances the Government of the United States decided at that point as did certain other governments especially concerned, that discontinuance of trade with Japan had become an appropriate, warranted, and necessary step—as a warning to Japan and as a measure of self-defense.

On July 26, 1941, President Roosevelt issued an Executive order freezing Japanese assets in the United States. This order brought under control of the Government all financial and import and export trade transactions in which Japanese interests were involved, and the effect of this was to bring about very soon the virtual cessation of trade between the United States and Japan.[11]

Japan's action in Indochina was indeed an "act of aggression" though neither as "overt" nor as "flagrant" as many other such imperialistic actions in the history of the world. On paper at least, the French had voluntarily agreed to the admission of Japanese forces; a formal agreement between the two powers was signed. This hardly disguised the fact that the French were faced with an either/or situation: either negotiate those terms the Japanese demanded or have the Japanese seize control by force of arms, with all the additional humiliation that would have bestowed upon an already downtrodden France. In all fairness, however, one must ask whether the French expansion into this part of the world was itself much short of the same thing: weaker power(s) yielding to the demand of a stronger external nation. If it was moral for the French to act as imperialists in Indochina, why was it any worse for the Japanese to do the same? Both were playing the empire-building game in defiance of preexisting regimes.

Dominant opinion in both Britain and France obviously saw nothing immoral in having a globe-circling empire, provided it was their own. In the United States, however, anti-imperialism had already become dominant. In an action which neither the British, French, nor Japanese colonialists could fully comprehend, the United States had already announced a time table for granting the Philippines its independence. The colonialism practiced by the two European powers was clearly frowned upon by the top American leadership, opposition that FDR handled quite gingerly in light of Churchill's determination to preserve his own nation's empire.

In spite of the dramatic shift of American opinion against empire-building, no one in authority was about to demand that the Europeans roll back their empires, as opinion demanded of Japan. Nor was anyone about to suggest a general freezing of the colonies of all powers. Not only would such a demand have been promptly rejected, it would have wrecked any chance of maintaining a British-American front against the Tripartite powers. In light of Americans' understandable unwillingness to apply the new anticolonialist sentiments uniformly, the Japanese could hardly see in American moral lectures anything but the gravest inconsistency, if not outright hypocrisy.

Disavowing the Linkage Between Embargo and War 209

The State Department insisted that "Japan's constant expansion of its military position in the southwest Pacific had already substantially imperiled the security of the United States along with that of other powers." One could clearly recognize a potential danger to Western colonies in that part of the world, but unless one defines "national security" as including possession of foreign colonies—themselves secured by chicanery and military force—one has difficulty embracing this argument. One would be even more hard-pressed to define such losses as threats to the existence or independence of the mother lands themselves.

One could more meaningfully point to the vital resources of the region (such as rubber) and how such losses would harm the ability of Britain and the United States to defend themselves. Such losses would obviously hurt, but it should be remembered that even after the loss of these resources, those two powers managed to defeat decisively both the Germans and the Japanese within four years. When such harm was to be inflicted upon the Western powers, such actions were abhorrent. On the other hand, when even a vaster trade loss was imposed upon the Japanese, they were supposed to bear such policies quietly and, preferably, reverse their existing national policies. Are we dealing here with legitimate argumentation or the age-old question of whose ox is being gored? Furthermore, from a military standpoint, just how dangerous was this latest Japanese move? Had it dramatically increased their potential for military mischief or were they actually in a very exposed position themselves? The latter scenario deserves examination, as it was raised at the time.

Although the Japanese could use Indochina fairly safely as a launching point for the takeover of Thailand, Major George Fielding Eliot wrote in July 1941 that it would be extremely hazardous for them to launch more extensive operations southward (that is, into the areas the United States was most concerned with). In spite of Japan's occupation of much of China, he noted: "the communications of the Japanese forces in Indo-China are not land communications, but maritime. These forces are wholly dependent, therefore, on the ability of the Japanese navy to maintain command of the route from the nearest point in Japan—let us say the naval base at Sasebo—to Saigon. This is a distance of 2,000 nautical miles, or say eight days' steaming for average supply ships and transports."[12]

Throughout such resupply journeys, Japanese vessels would be subject to vigorous assault from British bases in Hong Kong and American bases in Manila, both located some nine hundred nautical miles from the same Indochinese point.

Hence, even though the Japanese expansion was certainly a cause of concern, the Japanese themselves were in an exposed position, in a location where forceful Western opposition should have been able to hinder or stop the effective utilization of Japanese power. Of course this perception represents the perspective available to those at the time and does not reflect our postevent recognition that the Japanese were able to sweep away those bases that could have been used against Indochina. That they could have done so—especially so quickly and with such minimal cost—was unimaginable to contemporaries. In fact, even today one should remain horrified that the Japanese were able to accomplish so much, so quickly, so efficiently. Even so, what was known in 1941 or could reasonably have been known at the time should be the standard of evaluation. Using that standard, was not the danger posed by the Indochinese expansion far less significant than Roosevelt desired Americans to believe? This expansion posed a danger to the Western powers, but it could create problems for Japan as well.

One final State Department observation deserves comment: "By this further expansion of its field of aggression Japan virtually completed the encirclement of the Philippine Islands and placed its armed forces within striking distance of vital trade routes." Since the Japanese already had the northern half of Indochina in their hands in 1940, could not almost the identical statement have been made a year earlier? Had the facts really changed all that much or had there been a decision not to put up with those facts any longer?

Furthermore, a look at the map would be helpful. Japan is located to the north of the Philippines, Indochina to the west, the Dutch East Indies, New Guinea, and Australia to the south, and Hawaii to the east. Is this "encirclement" in the normal sense of the term? Perhaps the State Department author had in mind some of the mandated islands Japan administered on behalf of the League of Nations as constituting part of the encirclement, making it more complete than it would at first sound. That these islands had much power to isolate the Philippines seems unlikely; they clearly played no significant role in the actual conquest that occurred in 1942.

Saying that Japan's occupation of Indochina (to the west of the Philippines) put Japan "within striking distance of vital trade routes" doesn't make a whole lot of sense in regard to United States shipping routes. The geographical relationship of Indochina to the Philippines would suggest that British trade routes were under consideration. If this is what was really in the policymakers' minds (and it appears to be the only way to make a viable argument out of their reference to trade), then it also constitutes an admission that the United States undertook a potentially war-making action (the total embargo) not out of its own economic interests but to protect those of Britain. The pro–British slant of official government policy adds a certain additional credibility to this conclusion. On the other hand, the administration could hardly state explicitly that it was undertaking a dangerous policy to assist a nation that perhaps an outright majority did not want to risk war for; such an admission would have fueled speculation that

American Oriental policy was being shaped to get the nation into a war in the Pacific.

As debaters' points go, the government case is an effective one. This is only because it carefully disguises the apparent government desire to assist the British and does not discuss how the embargo turned a potential war situation into one where Japan felt no choice but to launch a retaliatory war.

The American ambassador, Joseph C. Grew, had a lot to say relevant to the question of the embargo and the outbreak of the conflict, and he provides a valuable additional example of how an intelligent government official attempted to handle the question without conceding at least partial American responsibility for the war. In an early August 1941 entry in his diary, he wrote of the results of the tightened trade freeze: "The vicious circle of reprisals and counter reprisals is on. . . . Unless radical surprises occur in the world, it is difficult to see how the momentum of the downgrade movement can be arrested, or how far it will go. The obvious conclusion is eventual war."[13]

In postwar testimony before Congress, the ambassador presented a far more optimistic interpretation of the embargo. He insisted that it had acted as a restraining influence upon Japanese foreign policy.[14] Grew appealed to a September 29, 1941, telegram that he had dispatched to the State Department. After reading a publicly available paraphrase of the text (he did not have the original available), Congressman Frank B. Keefe from Wisconsin challenged the relevance of the citation to the point Grew was making: "I must confess that the reading does not in any sense answer the question which I asked you. I would like to have you point out, if you can, either from this message or from any fact within your knowledge any specific fact which demonstrates that Japan was deterred in its militaristic policy of expansion and aggression by the imposition of economic sanctions."[15]

At this point Grew fell back upon what impact he thought the ending of trade had upon the prime minister, Prince Konoye. In spite of "his appalling record," Grew was convinced that Konoye was well aware of America's potential. Konoye was "intelligent enough, I think, to see the handwriting on the wall and to realize that Japan had got herself into an exceedingly dangerous position and that there were only two ways out: One way was by war and the other way out was an arrangement with the United States."[16]

Congressman Keefe listened and then challenged Grew: "Well, now, can you point to one single objective of the Japanese war lords or militarists who were in control that they receded from or refrained from carrying out as a result of the imposition of economic sanctions?"[17] In answer, Grew appealed to a September 6, 1941, conversation with the prime minister in which Konoye expressed interest in having a face-to-face meeting with President Roosevelt. Keefe interrupted again:

Mr. Keefe. For the purpose of getting a clear answer may I state this at this time: During the summer of 1941 and in the fall and especially in September Japan steadily continued her march to the south and her infiltration into Indo-China.
Mr. Grew. That is absolutely true.
Mr. Keefe. Which caused you and the State Department and the President growing concern.
Mr. Grew. Certainly.
Mr. Keefe. So that the imposition of economic sanctions did not stop Japan from going on down into Indo-China.
Mr. Grew. It did not. It had not up to that point. The question arose at that time whether at the point I am now speaking about it was going to be possible to stop that expansion.[18]

Congressman Keefe pointed out that as early as January of 1941 the Japanese began discussions about an attack upon the United States. Grew dismissed these discussions as what we today would call contingency planning. Keefe reminded him that throughout this period the Japanese "continued right on with their aggressive war in China, and with the infiltration into Indochina and down to the south, one step at a time."[19]

Mr. Grew. That is correct.
Mr. Keefe. Now, what I have asked you to do is to point out, if you will, to me, any particular act that was stopped or retarded as the result of the imposition of these economic sanctions.
Mr. Grew. I cannot point out any specific act that actually did stop that procedure, but I can point out, as is perfectly clear on the record, that we in Tokyo at that time felt if the Prime Minister and the President of the United States could meet face to face, it might be possible to put a stop to that movement.
Mr. Keefe. It was all guesswork?
Mr. Grew. We could not tell, but that is my answer to your question.
Mr. Keefe. That was an expression of a pious hope that would take place, was it not?.
Mr. Grew. That was an expression of a pious hope....[20]

Even Grew conceded that this proposed meeting was but a fleeting window of opportunity and that it vanished when Tojo took over. "He [Tojo] was not deterred by any economic sanctions, was he, after he came into control?" inquired the congressman from Wisconsin. "Not for a moment." At this point, Keefe received the admission he was apparently seeking. "No; and nobody was deterred before he came into control, so far as their actions disclosed?" Keefe asked. Grew replied, "That is correct."[21]

In all fairness to the ambassador, things might have yet had a peaceful resolution. With greater flexibility on the part of the United States either in compromising with Japan on her Asian continent conquests or in permitting limited exports while prolonging negotiations beyond the point where even the most optimistic militarist would have conceived war as a reasonable option, the administration would have been able to look back upon the embargo as playing the decisive role in forcing Japan to reconsider and revise her policy. In such a case, immense credit would have legitimately gone to the Roosevelt administration for its dramatic foreign policy victory. Hence it is only fair that the blame also be aportioned to it for the failure of that policy to accomplish a peaceful outcome. In essence, Japan was provided only two options: surrender or war. Roosevelt gambled that she would choose some form of the first. His miscalculation resulted in the very Pacific war he desired to avoid.

The ambassador preferred to view a Japanese policy reversal as just as possible as open conflict if not more so, thereby removing any potential stigma from the embargo as being the cause of the war or at least a major cause of it. The Army Pearl Harbor Board pressed him upon this point:

> Colonel Toulmin. Well, at the beginning of the enforcement of the embargoes you were in the last stage of your relationships, were you not, because if you were not successful with such embargoes you only had one other alternative; two alternatives: either to withdraw them or to precipitate a conflict. Is that correct?
> Mr. Grew. No, I don't think we argued it that way. Of course, there were not only the freezing order and the denunciation of our treaty and commerce with Japan, which had taken place considerably earlier; several steps one after another. ...
> Colonel Toulmin. Well, I am interested in the effect on Japan, as you observed it, the factual matter as far as you determined it to be a fact, when the embargoes had become sufficiently severe to precipitate a critical issue between Japan and the United States.
> Mr. Grew. Yes; the embargoes, I will say, especially plus the freezing order, did undoubtedly greatly increase the tension at that time.
> Colonel Toulmin. And about what time did that reach its peak?
> Mr. Grew. It was progressive, and continuously progressive up to the end.
> Colonel Toulmin. Increasingly as you applied each sanction one after the other?
> Mr. Grew. I would say so, yes.
> Colonel Toulmin. And the effects became apparent?
> Mr. Grew. The effects became apparent.
> Colonel Toulmin. So that the relationship under the economic sanctions was gradually narrowing to a point of some decision by one government or the other that something must be done about it; isn't that a fair statement?
> Mr. Grew. Yes, I would say that is a fair statement, Colonel. I do not mean to say, when you say something had to be done about it, that it had to be war, because there were other things to do about it besides war. The Japanese at that time could have taken steps to meet some of our views in connection with their expansion through the Far East. They could readily have done that, and if they had done that we might, for our part, have relaxed some of the economic pressure which we were placing on them. I think that would have been a perfectly logical thing to have happened, but it didn't happen.[22]

That the Japanese could have reversed their foreign policy, is, of course, quite true. There was, however, much to be said against this being a realistic possibility. The army radicals constituted a hard core of opposition to any such change. It was extremely easy for those opposed to the American approach to argue that the Americans were demanding nothing short of a disguised surrender. Indeed, since American policy called for the giving up of most if not all of Japan's foreign conquests, this was a quite comprehensible accusation. In addition, a foreign policy, once adopted, has the power of inertia behind it: it requires a conscious act to alter it. For all these reasons, to picture a Japanese foreign policy reversal as equally likely as war seems optimistic rationalization at the best. As we have previously conceded, in spite of all such obstacles it might have happened, but that is yielding little when one considers the degree of Japanese "face" committed to its then existing foreign policy course and the persistent unwillingness of the American side to make an offer that overcame Japanese wariness.

The best way (and perhaps the only way) to have overcome these obstacles would have been to somehow convincingly show that Japan's possession of its foreign territories was dangerous to its own long-range prosperity and security. The United States did make efforts in this direction, but with the imposition of a total embargo, the "coercive" element drowned out the appeal to enlightened self-interest. An ongoing realistic, pragmatic critique might have accomplished what a retributive "moralistic" policy could not. It would have allowed the Japanese the option of forging a policy of limited (or total) withdrawal from China in terms of their own interests rather than in terms of "giving in" to the Americans. Combined with precise, ironclad guarantees of foreign supplies of needed resources, this could have made the critical difference. Perhaps such an approach would have failed to maintain the peace (would the British have given up their empire on such terms?); all we know for certain is that the embargo failed to preserve the peace.

Furthermore, the most that Grew could offer in the Army Pearl Harbor Board investigation is that if the Japanese had "taken steps to meet some of our views in connection with their expansion" then "we might, for our part, have relaxed some of the economic pressure which we were placing on them." It would be hard for the cynical Japanese not to read words such as these in light of long-established Western racism (carefully overlooking similar elements in its own culture) and to interpret Grew's vague remarks to mean, "If you are good little children we might, perhaps, just let you have a little snack." This is the rhetoric of the powerful to the inferior and a dagger in the pride of an Oriental nation vying for continued world-power status.

NOTES

1. William L. Langer and S. Everett Gleason, *The Undeclared War: 1940–1941* (New York: Harper & Bros., 1953), 655.

2. William K. Klingman, *1941: Our Lives in a World on the Edge* (New York: Harper & Row, 1988), 345.

Disavowing the Linkage Between Embargo and War   215

3. Richard Overy and Andrew Wheatcroft, *The Road to War* (London: Macmillan, 1989), 252. Perhaps the two authors were thinking of the immediate situation in July rather than the results during the coming months.

4. Gordon W. Prange, with Donald M. Goldstein and Katherine V. Dillon, *Pearl Harbor: The Verdict of History* (New York: McGraw Hill, 1986), 153.

5. Joseph Alsop, *FDR: A Centenary Remembrance* (New York: Viking, 1982), 233. Although I dissent from Alsop on this point, this volume should be recommended to all who wish to better understand the interwar period in America. For those of us who were not adults at the time, it provides an invaluable "feel" for how life went on (at least in politics and in the nation's capital) during that period.

6. Ibid., 234.

7. Walter Millis, *This Is Pearl! The United States and Japan—1941* (New York: William Morrow, 1947), 115. Japanese aggression against British colonies would almost certainly have had catastrophic effects on any prospect of a successful conclusion to the European war, not to mention the horror of a calamitous withdrawal from the Pacific under fire. As Millis wrote shortly after the war:

> We had staked our world policy and our national future on the success of one side in the struggle [in Europe]. The loss to that side of Australia and New Zealand, of all the Far Eastern colonies and resources and very probably of India as well, the sacrifice of China and the doubtless prompt reappearance of an enormously strengthened Japan on Russia's Siberian flank, would have constituted a blow too crushing both materially and morally for our friends to have survived.

8. For example, on December 2, 1941, President Roosevelt ordered the commander of the Asiatic fleet to send three small chartered vessels—armed and with military personnel—for a reconnaisance mission off the Indochina coast. (For a photographic reproduction of the order, see Layton, *"And I Was There,"* 525). This has sometimes been called "the fishbait mission" and been considered a method of provoking a Japanese military response that would justify American military intervention against Japan. Layton is more restrained: "The sacrificial nature of the operation ... which required expendable vessels with Filipino crews" was carried out in order to assure that Filipino opinion would back the American side in the war with Japan (247). In my judgment both Layton and the more extreme conspiratorialists err, but that does not change the fact that an incident could have been arranged if so desired. The Japanese record of finding the needed incidents to excuse their expansionism in China would surely have alerted them to the fact that a suitable excuse could be manufactured to justify an American intervention even if only the British and Dutch were attacked.

9. Ronald Lewin, *Churchill As Warlord* (London: B. T. Batsford, 1973), 120.

10. Ibid., 121–22.

11. Department of State, *Peace and War: United States Foreign Policy, 1931–1941* (Washington, D.C.: U.S. Government Printing Office, 1943), 126–27. This comes from the expository analysis of American policy found in the first section of the book. The numbered extracts (which we have quoted from a number of times) constitute the remainder of the volume.

12. "Advantages Scant in Japanese Move," *Los Angeles Times*, 27 July 1941, I-5.

13. Herbert Feis, *The Road to Pearl Harbor: The Coming of War between the United States and Japan* (1950; reprint Princeton: Princeton Paperback Edition, 1971), 248.

14. Joint Committee on the Investigation of the Pearl Harbor Attack, *Pearl Harbor Attack, Hearings Before the Joint Committee on the Investigation of the Pearl Harbor Attack* (Washington, D.C.: U.S. Government Printing Office, 1946). See especially 2/710–12.

15. *PHA* 2/712.

16. Ibid.
17. Ibid.
18. *PHA* 2/713.
19. *PHA* 2/714.
20. Ibid.
21. *PHA* 2/720.
22. *PHA* 29/2152–53.

CONCLUSION

This study has documented how rightful resentment of an Oriental imperialism so affected this nation's leadership that it embraced a policy of total boycott that left the Japanese little choice (from their standpoint) but to launch a preemptive strike against their tormenter. As a result, the United States did gain the opportunity to confront Germany openly on the battlefield. But that was virtually inevitable anyway, and a two-ocean war created the dangerous risk of misallocating resources between the two theaters of war.

Perhaps war would have occurred the following year anyway. The Japanese could have read American willingness to continue trade as evidence that there was precious little they could do to provoke a dangerous reaction. Yet the "limited" embargo had grown markedly stronger. Even without the official asset freeze, no new petroleum licenses had been issued for months. In light of such tangible signs of American anger, it seems unlikely that a policy of continued limited trade would have led to any such misbegotten conclusions—but even if it had, a delay of even six months would have been immensely beneficial. The United States would have been much better prepared militarily. The Philippines would have been sufficiently reinforced to the point that the dramatic Japanese sweep southwards would either have been gravely hampered or permanently halted without the fall of the Philippines.

That is a pessimistic conclusion but a realistic one. The optimistic conclusion is that war might not have occurred at all. With Japan in continued occupation of part of China, would a Maoist revolution have been possible at all? And if the Maoist revolution had been avoided, our history would have eliminated two major wars (and their nonvictories, if not outright defeats) in Korea and Vietnam. Instead of looking back upon a blood-drenched Pacific during the second half of the twentieth century, we could be looking back upon an incredible half-century of American peace.

True, there would have been a Japanese militarist regime still in power. But how could that have been much worse for China than the Maoist ideological straitjacket worn for so many years by that country?

Today we still speak of the possibility that a "pragmatic" Communist regime in China may one day evolve toward Western-style democracy. Is there some kind of ideological rigidity in our own thinking that forbids us to grant the possibility of that having occurred in a Japanese system that dominated China? Japan in the thirties had already created some of the trappings of democracy, however much the substance may have been bent or misunderstood. Yet that is far more than the Maoist successors in China have yet permitted.

Even if Mao had been able to come to power, that would still have left Japan in control of Korea and Indochina, as well as Manchuria. Hence any Korean war would have been a Sino-Japanese conflict, as would any Indochinese war. In such a scenario the United States would have been a mere bystander watching two dictatorships bleed each other. As in the Iraq-Iran War of the 1980s, two unsavory foes would have dueled, and the United States would have had no need to intervene.

All of these are "might have beens." Which one accepts (if any) is unimportant, but all constitute reasonable, conceivable, rational alternative histories if the total boycott had not been utilized. What is not in the category of speculation is the fact that the United States knowingly and intentionally imposed economic strangulation upon Japan. Furthermore, it persisted in that policy while being aware that the Japanese economy was being wrecked to a degree that would have been intolerable if this nation had been on the receiving end. President Roosevelt had even publicly stated that the embargo had not previously been imposed because of the belief that it would result in Japan conquering the Dutch East Indies. What had happened in the few days between this remark and his imposition of the asset freeze? Not one single thing had changed in the statements, attitudes, or policies of the Japanese leadership. Japan was just as likely to strike out militarily as it had been forty-eight or seventy-two hours earlier.

What *had* altered was the attitude of the American leadership. It was no longer willing to avoid playing its most volatile card (a total embargo) or to accept unpleasant realities (the expansion of the Japanese empire) as it had in the past. Its sense of exasperation had become stronger than its realistic prediction of upcoming war. The administration embraced a policy knowing full well its probable result. Hence, in a very real sense, the Pacific war was caused by the United States launching a policy of economic destruction against the Japanese nation.

As has been repeatedly stressed, if the United States had been on the receiving end of such treatment, war would have clearly been the result. Indeed, few Americans would have felt any guilt over "firing the first shot" and little compunction would have been attached to initiating the war with a "sneak attack." Yet because Japan was the culprit who did these things, it has borne the sole blame when, in reality, at least a major proportion of the responsibility must be placed upon other shoulders as well.

Whether one calls the American-led total boycott a "co-cause" of the Pacific war or "the" cause makes little practical difference. In either case, without the boycott the war would not have erupted when it did, if it had at all. Thousands of American servicemen died needlessly. In this we have an abiding lesson of Pearl Harbor that has been little noticed: Never inflict upon another major military power a policy which would cause you yourself to go to war unless you are fully prepared to engage that power militarily. And don't be surprised that if they do decide to retaliate, that they seek out a time and a place that inflicts the maximum harm and humiliation upon your cause.

BIBLIOGRAPHY

Primary Sources: Books

Cadogan, Sir Alexander. *The Diaries of Sir Alexander Cadogan, O.M., O.M., 1938–1945.* Edited by Fred L. Israel. Lincoln: University of Nebraska Press, 1966.
Clapper, Raymond. *Watching the World.* Edited by Mrs. Raymond Clapper. New York: McGraw-Hill/Whittlesey House, 1944.
Emmerson, John K. *The Japanese Thread: A Life in the U.S. Foreign Service.* New York: Holt, Rinehart and Winston, 1978.
Holmes, W. J. *Double-Edged Secrets: U.S. Naval Intelligence in the Pacific during World War II.* Annapolis, Md.: Naval Institute Press, 1979.
Hull, Cordell. *The Memoirs of Cordell Hull.* Vol. 2. New York: Macmillan, 1948.
Ickes, Harold L. *The Secret Diary of Harold L. Ickes.* Vol. 3, *The Lowering Clouds, 1939–1941.* New York: Simon and Schuster, 1954.
Ike, Nobutake, trans. and ed. *Japan's Decision for War: Records of the 1941 Policy Conferences.* Stanford, Calif.: Stanford University Press, 1967.
Land, Emory S. *Winning the War with Ships.* New York: Robert M. McBride, 1958.
Layton, Edwin T., with Roger Pineau and John Costello. *"And I Was There": Pearl Harbor and Midway—Breaking the Secrets.* New York: William Morrow, 1985.
Long, Breckinridge. *The War Diary of Breckinridge Long: Selections from the Years 1939–1944.* Edited by Fred L. Israel. Lincoln: University of Nebraska Press, 1966.
Marshall, George C. *The Papers of George Catlett Marshall.* Edited by Larry I. Bland. Vol. 2, *"We Cannot Delay," July 1, 1939–December 6, 1941.* Baltimore: Johns Hopkins University Press, 1986.
[Morgenthau, Henry J., Jr.] Internal Security Subcommittee of the Committee on the Judiciary, United States Senate. *Morgenthau Diary (China).* Vol. 1. Washington, D.C.: U.S. Government Printing Office, 1965.
Richardson, James O. *On the Treadmill to Pearl Harbor: The Memoirs of Admiral James O. Richardson.* Washington, D.C.: U.S. Government Printing Office, 1973.
Roosevelt, Franklin D. *The Public Papers and Addresses of Franklin D. Roosevelt.*

Edited by Samuel I. Roseman. 1941 volume: *The Call to Battle Stations.* New York: Harper & Bros., 1950.

Ugaki, [Admiral] Matome. *Fading Victory: The Diary of Admiral Matome Ugaki.* Translated by Masataka Chiga. Edited by Donald M. Goldstein and Katherine V. Dillon. Pittsburgh, Penn.: University of Pittsburgh Press, 1991.

van Mook, H. J. *The Netherlands Indies and Japan: Their Relations, 1940–1941.* London: George Allen & Unwin, 1944.

Welles, Sumner. *Seven Decisions That Changed History.* New York: Harper & Bros., 1950, 1951.

Primary Sources: Contemporary U.S. and British Government Records and Studies

British

[Halifax, Lord, a.k.a., Edward Frederick Lindley Wood.] *Confidential Dispatches: Analyses of America by the British Ambassador, 1939–1945.* Evanston, Ill.: New University Press, 1974. Reprint with new introduction. London: H.M.S.O., 1975.

United States

Anderberg, Edward, Jr. *The Overseas Trade of Japan Proper, Including a Summary of the Prewar Trade and a Discussion of Postwar Problems* (prepared for the Foreign Economic Administration of the United States Tariff Commission, October 1945). Reprint. Ann Arbor, Mich.: University Microfilms, 1980.

Department of Commerce. *Economic Review of Foreign Countries: 1939 and Early 1940.* Economic Series No. 9. Washington, D.C.: U.S. Government Printing Office, 1941.

––––––––. *Foreign Commerce and Navigation of the United States.* Washington, D.C.: U.S. Government Printing Office. Annual volumes 1935–1941.

Department of State. *Peace and War: United States Foreign Policy, 1931–1941.* Washington, D.C.: U.S. Government Printing Office, 1943.

Joint Committee on the Investigation of the Pearl Harbor Attack. *Pearl Harbor Attack: Hearings Before the Joint Committee on the Investigation of the Pearl Harbor Attack.* Washington, D.C.: U.S. Government Printing Office, 1946. 39 volumes, including the text of earlier governmental investigations. A fortieth volume provides the panel's conclusions.

"Records of the U.S. Department of State Relating to the Internal Affairs of Japan, 1940–1944 – Decimal File 894." Scholarly Resources Microfilms: 20 reels.

Strategic Bombing Survey. *Japan's Struggle to End the War.* Washington, D.C.: U.S. Government Printing Office, 1946.

––––––––. *Oil in Japan's War.* Washington, D.C.: U.S. Government Printing Office, 1946.

———. *Oil in Japan's War (Appendix)*. Washington, D.C.: U.S. Government Printing Office, 1946.
Tariff Commission. *Petroleum*. War Changes in Industry Series, Report no. 17. Washington, D.C.: U.S. Government Printing Office, 1946.
———. *United States Imports from Japan and Their Relation to the Defense Program and to the Economy of the Country*. Washington, D.C.: U.S. Government Printing Office, September 1941. (Includes a descriptive press release dated September 19, 1941.)

Secondary Sources: Books

Alsop, Joseph. *FDR: A Centenary Remembrance*. New York: Viking, 1988.
Anderson, Irvin H., Jr. *The Standard-Vacuum Oil Company and United States East Asian Policy, 1933–1941*. Princeton: Princeton University Press, 1975.
Asahi Shimbun [staff of]. *The Pacific Rivals: A Japanese View of Japanese-American Relations*. New York: Weatherhill/Asahi, 1972; English translation first edition, 1972.
Baker, Leonard. *Roosevelt and Pearl Harbor*. New York: Macmillan, 1970.
Baldwin, Hanson W. *World War One*. New York: Grove, 1962.
Barlow, Jeffrey G. "World War II: U.S. and Japanese Naval Strategies." In *Seapower and Strategy*, edited by Colin S. Gray and Roger W. Barnett. Annapolis, Md.: Naval Institute Press, 1989.
Barnhart, Michael A. *Japan Prepares for Total War: The Search for Economic Security, 1919–1941*. Ithaca, N.Y.: Cornell University Press, 1987.
Beard, Charles A. *President Roosevelt and the Coming of the War, 1941: A Study in Appearances and Realities*. New Haven: Yale University Press, 1948.
Bell, Roger J. *Unequal Allies: Australian-American Relations and the Pacific War*. Melbourne: Melbourne University Press, 1977.
Boyle, John Hunter. *China and Japan at War, 1937–1945: The Politics of Collaboration*. Stanford, Calif.: Stanford University Press, 1972.
Cohen, Jerome B. *Japan's Economy in War and Reconstruction*. Minneapolis: University of Minnesota Press, 1949.
Cole, Wayne S. *Roosevelt & the Isolationists, 1932–1945*. Lincoln: University of Nebraska Press, 1983.
Collier, Basil. *The War in the Far East, 1941–1945: A Military History*. New York: William Morrow, 1969.
Collier, Richard. *The Road to Pearl Harbor, 1941*. 1981. Reprint. New York: Bonanza Books, 1984.
Drummond, Donald F. *The Passing of American Neutrality, 1937–1941*. 1955. Reprint. New York: Greenwood, 1968.
Fanning, Leonard M. *American Oil Operations Abroad*. New York: McGraw-Hill, 1947.
Feis, Herbert. *The Road to Pearl Harbor: The Coming of the War between the United States and Japan*. 1950. Reprint. Princeton: Princeton Paperback Edition, 1971.

Fuller, J. F. C. *The Conduct of War, 1789–1961.* New Brunswick, N.J.: Rutgers University Press, 1961. Reprint. [N.p.]: Minerva Press, n.d.
Goraski, Robert, and Russell W. Freeburg. *Oil & War: How the Deadly Struggle for Fuel in WWII Meant Victory or Defeat.* New York: William Morrow, 1987.
Graebner, Norman A. "Hoover, Roosevelt, and the Japanese." In *Pearl Harbor as History: Japanese-American Relations, 1931–1941,* edited by Dorothy Berg and Shumpei Okamoto. New York: Columbia University Press, 1973.
Halliday, Jon. *Political History of Japanese Capitalism.* New York: Pantheon Books, 1975.
Hart, B. H. Liddell. *History of the Second World War.* 1970. Reprint. New York: Perigee Books, 1982.
Heinrichs, Waldo. *Threshold of War: Franklin D. Roosevelt and American Entry into World War Two.* New York: Oxford University Press, 1988.
Hoyt, Edwin P. *Hirohito: The Emperor and the Man.* New York: Praeger, 1992.
Iriye, Akira. *Power and Culture: The Japanese-American War, 1941–1945.* Cambridge: Harvard University Press, 1981.
Jones, F. C. *Japan's New Order in East Asia: Its Rise and Fall, 1937–1945.* London: Oxford University Press, 1954.
Keegan, John. *The Second World War.* 1989. Reprint. New York: Viking, 1990.
Kernan, W. F. *Defense Will Not Win the War.* New York: Pocket Books, 1942.
Klingman, William K. *1941: Our Lives in a World on the Edge.* New York: Harper & Row, 1988.
Koginos, Manny T. *The Panay Incident: Prelude to War.* Lafayette, Ind.: Purdue University Studies, 1967.
Langer, William L., and S. Everett Gleason. *The Undeclared War: 1940–1941.* New York: Harper & Bros., for the Council on Foreign Relations, 1953.
Larsen, George Alexander. *The Strange Neutrality: Soviet-Japanese Relations during the Second World War, 1941–1945.* Tallahassee, Fla.: Diplomatic Press, 1972.
Lewin, Ronald. *Churchill As Warlord.* London: B. T. Batsford, 1973.
Maddox, Robert J. *The United States and World War Two.* Boulder, Colo.: Westview, 1992.
Martin, James J. *American Liberalism and World Politics, 1931–1941: Liberalism's Press and Spokesmen on the Road Back to War between Mukden and Pearl Harbor.* Vol. 2. New York: Devin-Adair, 1964.
Mason, R. H. P., and J. G. Caiger. *A History of Japan.* New York: Free Press, 1972.
May, Ernest R. "U.S. Press Coverage of Japan, 1931–1941." In *Pearl Harbor as History: Japanese-American Relations, 1931–1941,* edited by Dorothy Berg and Shumpei Okamoto. New York: Columbia University Press, 1973.
Medlicott, W. N. *The Economic Blockade.* 2 vols. Vols. 7 and 8 of the *History of the Second World War,* United Kingdom Civil Series, edited by W. Keith Hancock. London: H.M.S.O., 1952. Revised edition, including confidential source references, London: H.M.S.O./Nendeln, Liechtenstein: Kraus, 1978.
Millis, Walter. *This Is Pearl! The United States and Japan—1941.* New York: William Morrow, 1947.

Morgenstern, George. *Pearl Harbor: The Story of the Secret War*. New York: Devin-Adair, 1947.
Neumann, William L. *America Encounters Japan: From Perry to MacArthur*. Baltimore: Johns Hopkins University Press, 1969.
Overy, Richard, and Andrew Wheatcroft. *The Road to War*. London: Macmillan, 1989.
Parkinson, Roger. *The Origins of World War Two*. New York: G. P. Putnam Sons, 1970.
Partridge, P. H. "Depression and War, 1929–1950." In *Australia: A Social and Political History*, edited by Gordon Greenwood. 1955. Reprint. Sydney: Angus and Robertson, 1969.
Payton-Smith, D. J. *Oil: A Study of War-Time Policy and Administration*. London: H.M.S.O., 1971.
Prange, Gordon W., with Donald M. Goldstein and Katherine V. Dillon. *Pearl Harbor: The Verdict of History*. New York: McGraw-Hill, 1986.
Reese, Trevor R. *Australia, New Zealand and the United States: A Survey of International Relations, 1941–1968*. London: Oxford University Press.
Robertson, John. *Australia at War, 1939–1945*. Melbourne: William Heinemann, 1981.
Snyder, Louis L. *The War: A Concise History, 1939–1945*. New York: Julian Messner, 1960.
Utley, Jonathan D. *Going to War with Japan, 1937–1941*. Knoxville: University of Knoxville Press, 1985.
van der Vat, Dan. *The Pacific Campaign: World War II, the U.S.-Japanese Naval War, 1941–1945*. New York: Simoin and Schuster, 1991.

Secondary Sources: Articles

Anderson, Irvine H., Jr. "The 1941 De Facto Embargo on Oil to Japan: A Bureaucratic Reflex." *Pacific Historical Review* 44 (May 1975): 2091–2096.
Brune, Lester H. "Considerations of Force in Cordell Hull's Diplomacy, July 26 to November 26, 1941." *Diplomatic History* 2 (Winter 1978): 389–405.
Haight, John McVicker, Jr. "Franklin D. Roosevelt and a Naval Quarantine of Japan." *Pacific Historical Review* 40 (May 1971): 203–26.
Herzog, James H. "Influence of the United States Navy in the Embargo of Oil to Japan, 1940–1941." *Pacific Historical Review* 35 (August 1966): 317–28.
Utley, Jonathan C. "Upstairs, Downstairs at Foggy Bottom: Oil Exports and Japan, 1940–1941." *Prologue: The Journal of the National Archives* 8 (Spring 1976): 17–28.

Contemporary Newspapers and Periodicals

Although these would normally be considered secondary sources, they are used in this study as evidence of contemporary opinion and judgment and are thus far more in the nature of primary sources.

Newspapers: The entire press run of the following papers was examined for the late July to early December of 1941 period: *Washington Post, Los Angeles Times, Wall Street Journal.* The *New York Times* was consulted upon the basis of listings in the index for that publication. Late July–early August issues of the *Richmond* (Virginia) *Times Dispatch* were also consulted. The *Japan Times and Advertiser* for August to December was an invaluable source for Japanese opinion.

Magazines and periodicals: Based upon various indexes and consultation of issues at the time of the inauguration of the embargo, these publications were consulted: *Asia, Christian Century, Current History, Foreign Affairs, Harpers, Nation, Newsweek,* and *Time.*

INDEX

Acheson, Dean: dodges commitment to issue specific level of import licenses 69; implemented severer trade restrictions than admitted to U.S. allies 85; major proponent of anti-Japan petroleum restrictions 84; official British and Dutch restrictions on trade equivalent to U.S. unofficial ones 88–89; proposes export license requirements 47; rebuked for being more rigid on trade 85
AFL-CIO: endorses boycott of Japanese-made products 18
Africa: trade with Japan 116 (Table 7.2), 118 (Table 7.3), 120 (Table 7.4)
Agriculture and Forestry Ministry (Japan) 146
airplanes: ban of exporting bombers to Japan 18, 34 101; ban on parts exports 26; ban on export of plans showing how to build airplane engines 37
Alaska: American military bases in 145
aluminum exports to Japan 183
America First Committee 72; charges U.S. demands on Japan restrictions not applied to itself 79n51
American Committee for Non-Participation in Japanese Aggression 29
American Iron and Steel Institute 35–36
American Maritime Commission 48–49, 51, 52

Argentina 92
Army-Navy Munitions Board 29
Australia: 12, 50, 80n75, 102, 204, 210, 215n7; changing attitudes on embargo measures 75–76; degree of Japan's reliance upon imports from 108, 116 (Table 7.2), 118 (Table 7.3), 120 (Table 7.4); food exporter to England 199; minimal post-embargo trade 89; views of ambassador to U.S. 172; war role in Near East 199
Axis 39, 47, 55, 167, 181, 182, 187

B17s 90
Bain, H. Foster 131–132
Baltimore, Maryland 51
Bangkok, Thailand 111
Batavia (Dutch East Indies) 76
Beard, Charles A. 188
Belgium 96 (Table 5.3)
Berlin 39, 166
Borneo, as oil exporter 127
brass exports to Japan 46
Bratton, R. S. (chief, Far Eastern Section, U.S. Army Military Intelligence) 180
Brewster, Owen (U.S. Senator) 195
Britain: 68, 73, 75, 108, 109, 111, 142, 159, 164, 177, 179, 180, 199, 207; ambassador to U.S. on damage inflicted by western embargo 5; attitude toward U.S.-Japan war 168; danger of a war with Japan 5, 30; economic comparison with Japan 115; evaluates potential impact of 1941 total

227

embargo 107; export licenses for Japanese shipments 70; importance of participation in embargo against Japan 182; iron and steel scrap purchases from U.S. 37, 138; Japanese trade with 116 (Table 7.2), 118 (Table 7.3), 120 (Table 7.4), 141; joins in 1941 total embargo 74; limits Japanese use of British-flag petroleum tankers 34–35; petroleum received from U.S. 32 (Table 2.1), 49, 96 (Table 5.3); rubber imports 209; shipping crunch 48–53; skepticism concerning role in bringing U.S. into World War I 27, 54; tanker shortage 49; unable to pin down U.S. to exact trade restrictions concerning Japan (Spring 1941) 46; U.S. aid to 137; U.S. tankers legally unable to enter in war-time 51; views of ambassador to U.S. 172; would go to war if Dutch East Indies invaded 200; *see also* England
British Commonwealth 5, 88, 189, 204; nervous because of war-potential of a total embargo against Japan 74–75
British Empire 76, 102, 108, 148, 178, 179, 204, 208; petroleum exports to 82, 84; petroleum tankers available to 34
bronze exports to Japan 46
Buck, Pearl 13
Bureau of Mines (U.S.) 31
Burma 75

Cadogan, Sir Alexander 74
California: fear of fifth-column activities in 64; indignation over large oil shipments to Japan 197; tanker shipments from 33
Canada 34, 102, 108, 204; eliminates Japanese trade 89; endorses embargo against Japan 74; petroleum exports to 95 (Table 5.2), 96 (Table 5.3); scrap metal exports to 37
Cape Horn 69
Caribbean 49, 51, 53, 69

Caribbean Defense Command 57
Caroline Islands 7
Cathay Hotel (Shanghai, China) 13
Cavite (U.S. naval base, Philippines) 91
Central America 64, 141; Japanese trade with 116 (Table 7.2), 118 (Table 7.3), 120 (Table 7.4)
Chicago, Illinois 16
Chile 92
China x, 2, 10, 76, 104, 107, 111, 115, 129, 166, 177, 180, 212, 214, 215n7, 217; American missionaries and humanitarian efforts within 12, 28; Central Bank of 65; cotton exports of 160; explanations and rationalizations for Japanese expansion in 8, 10; Japan "over-extended" in 181; Japanese violation of U.S. trade rights in 19–20, 139; Japan's ability to continue war in after petroleum boycott 131, 182; newsreels of war shocked western viewers 13; petroleum for Japanese-occupied sectors limited to low octane grades 46; rationale for including shipments to in anti-Japan embargo 64–65; secondary role in victory over Japan 11; significance of continued resistance by 110; trade with Japan 115, 116 (Table 7.2), 118 (Table 7.3), 120 (Table 7.4); U.S. assistance to government 39, 63, 195; widespread corruption 65; withdrawal from "suicidal" for Japan 161
"China Affair" 10, 11, 179
"China Incident" 15, 110, 180
Chosen 149
Christian Century: opposes official embargo 28, 29; supports expansion of moral embargo 26
chromite exports to Japan 47
Churchill, Winston 207, 208
coal, Japan's reserves of 184
coconut oil exports to Japan 47
Columbia 92
Conally, Tom (Senator) 58
copper exports to Japan 27, 101; amount of 28; from Philippines 47; licenses for 41, 46

cotton supplies for Japan: China as secondary source 160; exports to Japan 26, 39, 57, 89, 101, 108 (Table 7.1), 111, 158, 182; India as source 195; inferior Asian product 146; labor force used in processing 115; Latin America as potential source 92, 184

Crete 50, 51

Czechoslovakia 54

Domei (Japanese news agency) 87, 137, 140, 143, 148

Dutch East Indies 5, 12, 34, 55, 56, 67, 90, 101, 111, 148, 149, 177, 180, 189, 191, 194, 210, 218; cut-off of petroleum exports to Japan 70, 123, 182; danger of war/invasion due to oil cut-off 17, 30, 58, 73, 146, 147, 189, 197–200; exports of petroleum to Japan 173, 195; invasion of, would escalate into war with western powers 200; negotiations with Japan 81n92; oil fields mined to prevent Japanese use 77; petroleum of essential to Japanese war effort 132, 160, 161; recipient of U.S. exports 96 (Table 5.3); trade with Japan 116 (Table 7.2), 118 (Table 7.3), 120 (Table 7.4)

economic and oil boycott of Japan: advocated during "moral embargo" phase 21–22; allies misled as to degree of trade freeze U.S. implementing 85; American evaluations of impact 175–185 (chapter 12); as means of assuring adequate defense build-up supplies for U.S. 28; attempts to delink embargo and outbreak of war 203–214; church leaders and 28; dependence of Japan on foreign imports 108 (Table 7.1), 116 (Table 7.2), 118 (Table 7.3), 120 (Table 7.4); downplaying of among historians 3; five interlocking roadblocks to new shipments to Japan 85, 97n11;

impact of 1940 embargo measures 100–106; impact of 1941 embargo measures 107–122; importance of foreign trade to Japanese economy 115; interpretation of by U.S. diplomats in Japan 4; Japan warns of danger of non-shooting economic warfare 171; maximalists in State Department win out over moderate trade restrictionists 46; 1918 successful embargo precedent 39–40; public announcement of 63; public stance of Japanese government 136–152; shipment of small drums of oil prohibited 44; Sumner Welles feared war if adopted in 1940 30; total cut-off of oil 88; U.S. ambassador to Japan feared war over 176; U.S. opinion underestimated degree of damage inflicted by 5, 114

Economic Defense Board 85

Eden, Sir Anthony 189–190; resigns as British foreign secretary 17; warns that embargo must be backed up by force (1937) 16

England 32, 55, 147, 166, 167; Australia as food source for 199; see also Britain

Federation of Cotton Spinning Companies 178

Foley, Edward H., Jr. 69

Foreign Policy Association 113

Formosa 125; Japanese trade with 117, 118 (Table 7.3), 120 (Table 7.4)

France 32, 199; empire of 208; trade with Japan 116 (Table 7.2); ultimatum to by Japan 56; U.S. petroleum exports to 32 (Table 2.1), 96 (Table 5.3)

French Indochina see Indochina

fuel, aviation quality 82–83, 101; ability to upgrade lower quality supplies 32, 33, 34; contradictory U.S. government figures on amount exported 33–34; existing exportation licenses revoked 84; redefined downward to limit supply to Japan 31; reprocessing vegetable oils into 140; Sumner Welles on rationale for limiting exports to Japan 31; technical definition of exportable fuel 42*n13*; U.S. exports to Japan 104 (Table 6.3)

Gallup Poll 11–12, 12, 23*n9*, 203
Gearhart, Bertrand W. (Congressman) 196
Germany 32, 38, 39, 54, 55, 64, 180, 217; as "have not" nation 148; invasion of/war with Soviet Union 166, 191; Japanese trade with 116 (Table 7.2), 118 (Table 7.3), 120 (Table 7.4), 137; speculation as to exact relationship of with Japan 55; U.S. petroleum exports to 96 (Table 5.3)
Great Britain *see* Britain; England
Greater East Asia Co-Prosperity Sphere 179; fundamental premise of Japanese official policy 140; as response to western economic trade restrictions 143
Greece 50
Grew, Joseph (Ambassador) 169–170; attempts to delink embargo and outbreak of war 211–212, 213; originally opposed stiff embargo measures against Japan 176; reports from Grew and staff on impact of economic embargo 175–180; reverses anti-embargo stance 177; surveys South American diplomats to gauge attitude toward U.S. embargo 92
Gulf of Mexico 84

Hall, Noel F. 85
Hawaii *see* Hawaiian Islands
Hawaiian Islands 1, 57, 91, 193, 206, 210; potential for fifth-column type activities in 64
hemp exports to Japan 47
Hiraide, Hideo (Captain) (Japanese navy spokesman) 142
Hirohito (Japan's emperor): attitude toward expansion in Manchuria and China 9; theoretical versus actual power of 9
Hitler, Adolph 29, 55, 109, 164, 192, 200
Holland 207; *see also* Netherlands
Hong Kong 75, 147, 191, 209
Honolulu 40
Hopkins, Harry 50
Hornbeck, Stanley K.: advises petroleum companies on how to dodge Japanese demands for larger supplies 44; "hardliner" on relations with Japan 21
House Resolution 9850 ("To Expedite the Strengthening of the National Defense") 29–30
Howard, Clinton M. 114
Hull, Cordell 164, 165, 170, 198; discourges strong Congressional trade limitation legislation 29; downplays degree of western coordination of embargo measures 90; endorses moral embargo 18; opposes embargo measures that could lead to war 40, 100; rebukes Japanese double standard 40; trade limitations forced more cautious expansionary policy by Japan 101; urges Japan to withdraw from Tripartite Pact 172

Ickes, Harold 32, 40, 84; unilaterally restricts lubricating oil from going to Japan but forced to back off 47; upset Roosevelt would not move faster against Japan 62
Imperial Conferences (Japanese government) 157–162
India 145, 102, 108, 195; degree of post-embargo trade with Japan 89; iron ore exports 104; pre-embargo trade with Japan 116 (Table 7.2), 118 (Table 7.3), 120 (Table 7.4)
Indochina 2, 17, 66, 67, 69, 75, 76, 104, 199, 207, 208, 210, 212; American retaliation anticipated in response to Japanese expansion within 158; expansion of Japanese forces into southern half 54, 57, 62, 147, 189; "fishbait mission"

to 215n8; justifications for Japanese control of 164, 166–167; occupation of northern half 37; as potential jumping off point for further Japanese expansionism 55, 164–165, 209; proposal of Japanense withdrawal and western cancellation of economic boycott 172; as protection for Japanese supply lines 160; size of Japanese occupation force 192; U.S. rejects Japanese defense of interventionism in 168
Interdepartmental Foreign Funds Control Committee 85
Iraq-Iran War 218
iron/iron scrap exports to Japan 92, 101, 139; degree of dependence upon 28, 108 (Table 7.1), 183; from Malaya 89; from Philippines 47; impact of restrictions 184; Japanese industrial expansion restricted by limited supply of 35; July 1940 restrictions on 138; possibility of including as part of "moral embargo" 26; reliance upon American sources 102 (Table 6.1), 103 (Table 6.2); reserves of 104; September 1940 restrictions on 138
Isoda, Saburo (Major General) 180
isolationism/isolationists: support discretionary trade limitation power for President 30; wide support among for strong anti–Japan stance 12, 71, 72, 74, 169, 203
Italy 32, 38, 39, 64; recipient of U.S. petroleum 96 (Table 5.3)

Janeway, Eliot 73
Japan 64, 90, 92, 93, 95, 115; accused of foreign policy inconsistencies 139; appeals to anti-white race sentiments 10; cities open to massive fire-bombing 72; coded diplomatic messages to its Washington embassy 163–173 (chapter 11); denied use of U.S. tankers 60n46; domestic sources of oil 124–125; economic costs of war in China 102; economic weaknesses when contrasted with U.S. 100; Foreign Ministry 137; heavy cost of using foreign-owned tankers 53; liaison and imperial conferences of Japanese government 157–162 (chapter 10); limited supply of petroleum tankers 34; merchantmen ordered to operate only in Pacific Ocean 53; militarism 8, 9, 203; more reliance on foreign trade than Britain 115; neutrality pact with Soviet Union 168; number of oil wells in production (1941) 123; petroleum imports from Dutch East Indies 123, 127; petroleum imports from United States 32 (Table 2.1), 126 (Table 8.3), 127 (Table 8.4), 128 (Table 8.5), 129; petroleum reserves 130, 131 (Table 8.6), 132, 133, 159, 160, 178, 182, 184; as potential transshipper of goods to Germany 47; reliance upon imported metals 28, 183; reliance upon imported oil 123, 124 (Table 8.1), 125 (Table 8.2), 128, 183; reliance upon imported raw materials 108 (Table 7.1), 110; reservists called to duty 54; rice production of 100; steel production of 100; trade with South America 141; types of imperialists 8–9; war with as potential door into European war 198; World War I era expansionism 7
Japan Chamber of Commerce and Industry 151
Japan Times and Advertiser: English-language publication 65; status as semi-official organ of Japanese Foreign Office 154n53
Johnson, Hiram (U.S. Senator) 12
Judd, Dr. Walter H. (medical missionary to China) 28

Kai-shek, Chiang (Generalissimo) 63, 66, 110
Kaufman, Samuel H. 193
Kaya, Okinori (Finance Minister, Japan) 151, 152

Keefe, Frank B. (Congressman) 211–212
Kernan, W. F. 187
kerosene 95 (Table 5.2)
Kimmel, H. E. (Admiral) 193–194
Knox, Frank (Secretary of Navy) 32, 40; criticized by Japanese press 150; estimates of Japanese petroleum reserve 132, 133; supports drastic lowering of permissible octane level of fuel exports to Japan 38–39
Konoye, Fumimaro (Prince; Prime Minister, Japan) 171; recognized America's immense war-making potential 211; summit conference with Roosevelt proposed 167, 211
Korea 10; Japanese occupation of 1; Japanese trade with 117, 118 (Table 7.3), 120 (Table 7.4)
Korean Conflict/War 217
Kresege (retail stores) 18
Kress (retail stores) 18
Kurusu, Saburo (special diplomatic envoy to U.S.) 113, 170, 172
Kwantung Leased Territory 116 (Table 7.2), 118 (Table 7.3), 120 (Table 7.4)

Layton, Edwin T. 194
lead exports to Japan 183
League of Nations: ceasefire in China, May 1932 8; failed sanctions against Italy 22; "moral embargo" policy of 101; skepticism toward institution 22
Leahy, William (Admiral) 13
Lend Lease 101
Liaison Conferences (Japanese government) 157–162; attendees 157
London 57, 70, 76, 91, 108
Long, Breckinridge 197–198; on cycle of U.S.-Japanese retaliations 39
Los Angeles, California 86
Loudon, Dr. Alexander 76–77
lumber exports to Japan 158

Mabuchi, Hayato (Colonel) (Chief, Japanese Army press section) 142, 154n41
MacArthur, Douglas (General): difficulties faced in Philippines 91; recalled to active duty 90
McCroy (retail stores) 18
MacKenzie, W. L. (Prime Minister, Canada) 74
"Magic" (decryption program) 55, 173
Malaya/Malaysia 75; as mineral exporter 89; as oil exporter 127; as potential Japanese military target 17, 30, 194; as rubber exporter 149
Manchukuo 76, 111
Manchuria 2, 149; Japanese trade with 116 (Table 7.2), 118 (Table 7.3); press coverage of Japanese expansion in 8; as source of petroleum for Japan 124
"Manchurian Affair"/"Manchurian Incident" 8, 10, 11, 87, 146
manganese: exports to Japan 47, 89, 108 (Table 7.1); Japan's reserves of 184
Manila (Philippines) 91
Marco Polo Bridge "Incident" 9
Marshall, George C. (General, U.S. Army Chief of Staff): war danger from petroleum cut-off to Japan 30, 197
Marshall Islands 7
Matsushita, Masatoshi 111, 148
Mead, James M. (Senator) 58
Menzies, Robert G. 75
mercury exports to Japan 183
Mexico 32, 92
mica exports to Japan 183
Miles, Sherman (Brigadier General) 180, 181
milk 141
Miyako (Japanese newspaper) 89
molybdenum exports to Japan 183
Moore, Frederick (legal adviser to Japanese Embassy) 170
"moral embargo" of Japan 15–19, 136–137; criticized as inadequate 101; endorsed by Secretary of State 18
Morgenstern, George 188
Morgenthau, Henry, Jr. (Secretary of

Treasury) 40; advocates lower octane for exportable petroleum 56–57; blamed by Japanese press for inspiring the embargo 150; estimate of Japanese reliance on U.S. oil 128; Japanese ability to upgrade quality of petroleum it received 32; seeks evaluation of degree of damage caused by embargo 184; supports total scrap export ban for Japanese market 36
Moscow 143
"Mukden Incident" 7; see also "Manchurian Affair"
Munich 54

Nash, Walter (Finance Minister, New Zealand) 75
National Defense Act (1940) 30
National Defense Advisory Commission (NDAC) 35–36
National Industrial Conference Board 114
neocolonialism 204
Netherlands 30, 96 (Table 5.3), 142; ambassador to U.S. 172; possessions 68, 109; see also Holland
Netherlands East Indies see Dutch East Indies
New Guinea 210
New York 51, 111
New Zealand 12, 75, 215n7; war role in Near East 199
nickel exports to Japan 41, 46, 108 (Table 7.1), 183
Nitiel Maru 86, 97n18
Nomura, Kichisaburo (Admiral) 170, 171; appointed ambassador to U.S. 137; embargo by West could produce same results of a successful war against Japan 169; hope for reconciliation with U.S. 58; rebukes timing of expansion into southern Indochina 165; reports strong support for anti–Japan stance among Americans opposed to war with Germany 168, 169; suspects British want U.S.-Japan war to bring U.S. into European war 168; U.S. cabinet member warns him of government skepticism of Japanese intentions 170
Norris, George W. (Senator): ambivalent toward war with Japan 72; endorses moral embargo 19
Norway: shipping vessels and tankers 51, 52

Office of Arms and Munitions Control (U.S. State Department) 18–19
Ogura, Matasune (Finance Minister, Japan) 140
Ohashi, Chuichi (Vice Foreign Minister, Japan) 137
oil boycott of Japan see economic and oil boycott of Japan
Okamoto, Kiyofuku (Major-General) 148–149
Oregon 72
Otowasan Maru 86, 97n18

Palestine 199
Panama: tankers registered in 52, 53
Panama Canal: Japanese freighters denied transit through 69
Panay, assault upon 14, 18
Paraguay 92
Pearl Harbor, attack on ix, 1, 5, 6, 114, 115, 123, 162, 180, 187, 192, 206, 218
Pemberton, J. F. (oil industry spokesman) 27
Persian Gulf War (1991) 129
Peru 92
petroleum coke exports to Japan 46
Philadelphia, Pennsylvania 51
Philippines 6, 40, 57; American build-up in x, 191, 217; assumption of prompt fall to Japanese reversed to policy of vigorous defense 47–48; danger of expanding U.S. defense perimeter to Philippines 91; as jumping off point for potential anti–Japanese military action 48, 90, 91, 206; militia called into U.S. service 90, 192; pre-embargo trade with Japan 116 (Table 7.2), 118 (Table 7.3), 120 (Table 7.4);

promised independence 204, 208; shifting dates for completion of ability to repel invasion 48; as target for Japanese expansionism 17, 90, 194, 207, 210; transshipment of embargoed goods to Japan prohibited 47
Pratt, William V. (Admiral) 169, 191–192
Privy Council (Japanese) 160

Quezon, Manuel (President of Philippines) 47

radar 1
Rainbow 5 (U.S. war plan) 47–48, 91
"Red Sea project" 51
Richardson, James O. (U.S. Pacific Fleet Commander-in-Chief) 35; on possible naval blockade to enforce embargo (1940) 40–41
Rome 39
Roosevelt, Eleanor 198
Roosevelt, Franklin Delano 167; avoiding war with Japan assisted Britain 199; determination to involve U.S. in war with Germany 5; embargo intentions broadened by administrators 4, 63, 78n30; limited intentions behind "total" boycott rhetoric 62, 66; pro- and anti-interpretations of role in outbreak of war vii, 187; public opinion supported anti–Japan actions 14, 203; "Quarantine the Aggressors" speech 16; rebukes Harold Ickes 47; rebukes war excesses 14; recognition that petroleum cut-off could lead to war 56, 112, 123, 150, 197–198, 198–199, 199–200; why conflict in China never officially branded a "war" 15
rubber exports: to Japan 108 (Table 7.1), 111, 183; to U.S. 149, 209
Russia 10, 39, 112, 166, 167, 181, 198; relative military strength of as a foe of Japan 190; as trade conduit between Japan and Europe 183
Russo-Japanese War 10, 56, 141, 148

Saigon 209
Sakhalin (Island), as source of petroleum for Japan 124
Sakonji, Seizo (Vice Admiral) 142
Salter, Sir Arthur 50
Samoa 40
Senate Foreign Relations Committee 170
Shanghai: currency exchange rates in 65; Japanese-controlled front businessmen 64; western economic boycott impact on trade in 146
Shell Oil Company 44, 45
Shimizu, Yoshitaro (political commentator) 148, 155n66
Short, Walter C. (General) 193
Siberia 10, 145, 215n7; air bases in 90; 1918 Japanese intervention in 39; potential Japanese military target 181
silk 39, 57; degree of damage to Japanese economy by U.S. freeze on 115, 146, 183, 189; degree of damage to U.S. economy by U.S. freeze on 93, 94; Japanese newspapers stress economic harm to U.S. caused by ban on Japanese silk 140; production of silk products for Japan's domestic market 184; replacements for silk 18
Singapore 12, 40, 75, 147, 191; military build-up at 73
South Africa 75
South America 37, 64, 68, 87, 141, 177; amount of trade with Japan 92, 116 (Table 7.2), 118 (Table 7.3), 120 (Table 7.4); Japanese ships using west coast ports 92; potential for using to avoid full impact of western embargo 91
Soviet Union 32, 145; Japanese trade with 102, 137; neutrality pact with Japan 168; *see also* Russia
Spain: bombings in 18; petroleum products received from U.S. 96 (Table 5.3)
Standard Oil Company 32

Stanvac/Standard-Vacuum Oil Company 33, 44, 45, 72
Stark, Harold R. (Admiral, Chief of Naval Operations) 199; conversations with General Marshall on embargo dangers 197; cut off of petroleum would result in war 30, 195–196
steel: exported to Japan 34, 103 (Table 6.2); Japanese industry hurt by limited supply 35, 111; Japanese reserve supplies 132, 182, 184
steel scrap exports to Japan 139, 101; July 1940 restrictions on 138; redefining downward permissible exports 36–37; reliance on imported 28, 102 (Table 6.1); September 1940 restrictions on 138
Stimson, Henry I. (Secretary of War): promotes embargo 40
Stimson Doctrine 149
Stirling, Yates, Jr. (Rear Admiral, Retired) 111–112, 123
Stone, I. F. 73
Strait Settlements 75, 199
Sweden 96 (Table 5.3)
Sweetland, Monroe 72
Syria 199

Taiwan *see* Formosa
Takemura, Tadao (Professor, Kei University) 145
tetraethyl lead 32
Thailand 111, 177, 209
Third Neutrality Act (1937) 15
Tidewater Oil Company 32
tin exports: to Japan 108 (Table 7.1), 183; to U.S. 149
titanium exports to Japan 46
Togo, Shigenori (Foreign Minister, Japan) 144; asserts that economic pressure more dangerous than military opposition 161; government positions simultaneously occupied by 183
Tojo, Hideki (Lieutenant General, Prime Minister, Japan) 144, 181
Tokyo 4, 8, 13, 39, 55, 76, 89, 92, 110, 111, 137, 141, 142, 149, 150, 151, 164, 167, 169, 171, 212

Tokyo Stock Exchange 141
Tominaga, Kametaro (Major) (spokesman, War Ministry's Press Bureau) 10, 146–147
Toyoda, Teijior (Vice Admiral) 137–138, 181
Treaty of Commerce and Navigation (1911) 21; withdrawn from to permit embargo measures 21, 23
Tripartite Pact 55, 64; contents of 38; embargo as means of forcing Japan to withdraw from 181; Japanese seek "flexibility" in application of 166; U.S.-British tensions in opposing 208; U.S. seeks Japanese withdrawal from 172
Tsingtao (Chinese city) 7
Turner, Raymond K. (Admiral) 194, 195

Ugaki, Matome (Admiral) 56
United States: Congress 175; differing means of treating repugnant regimes 2; double standard on colonialism 204; Japanese owned banks in 145; minimal internal impact of total embargo on Japan 93, 95; newspapers, anti-Japan attitudes of 170; oil wells in production (1941) 123–124; press coverage of war in China 13; public opinion hostile to Japan's expansionism 11–12, 14; public opinion hostile to large oil shipments to Japan 72–73, 200; public opinion more vehemently anti–Japan attitudes 204; types and amount of imports from Japan 94 (Table 5.1); viewed as less dangerous enemy than Russia by Japan 190
United States, petroleum exports: to Japan 129, 195; to Japan, May 1940 32 (Table 2.1); to Japan 1936–1941 126 (Table 8.3), 127 (Table 8.4), 128 (Table 8.5); worldwide figures, by type of product 95 (Table 5.2); worldwide figures, by volume 1931–1942 96 (Table 5.3)

United States Tariff Commission 93, 95
U.S.S.R. *see* Soviet Union

Vandenberg, Arthur H. (Senator) 21
van Mook, H. J. 76
Venezuela 92
Vichy regime (France) 164–165
Vietnam *see* Indochina
Vladivostok, U.S. shipments through: "petroleum products" sent to 168

Washington Monument 50
Wellborn, Charles, Jr. (Captain) 196
Welles, Sumner 57, 69, 76, 164; on motives behind "Quarantine the Aggressors" speech of Roosevelt 16; opposed embargo in 1940 due to danger of involving U.S. in war 30; supports aviation fuel export restrictions 31; supports minimalization of exports rather than absolute prohibition 87

wheat exports to Japan 158
Wheeler, Burton K. (Senator) 71, 79n44,46
White, H. D.: analysis of economic harm inflicted on Japan by embargo 184
White House 70, 82, 83
Williams, Frank S. (Commercial Attache in Japan) 178
wool exports to Japan 89, 108 (Table 7.1), 109
Woolworth (retail stores) 18
World War I 7, 203; Britain and American entry into 27
World War II, differences over whether it began first in Asia or Europe 11

Yamamoto, Isoroku (Admiral) 56
Yokohama Specie Bank 87

zinc exports to Japan 41, 464, 108 (Table 7.1)

www.ingramcontent.com/pod-product-compliance
Ingram Content Group UK Ltd.
Pitfield, Milton Keynes, MK11 3LW, UK
UKHW041940140426
5217IPUK00014B/577